W9-AEC-933

Woodbourne Library
Washington-Centerville Public Library
Centerville, Ohio

DISCARD

STAR WARS®
VECTOR

VOLUME ONE

KNIGHTS OF THE OLD REPUBLIC VOLUME 5   **DARK TIMES** VOLUME 3

PAST > > > > > > > PRESENT > > > > > > > FUTURE

KNIGHTS OF THE OLD REPUBLIC

The Old Republic
(25,000–1,000 years before the battle of Yavin)

The Old Republic was the legendary government that united a galaxy under the rule of the Senate. In this era, the Jedi are numerous, and serve as guardians of peace and justice. The *Tales of the Jedi* comics series takes place in this era, chronicling the immense wars fought by the Jedi of old, and the ancient Sith.

The events in this chapter take place approximately 3,963 years before the Battle of Yavin.

DARK TIMES

The Rise of the Empire
(1,000–0 years before the battle of Yavin)

After the seeming final defeat of the Sith, the Republic enters a state of complacency. In the waning years of the Republic, the Senate rife with corruption, the ambitious Senator Palpatine causes himself to be elected Supreme Chancellor. This is the era of the prequel trilogy.

The events in this chapter take place approximately nineteen years before the Battle of Yavin.

STAR WARS® VECTOR

VOLUME ONE

CHAPTER ONE	CHAPTER TWO
KNIGHTS OF THE OLD REPUBLIC VOLUME 5	DARK TIMES VOLUME 3

CHAPTER ONE

KNIGHTS OF THE OLD REPUBLIC VOLUME 5

Script
JOHN JACKSON MILLER

Pencils
SCOTT HEPBURN

Inks
JOE PIMENTEL
DAN PARSONS

Colors
MICHAEL ATIYEH

Lettering
MICHAEL HEISLER

CHAPTER TWO

DARK TIMES VOLUME 3

Script
MICK HARRISON

Art
DOUGLAS WHEATLEY
DAVE ROSS

Colors
DAVE McCAIG

Lettering
MICHAEL HEISLER

Front Cover Art **TRAVIS CHAREST**   Back Cover Art **DOUGLAS WHEATLEY**

Publisher MIKE RICHARDSON Collection Designer JOSH ELLIOTT Art Director LIA RIBACCHI Editor RANDY STRADLEY
Associate Editor DAVE MARSHALL Assistant Editor FREDDYE LINS

Special thanks to Elaine Mederer, Jann Moorhead, David Anderman, Leland Chee, Sue Rostoni, and Carol Roeder at Lucas Licensing

STAR WARS VECTOR Volume One
STAR WARS KNIGHTS OF THE OLD REPUBLIC Volume Five
STAR WARS DARK TIMES Volume Three

Star Wars © 2009 Lucasfilm Ltd. & ™. All rights reserved. Used under authori-
zation. Text and illustrations for Star Wars are © 2008, 2009 Lucasfilm Ltd. Dark
Horse Books® and the Dark Horse logo are registered trademarks of Dark Horse
Comics, Inc. All rights reserved. No portion of this publication may be repro-
duced or transmitted, in any form or by any means, without the express written
permission of Dark Horse Comics, Inc. Names, characters, places, and incidents
featured in this publication either are the product of the author's imagination or
are used fictitiously. Any resemblance to actual persons (living or dead), events,
institutions, or locales, without satiric intent, is coincidental.

This volume collects issues twenty-five through twenty-eight of the Dark Horse
Comics series *Star Wars: Knights of the Old Republic*, and issues eleven and
twelve of the Dark Horse Comics series *Star Wars: Dark Times.*

Published by
DARK HORSE BOOKS
A division of Dark Horse Comics, Inc.
10956 SE Main Street
Milwaukie, OR 97222

darkhorse.com
starwars.com

To find a comics shop in your area, call the Comic Shop Locator Service
toll-free at 1-888-266-4226

First edition: January 2009
ISBN: 978-1-59582-226-0

1 2 3 4 5 6 7 8 9 10   Printed in China

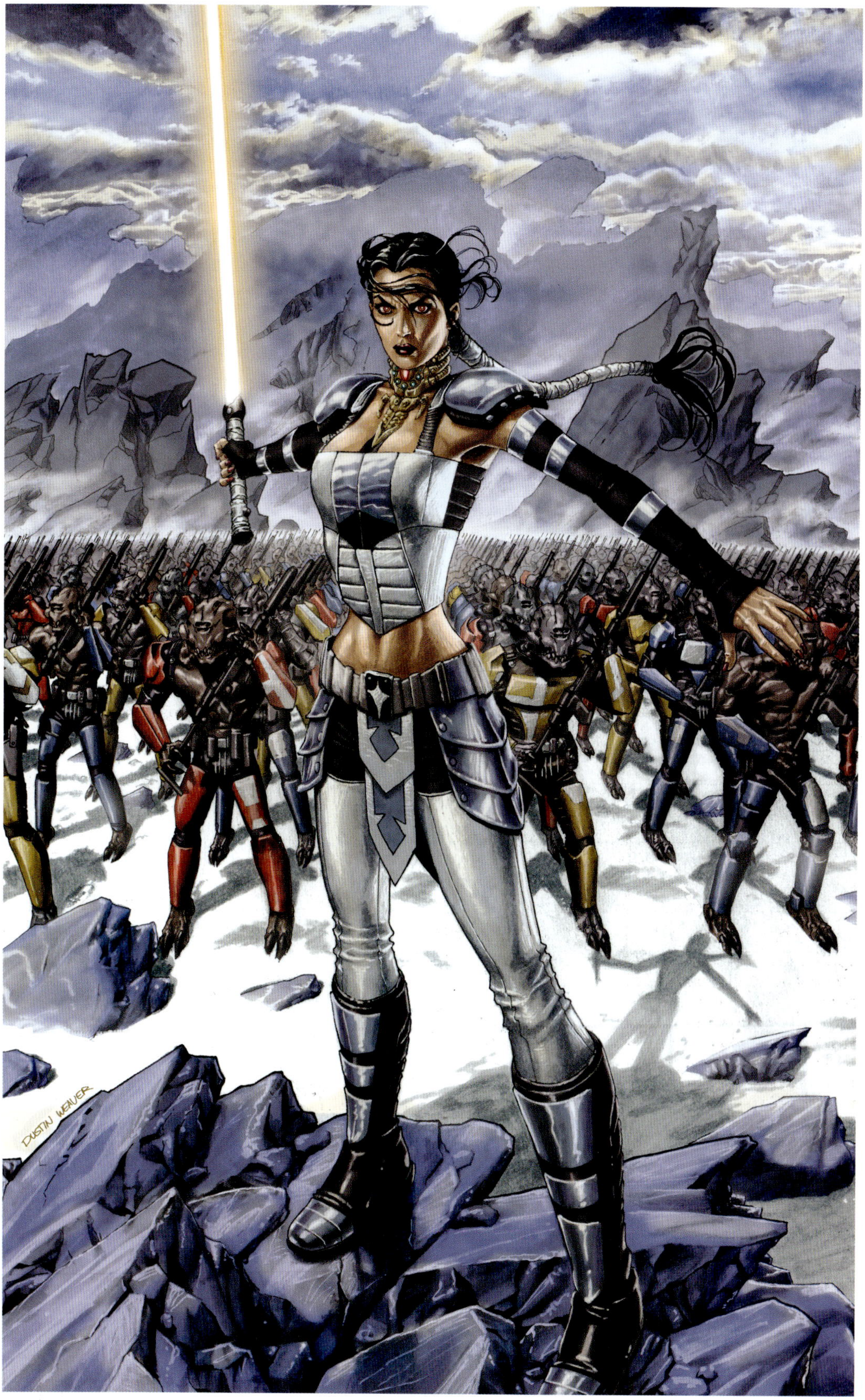
DUSTIN WEAVER

Illustration by **DUSTIN WEAVER**

HOW "VECTOR" CAME TO BE,
OR, CONFESSIONS OF A COMIC BOOK MONGER

I have a confession to make. Though it pains me to say it, I must admit that the story you're about to read has its roots (well, the very tips of them, anyway) in crass commercialism. It started with an observation made by fellow editor Chris Warner about the vast, multi-issue, multi-series crossover "events" which our competitors Marvel and DC roll out on an almost annual basis. "That's the comics industry for you," said Chris. "We never run out of the same idea."

He was right. But the reason behind this repetition of the "same idea" is solid: the crossovers always sell. And I got to thinking, *why can't we have the same idea with* Star Wars? *Why can't* Star Wars *comics generate some of that crossover money?* The continuity in *Star Wars* runs from thousands of years prior to Luke Skywalker's birth, to over one hundred fifty years beyond it. We had four regular series of titles, each set in a different era of *Star Wars* history; why couldn't we tell an epic story which touched upon each of the points we were exploring along the *Star Wars* timeline? Why *shouldn't* we? As long as we didn't contradict established events, it could work—and we could (hopefully) attract new readers to our comics.

So much for commercial concerns. I was sure we could find a way to make the logistics work, but I knew that in order to win over readers, the story also had to mean something to the characters in each of our comics series, while at the same time affecting the *Star Wars* mythos as a whole. A story played out on a massive stage, but with only a few characters in the spotlight at any one time. A big story that remained intensely personal. And there was one final caveat: each chapter of "Vector" had to be accessible to readers who might not know anything more about *Star Wars* than what they had seen in the films. What could be easier?

Fortunately, our team—writers John Jackson Miller (*Star Wars: Knights of the Old Republic*), Mick Harrison (*Star Wars: Dark Times*), Rob Williams (*Star Wars: Rebellion*), John Ostrander and his co-plotter and artist Jan Duursema (*Star Wars: Legacy*), editor Jeremy Barlow, and then–assistant–editor Dave Marshall (well, and myself)—made the task seem, if not easy, then at least possible. Our discussions began with months of email messages and eventually ended with a summit meeting attended by most of the principals. Everybody had suggestions, everyone contributed important plot or character points, and along the way that "same idea" became something new. Together we managed, I believe, to come up with a tale that is truly epic in its scope, while being personal in its focus. I hope you'll agree.

Randy Stradley
editor

P.S.—And, yes, the comics achieved their commercial goals.

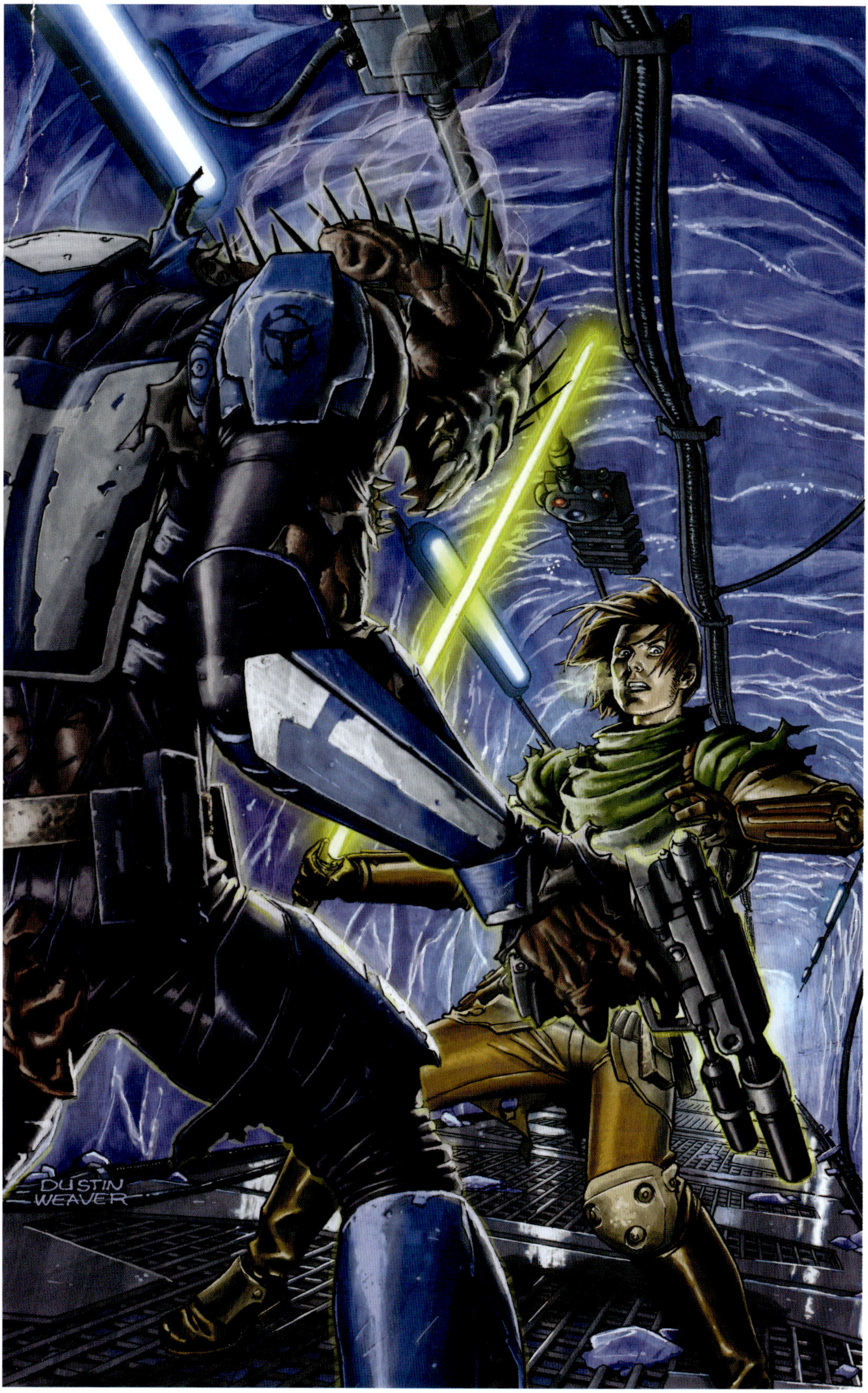
DUSTIN
WEAVER

Illustration by **DUSTIN WEAVER**

KNIGHTS OF THE OLD REPUBLIC

VOLUME 5 Weeks after the surprise attack by the nomadic Mandalorians, the forces of the Old Republic have fallen back to protect more populated systems—leaving Outer Rim worlds like Taris to fend for themselves.

The Jedi Knights reject official involvement in the war—a view applauded by the Covenant, a secret organization founded by the Order's greatest seers. The Covenant desires instead to predict and prevent the return of the Sith—and its prime suspect for triggering that event in the future is an unlikely one: Zayne Carrick, an undistinguished Padawan.

Even after being framed by his Masters for a crime he did not commit, Zayne proves hard to capture, fleeing with con artist Gryph and finding refuge with the Taris Resistance. But when a desperate stroke against the Mandalorians fails, the Taris defense shatters—and Zayne and Gryph learn there are worse things on Taris than Mandalorians . . .

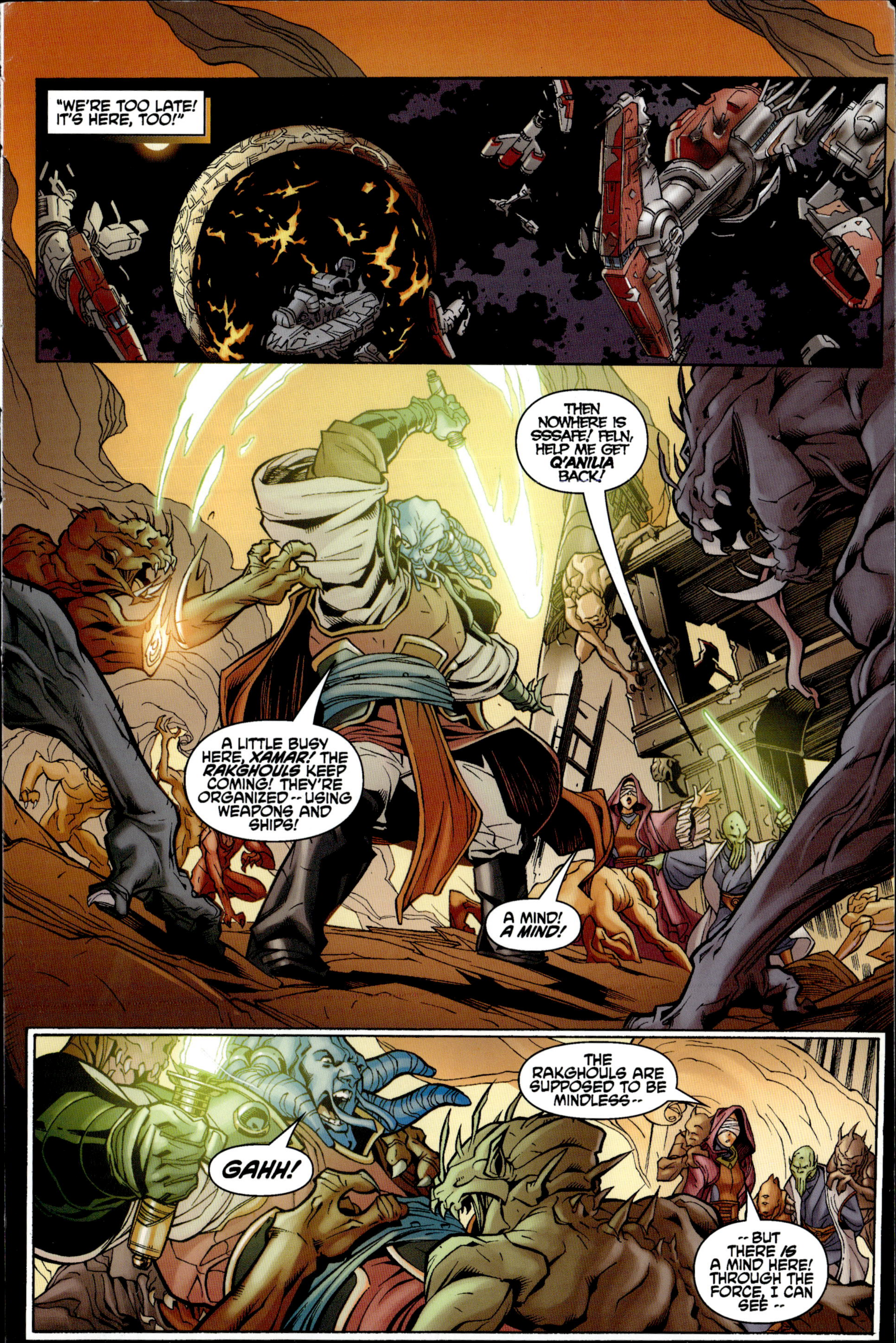
"WE'RE TOO LATE! IT'S HERE, TOO!"
THEN NOWHERE IS SSSAFE! FELN, HELP ME GET Q'ANILIA BACK!
A LITTLE BUSY HERE, XAMAR! THE RAKGHOULS KEEP COMING! THEY'RE ORGANIZED -- USING WEAPONS AND SHIPS!
A MIND! A MIND!
GAHH!
THE RAKGHOULS ARE SUPPOSED TO BE MINDLESS --
-- BUT THERE IS A MIND HERE! THROUGH THE FORCE, I CAN SEE --

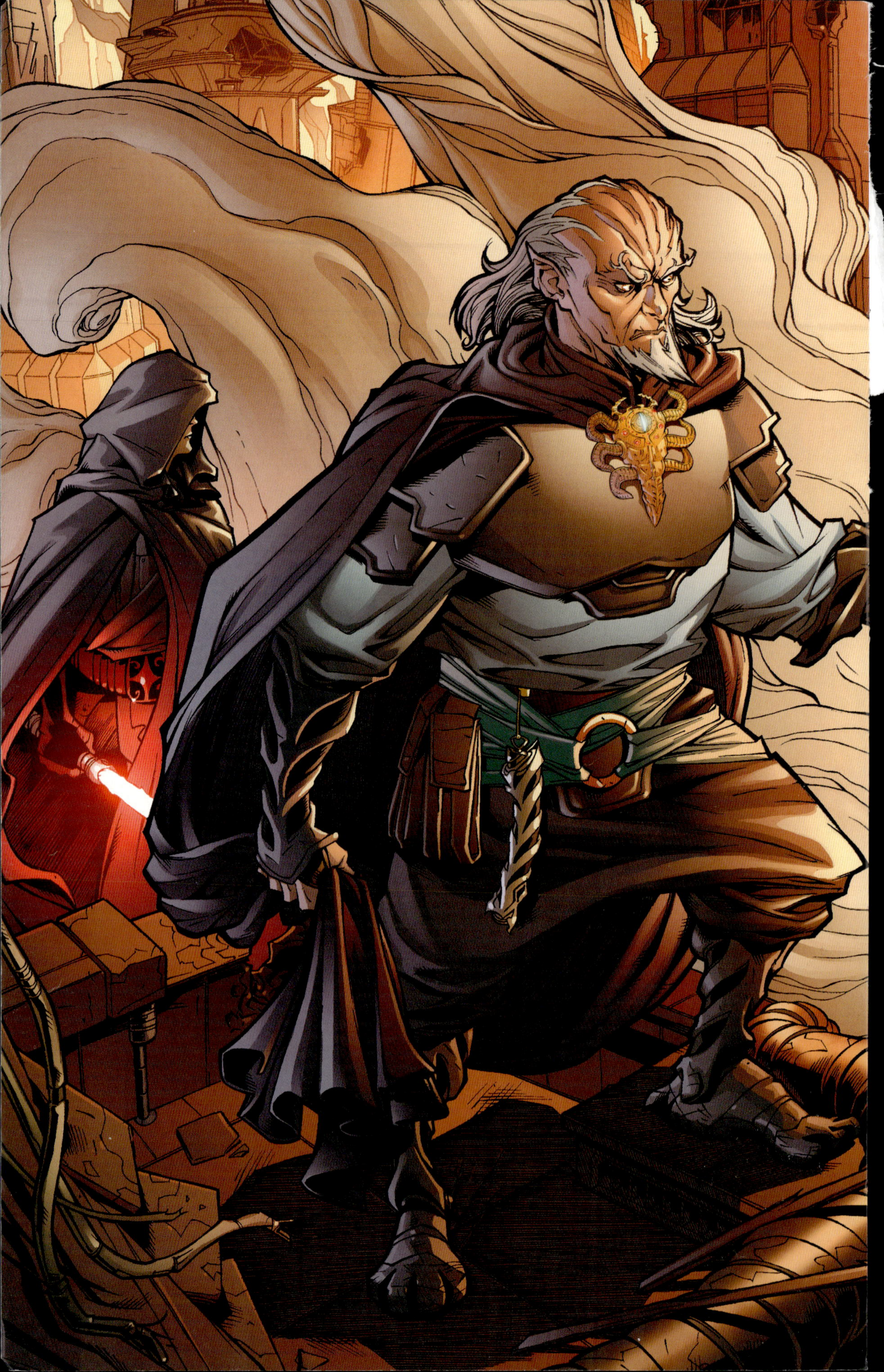

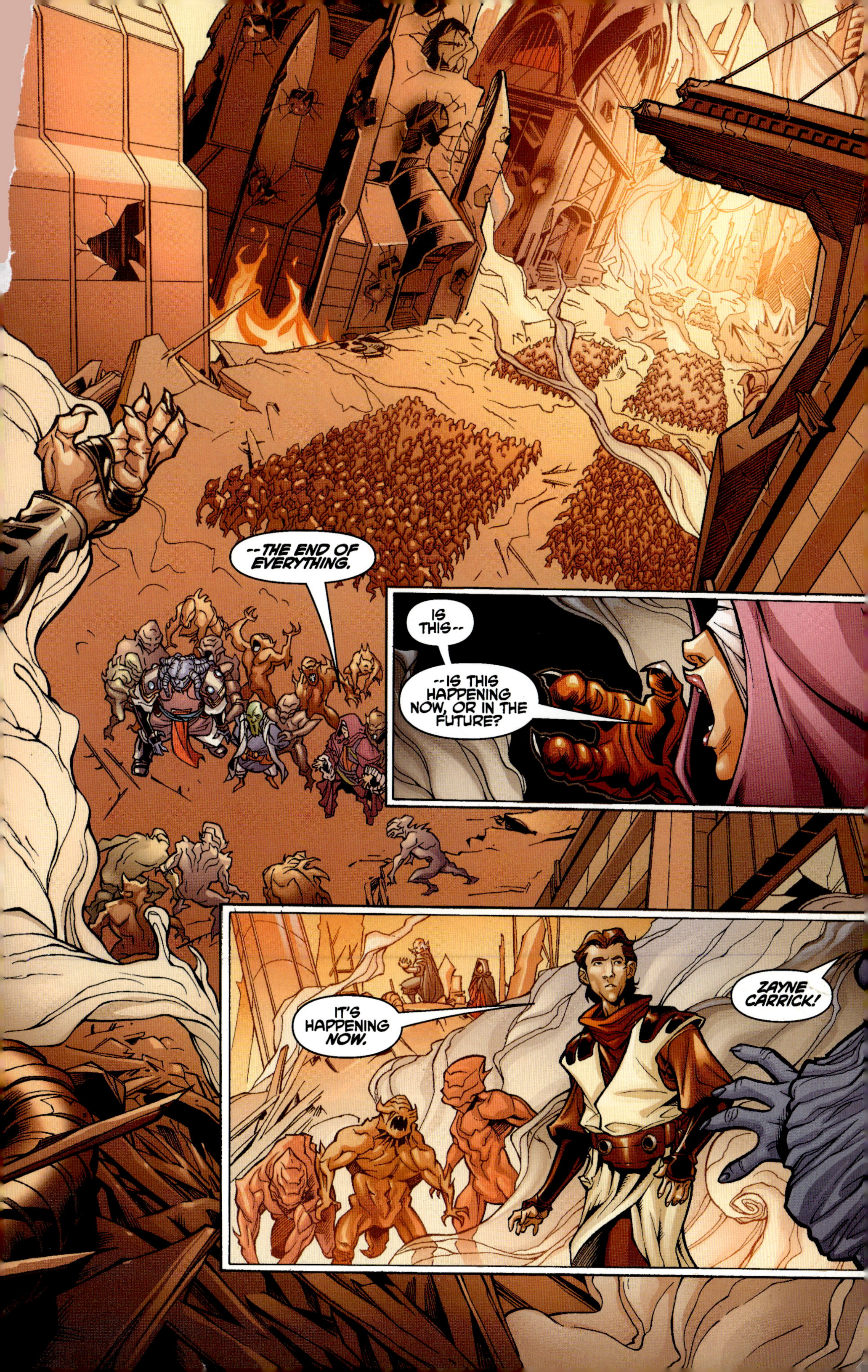
--THE END OF EVERYTHING.
IS THIS--
--IS THIS HAPPENING NOW, OR IN THE FUTURE?
IT'S HAPPENING NOW.
ZAYNE CARRICK!

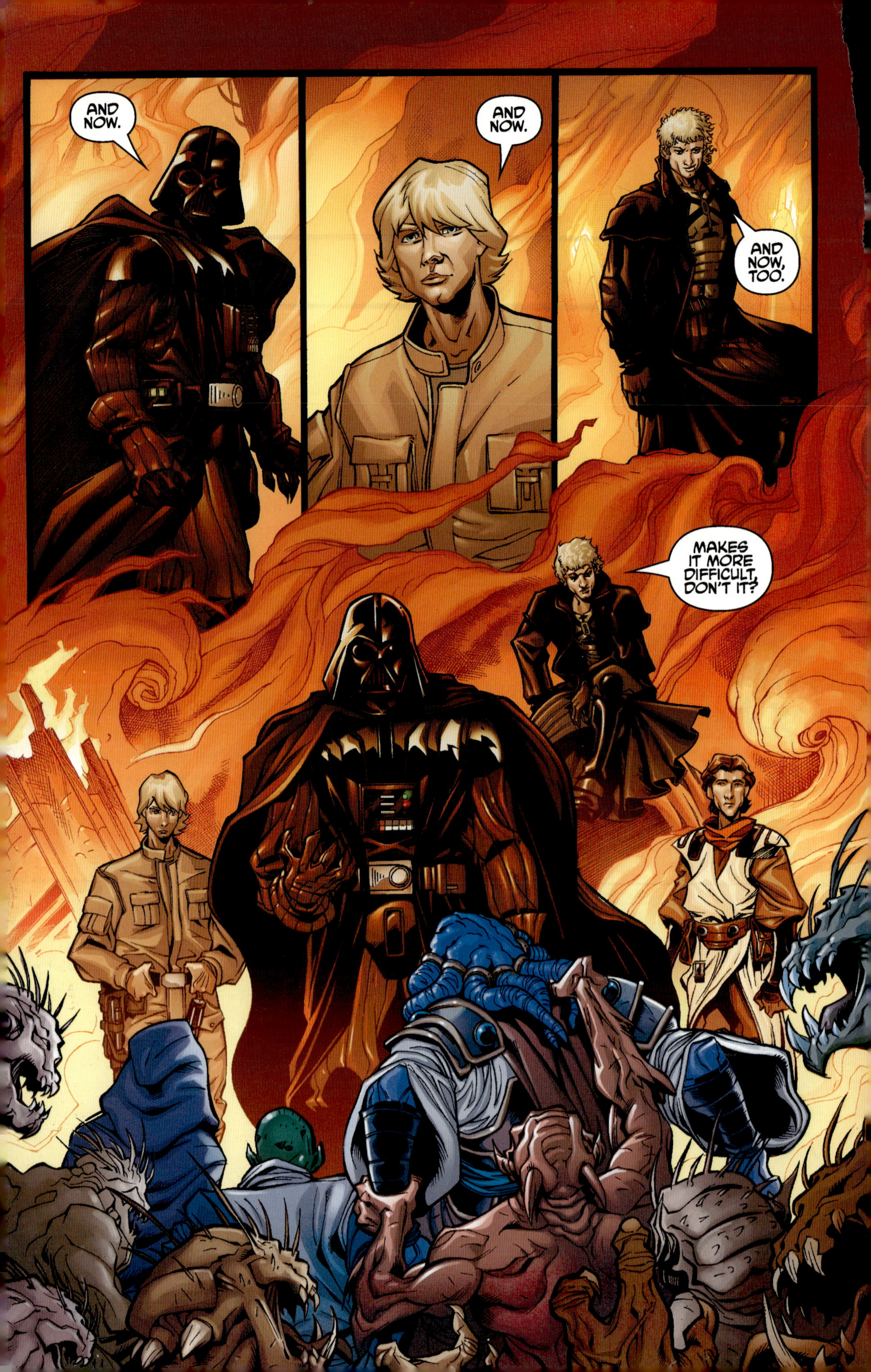
AND NOW.
AND NOW.
AND NOW, TOO.
MAKES IT MORE DIFFICULT, DON'T IT?

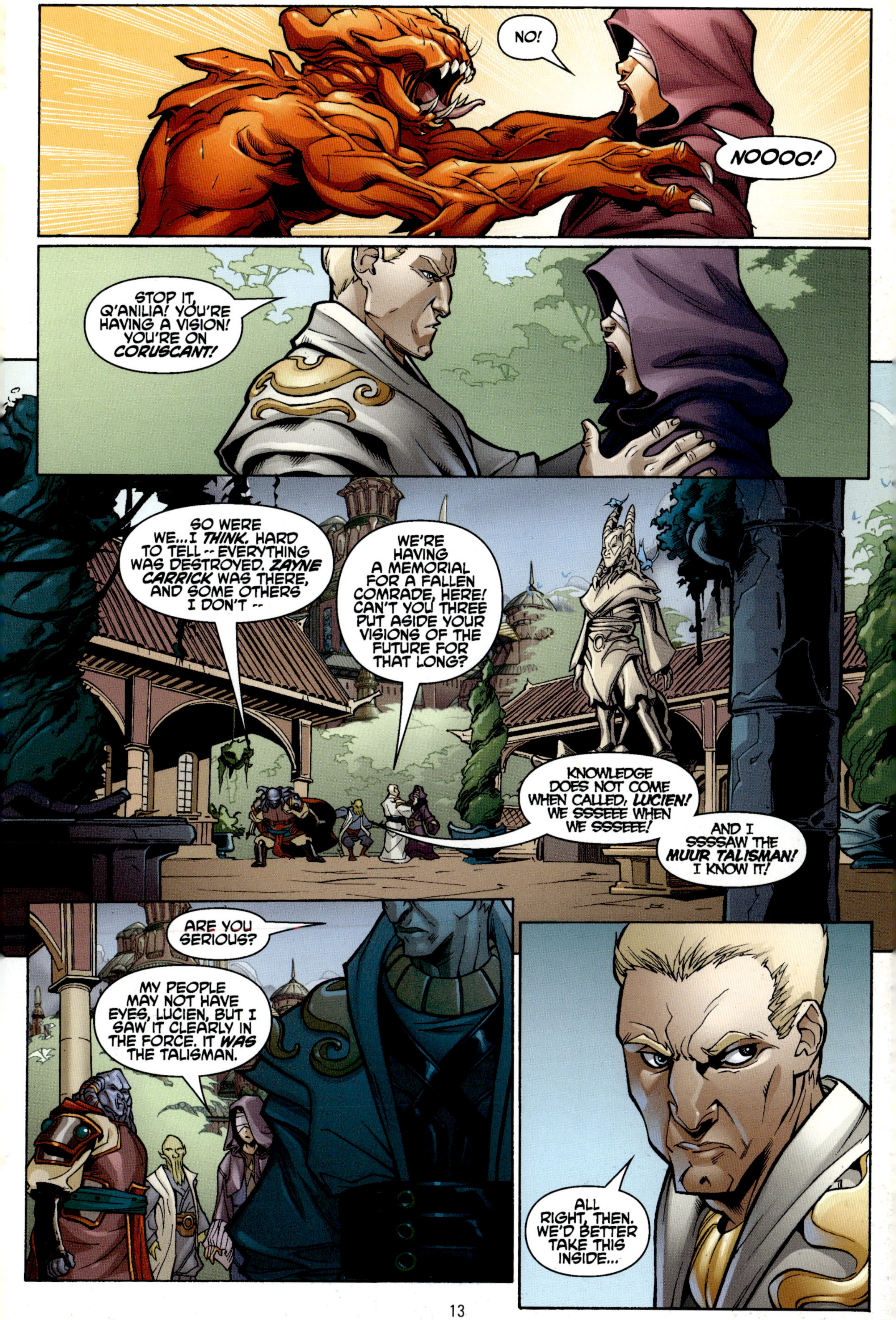
NO!
NOOOO!
STOP IT, Q'ANILIA! YOU'RE HAVING A VISION! YOU'RE ON CORUSCANT!
SO WERE WE...I THINK. HARD TO TELL -- EVERYTHING WAS DESTROYED. ZAYNE CARRICK WAS THERE, AND SOME OTHERS I DON'T --
WE'RE HAVING A MEMORIAL FOR A FALLEN COMRADE, HERE! CAN'T YOU THREE PUT ASIDE YOUR VISIONS OF THE FUTURE FOR THAT LONG?
KNOWLEDGE DOES NOT COME WHEN CALLED, LUCIEN! WE SSSEEE WHEN WE SSSEEE!
AND I SSSSAW THE MUUR TALISMAN! I KNOW IT!
ARE YOU SERIOUS?
MY PEOPLE MAY NOT HAVE EYES, LUCIEN, BUT I SAW IT CLEARLY IN THE FORCE. IT WAS THE TALISMAN.
ALL RIGHT, THEN. WE'D BETTER TAKE THIS INSIDE...

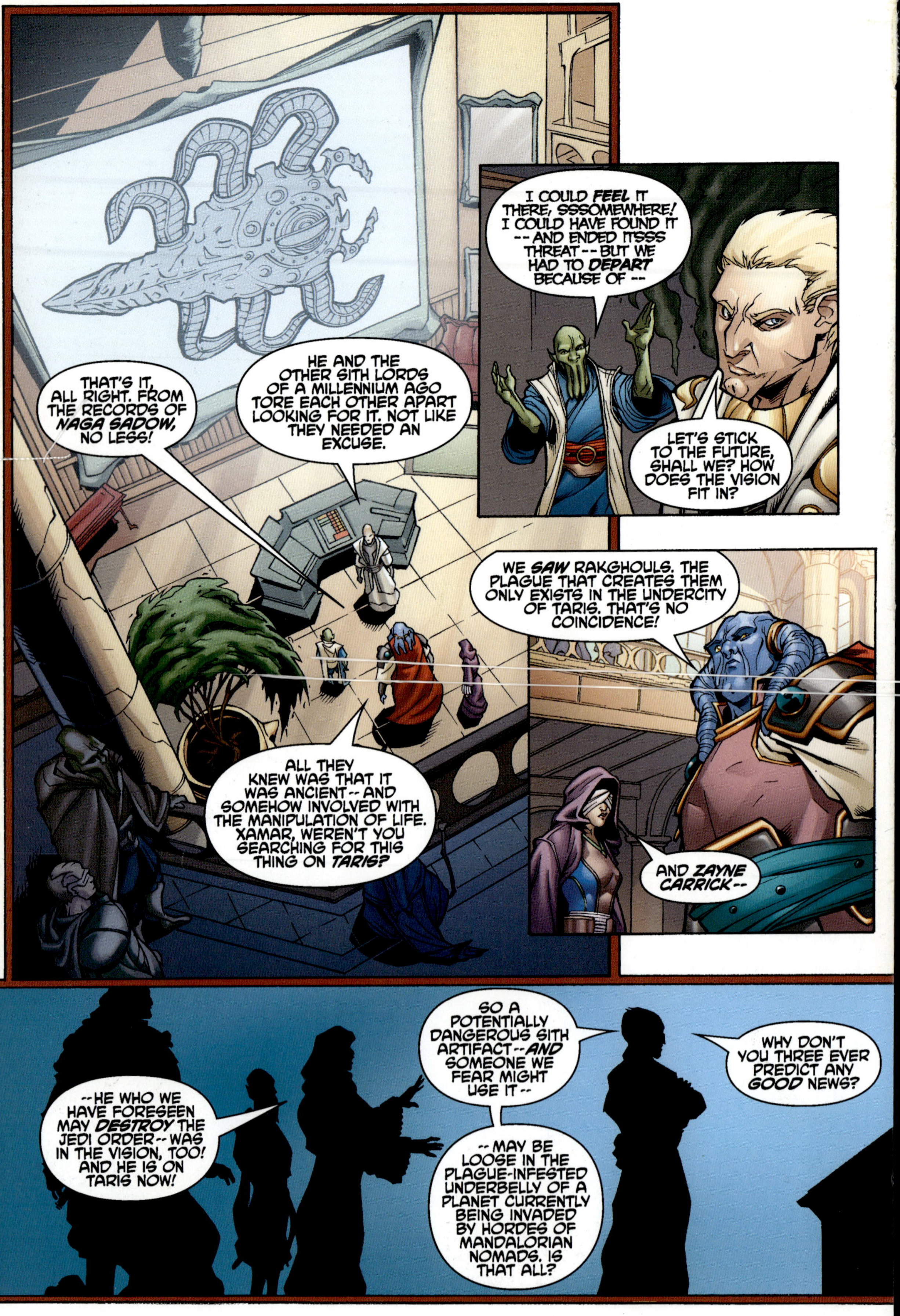

I COULD FEEL IT THERE, SSSOMEWHERE! I COULD HAVE FOUND IT -- AND ENDED ITSSS THREAT -- BUT WE HAD TO DEPART BECAUSE OF --
LET'S STICK TO THE FUTURE, SHALL WE? HOW DOES THE VISION FIT IN?
THAT'S IT, ALL RIGHT. FROM THE RECORDS OF NAGA SADOW, NO LESS!
HE AND THE OTHER SITH LORDS OF A MILLENNIUM AGO TORE EACH OTHER APART LOOKING FOR IT. NOT LIKE THEY NEEDED AN EXCUSE.
ALL THEY KNEW WAS THAT IT WAS ANCIENT -- AND SOMEHOW INVOLVED WITH THE MANIPULATION OF LIFE. XAMAR, WEREN'T YOU SEARCHING FOR THIS THING ON TARIS?
WE SAW RAKGHOULS. THE PLAGUE THAT CREATES THEM ONLY EXISTS IN THE UNDERCITY OF TARIS. THAT'S NO COINCIDENCE!
AND ZAYNE CARRICK --
--HE WHO WE HAVE FORESEEN MAY DESTROY THE JEDI ORDER -- WAS IN THE VISION, TOO! AND HE IS ON TARIS NOW!
SO A POTENTIALLY DANGEROUS SITH ARTIFACT -- AND SOMEONE WE FEAR MIGHT USE IT --
-- MAY BE LOOSE IN THE PLAGUE-INFESTED UNDERBELLY OF A PLANET CURRENTLY BEING INVADED BY HORDES OF MANDALORIAN NOMADS. IS THAT ALL?
WHY DON'T YOU THREE EVER PREDICT ANY GOOD NEWS?

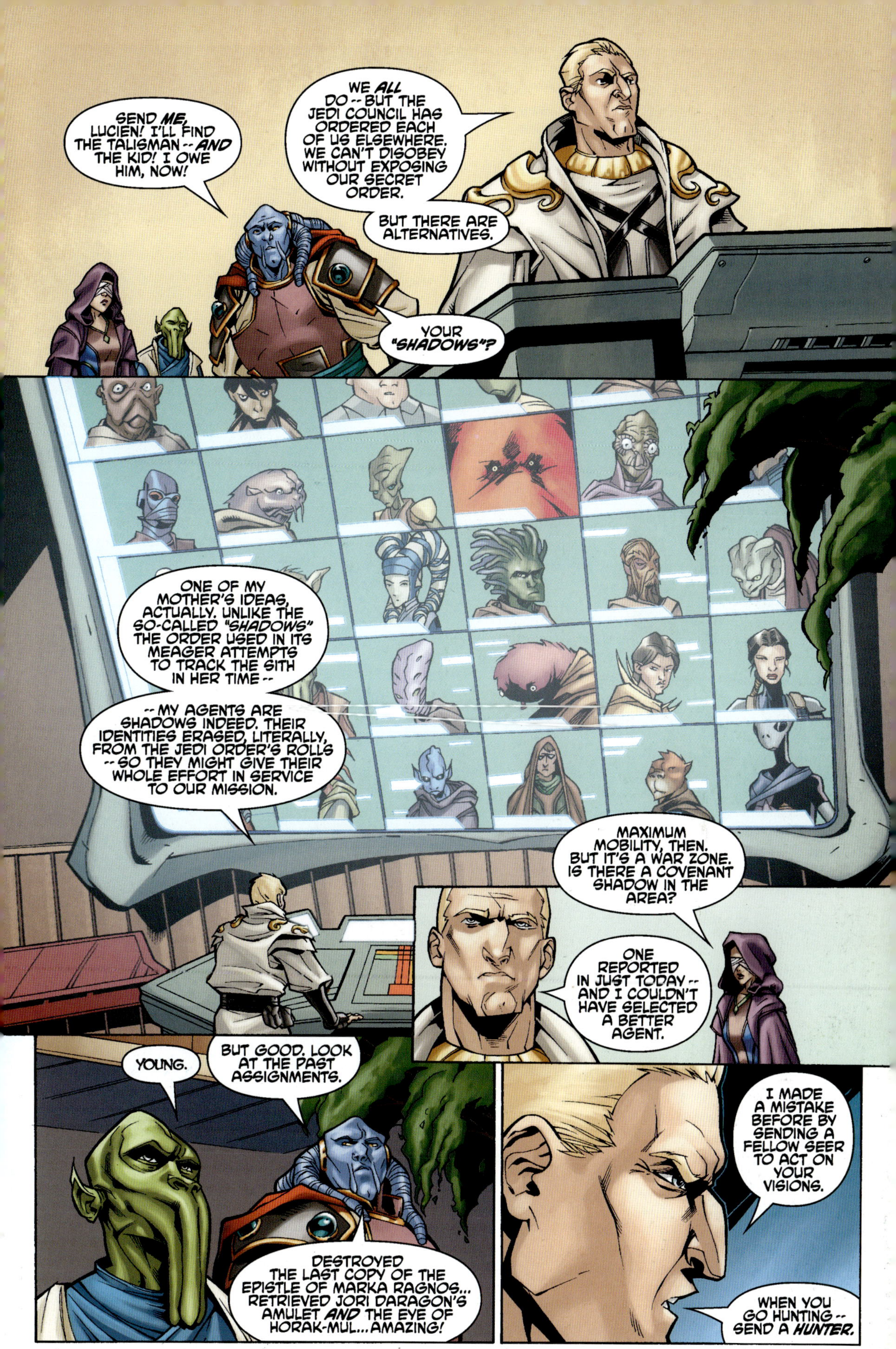

SEND *ME*, LUCIEN! I'LL FIND THE TALISMAN -- *AND* THE KID! I OWE HIM, NOW!
WE *ALL* DO -- BUT THE JEDI COUNCIL HAS ORDERED EACH OF US ELSEWHERE. WE CAN'T DISOBEY WITHOUT EXPOSING OUR SECRET ORDER.
BUT THERE ARE ALTERNATIVES.
YOUR *"SHADOWS"*?
ONE OF MY MOTHER'S IDEAS, ACTUALLY. UNLIKE THE SO-CALLED *"SHADOWS"* THE ORDER USED IN ITS MEAGER ATTEMPTS TO TRACK THE SITH IN HER TIME --
-- MY AGENTS ARE SHADOWS INDEED. THEIR IDENTITIES ERASED, LITERALLY, FROM THE JEDI ORDER'S ROLLS -- SO THEY MIGHT GIVE THEIR WHOLE EFFORT IN SERVICE TO OUR MISSION.
MAXIMUM MOBILITY, THEN. BUT IT'S A WAR ZONE. IS THERE A COVENANT SHADOW IN THE AREA?
ONE REPORTED IN JUST TODAY -- AND I COULDN'T HAVE SELECTED A BETTER AGENT.
YOUNG.
BUT GOOD. LOOK AT THE PAST ASSIGNMENTS.
DESTROYED THE LAST COPY OF THE EPISTLE OF MARKA RAGNOS... RETRIEVED JORI DARAGON'S AMULET *AND* THE EYE OF HORAK-MUL... AMAZING!
I MADE A MISTAKE BEFORE BY SENDING A FELLOW SEER TO ACT ON YOUR VISIONS.
WHEN YOU GO HUNTING -- SEND A *HUNTER.*

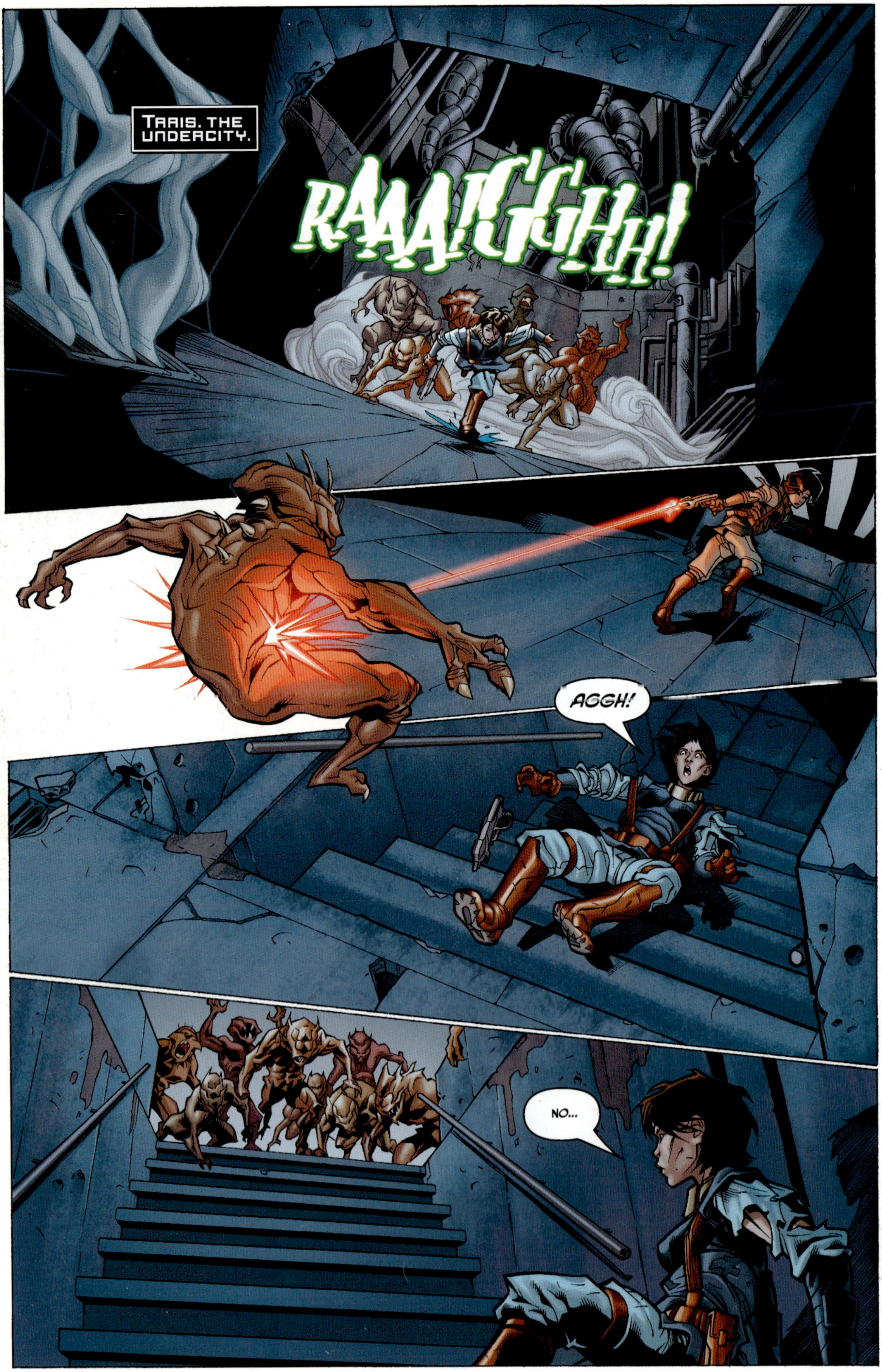
TARIS. THE UNDERCITY.
RAAAHGHH!
AGGH!
NO...

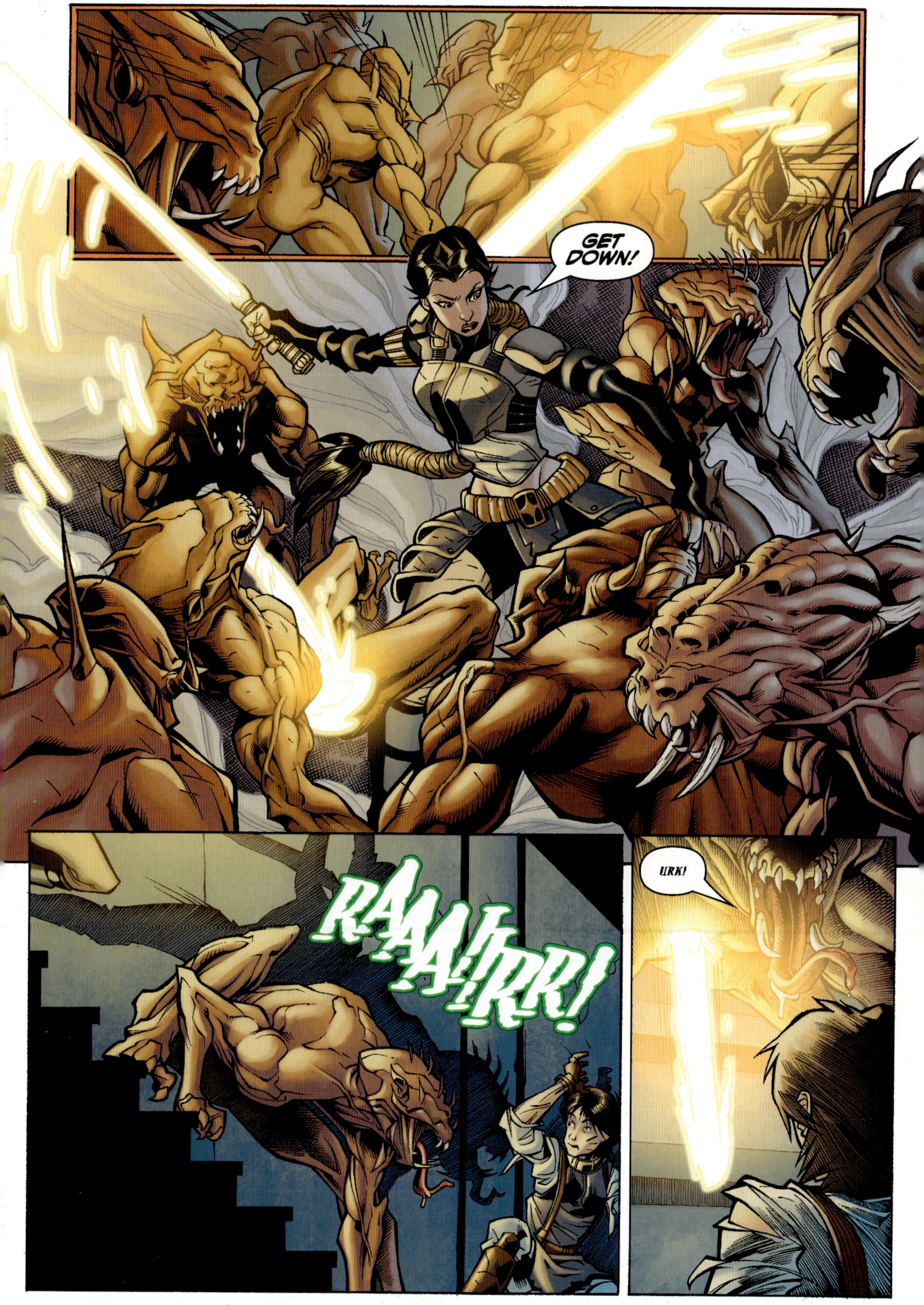
GET DOWN!
RAAAARR!
URK!

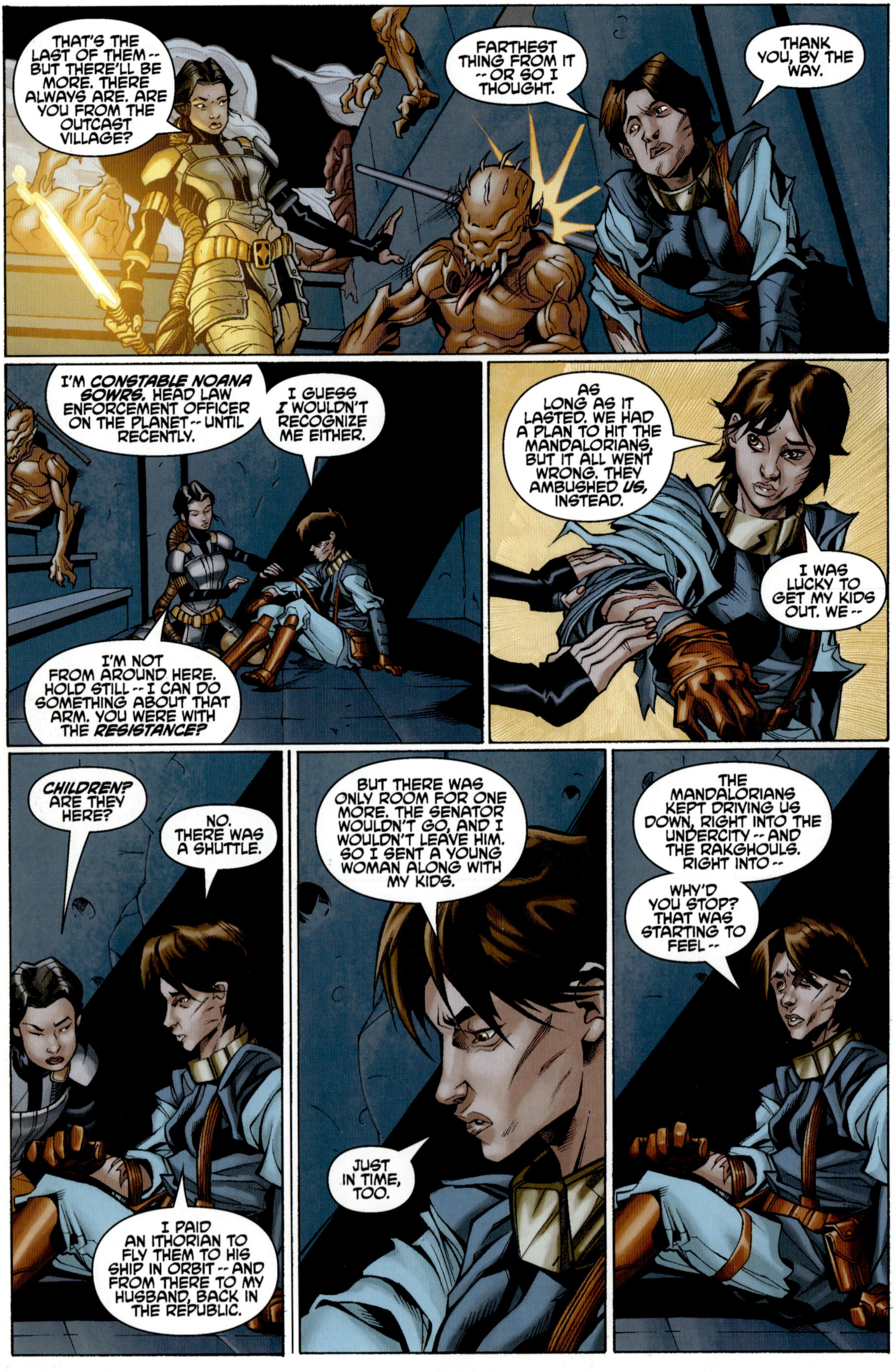
THAT'S THE LAST OF THEM -- BUT THERE'LL BE MORE. THERE ALWAYS ARE. ARE YOU FROM THE OUTCAST VILLAGE?
FARTHEST THING FROM IT -- OR SO I THOUGHT.
THANK YOU, BY THE WAY.
I'M CONSTABLE NOANA SOWRS. HEAD LAW ENFORCEMENT OFFICER ON THE PLANET -- UNTIL RECENTLY.
I GUESS I WOULDN'T RECOGNIZE ME EITHER.
I'M NOT FROM AROUND HERE. HOLD STILL -- I CAN DO SOMETHING ABOUT THAT ARM. YOU WERE WITH THE RESISTANCE?
AS LONG AS IT LASTED. WE HAD A PLAN TO HIT THE MANDALORIANS, BUT IT ALL WENT WRONG. THEY AMBUSHED US, INSTEAD.
I WAS LUCKY TO GET MY KIDS OUT. WE --
CHILDREN? ARE THEY HERE?
NO. THERE WAS A SHUTTLE.
I PAID AN ITHORIAN TO FLY THEM TO HIS SHIP IN ORBIT -- AND FROM THERE TO MY HUSBAND, BACK IN THE REPUBLIC.
BUT THERE WAS ONLY ROOM FOR ONE MORE. THE SENATOR WOULDN'T GO, AND I WOULDN'T LEAVE HIM. SO I SENT A YOUNG WOMAN ALONG WITH MY KIDS.
JUST IN TIME, TOO.
THE MANDALORIANS KEPT DRIVING US DOWN, RIGHT INTO THE UNDERCITY -- AND THE RAKGHOULS. RIGHT INTO --
WHY'D YOU STOP? THAT WAS STARTING TO FEEL --

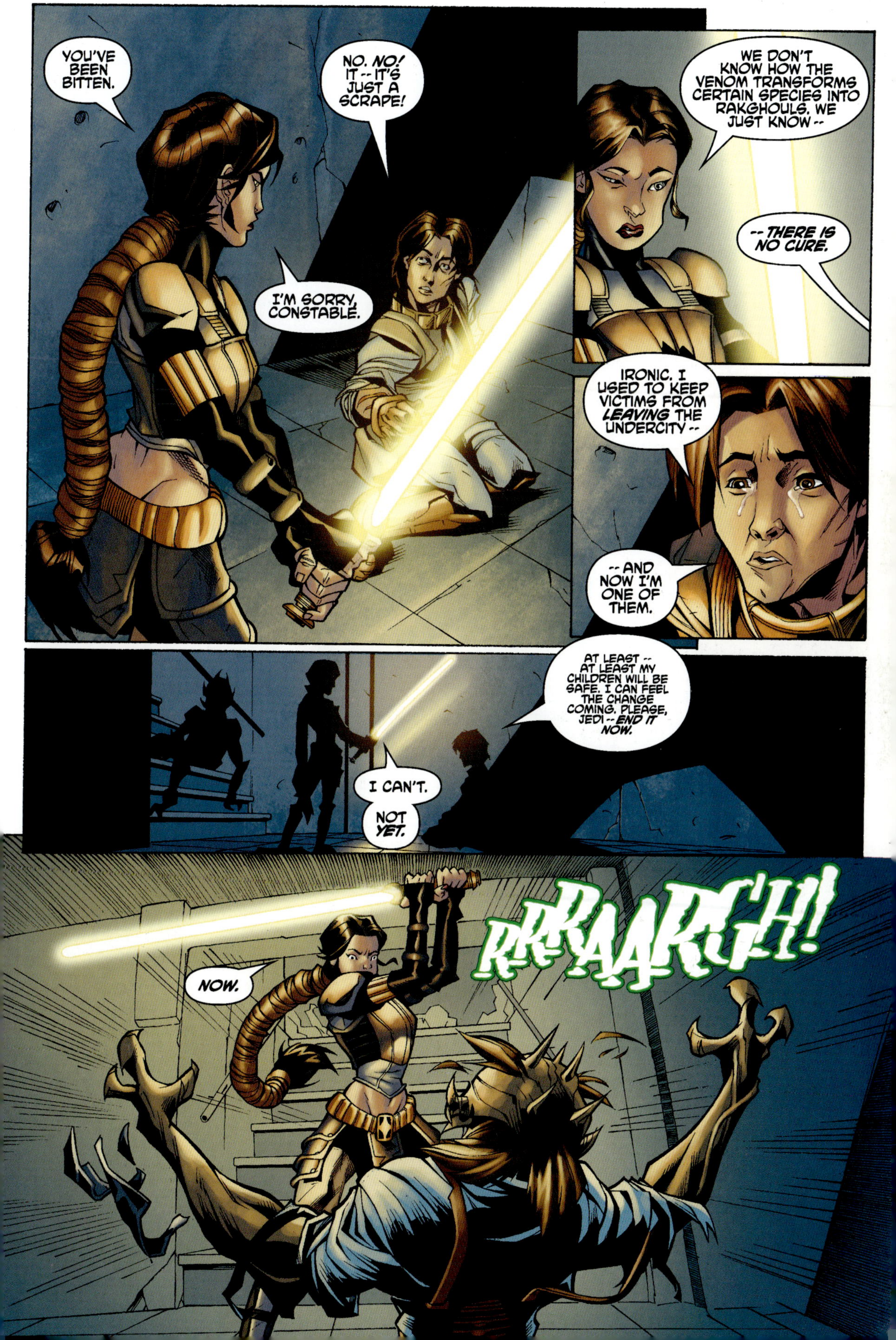
YOU'VE BEEN BITTEN.
NO. *NO!* IT -- IT'S JUST A SCRAPE!
I'M SORRY, CONSTABLE.
WE DON'T KNOW HOW THE VENOM TRANSFORMS CERTAIN SPECIES INTO RAKGHOULS. WE JUST KNOW --
-- *THERE IS NO CURE.*
IRONIC. I USED TO KEEP VICTIMS FROM *LEAVING* THE UNDERCITY --
-- AND NOW I'M ONE OF THEM.
AT LEAST -- AT LEAST MY CHILDREN WILL BE SAFE. I CAN FEEL THE CHANGE COMING. PLEASE, JEDI -- *END IT NOW.*
I CAN'T.
NOT *YET.*
NOW.
RRRAAARGH!

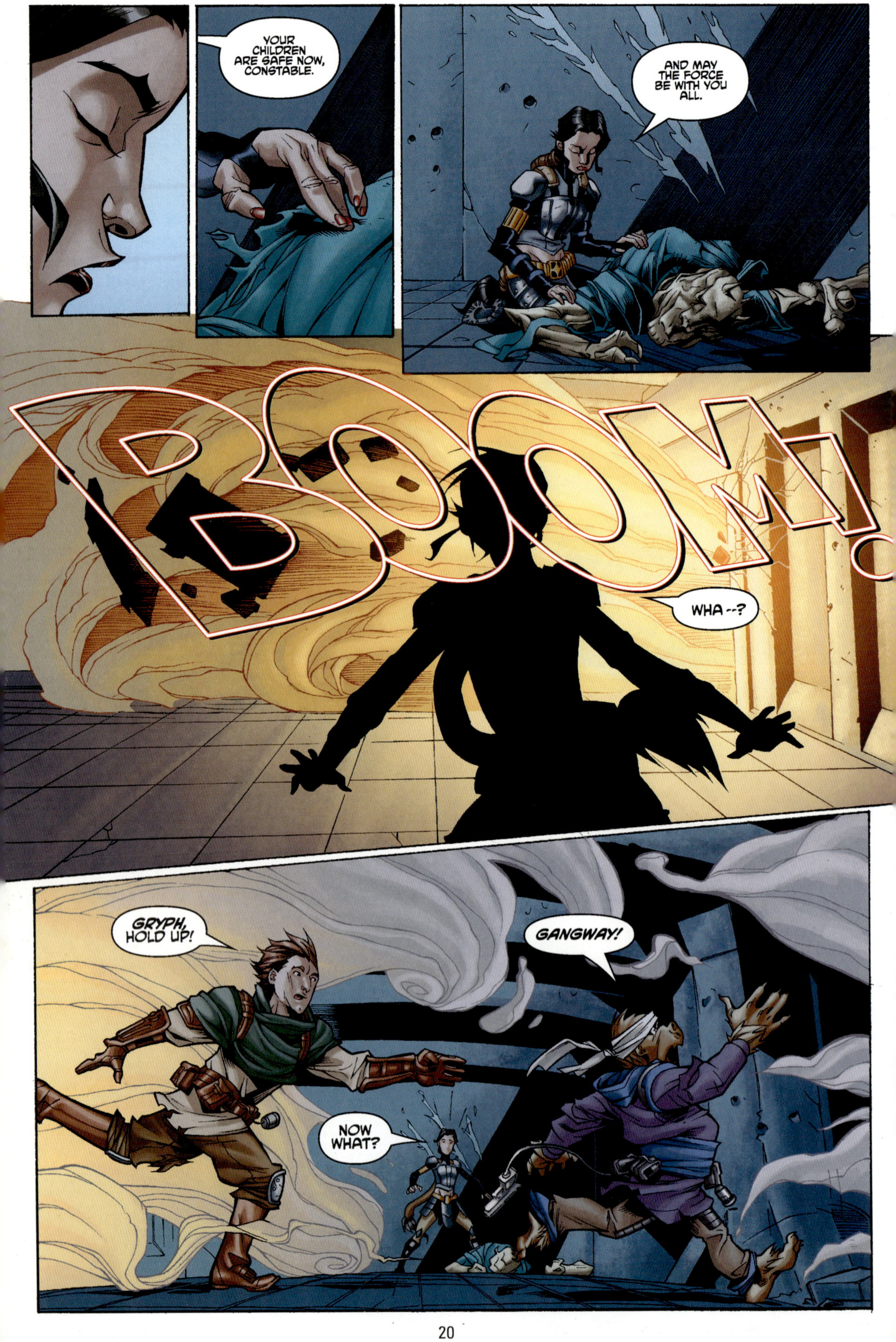

YOUR CHILDREN ARE SAFE NOW, CONSTABLE.
AND MAY THE FORCE BE WITH YOU ALL.
BOOM!
WHA --?
GRYPH, HOLD UP!
GANGWAY!
NOW WHAT?

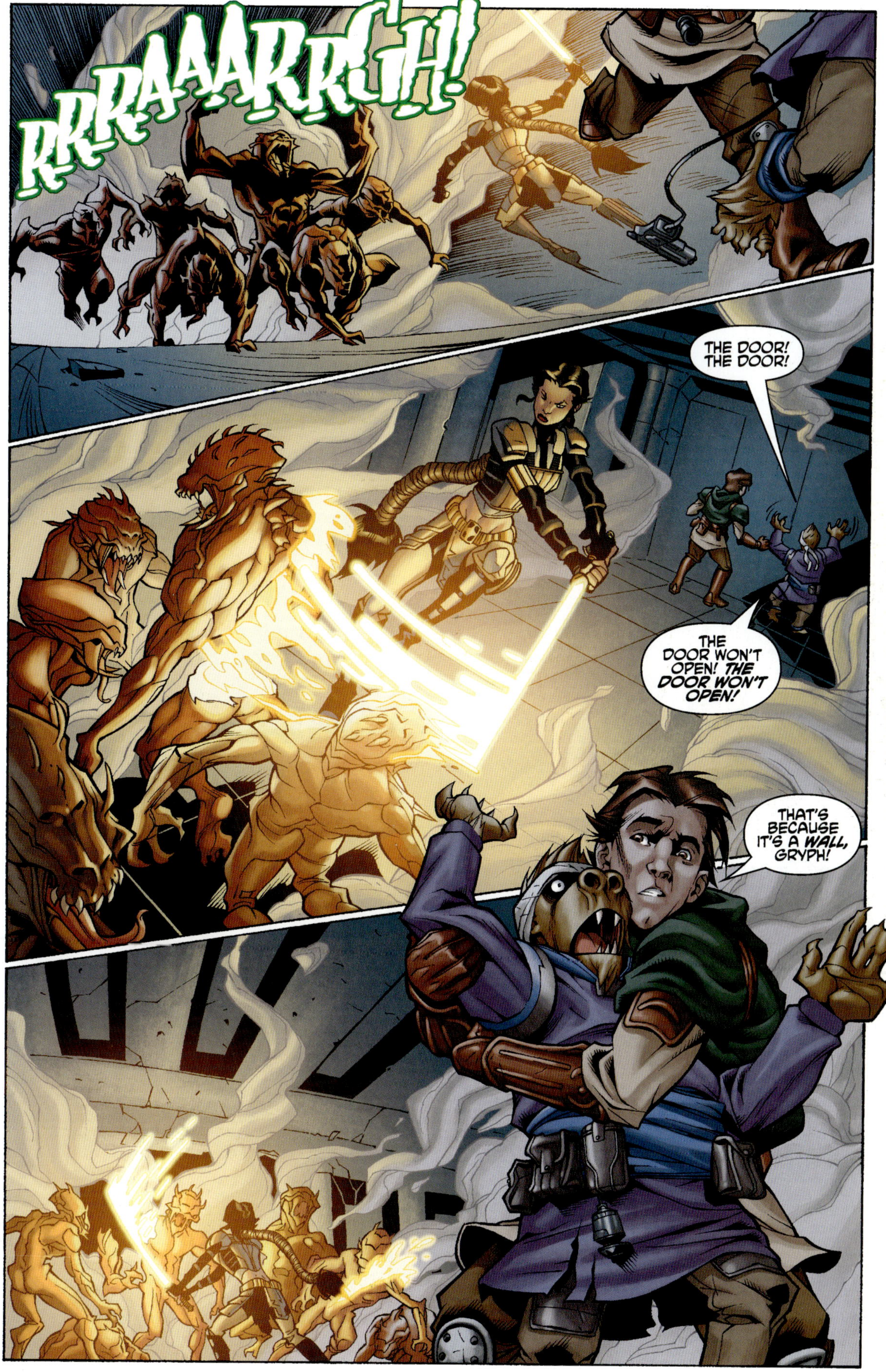
RRRAAARRGH!
THE DOOR! THE DOOR!
THE DOOR WON'T OPEN! *THE DOOR WON'T OPEN!*
THAT'S BECAUSE IT'S A *WALL*, GRYPH!

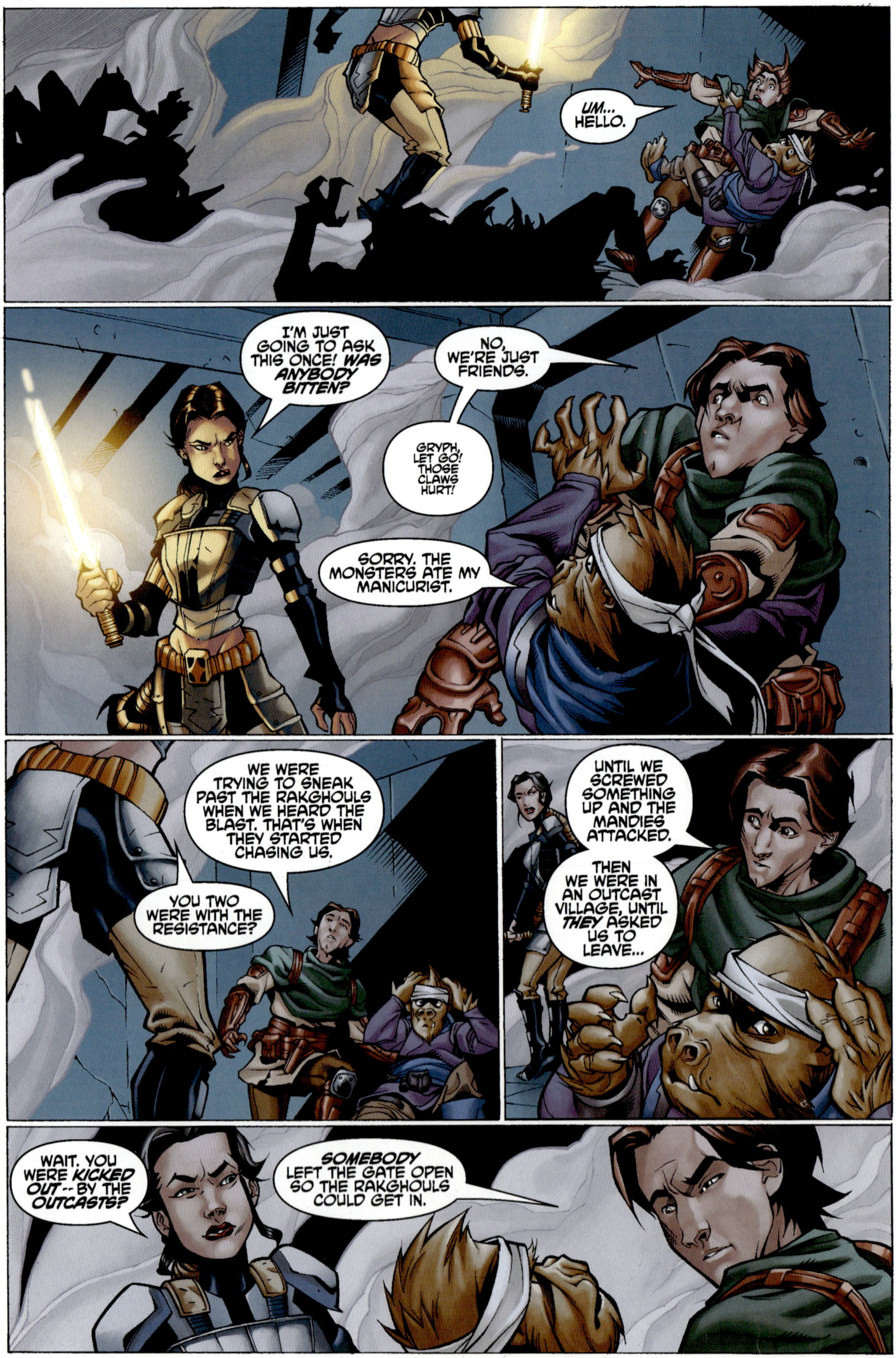
UM... HELLO.
I'M JUST GOING TO ASK THIS ONCE! WAS ANYBODY BITTEN?
NO, WE'RE JUST FRIENDS.
GRYPH, LET GO! THOSE CLAWS HURT!
SORRY. THE MONSTERS ATE MY MANICURIST.
WE WERE TRYING TO SNEAK PAST THE RAKGHOULS WHEN WE HEARD THE BLAST. THAT'S WHEN THEY STARTED CHASING US.
YOU TWO WERE WITH THE RESISTANCE?
UNTIL WE SCREWED SOMETHING UP AND THE MANDIES ATTACKED.
THEN WE WERE IN AN OUTCAST VILLAGE, UNTIL THEY ASKED US TO LEAVE...
WAIT. YOU WERE KICKED OUT-- BY THE OUTCASTS?
SOMEBODY LEFT THE GATE OPEN SO THE RAKGHOULS COULD GET IN.

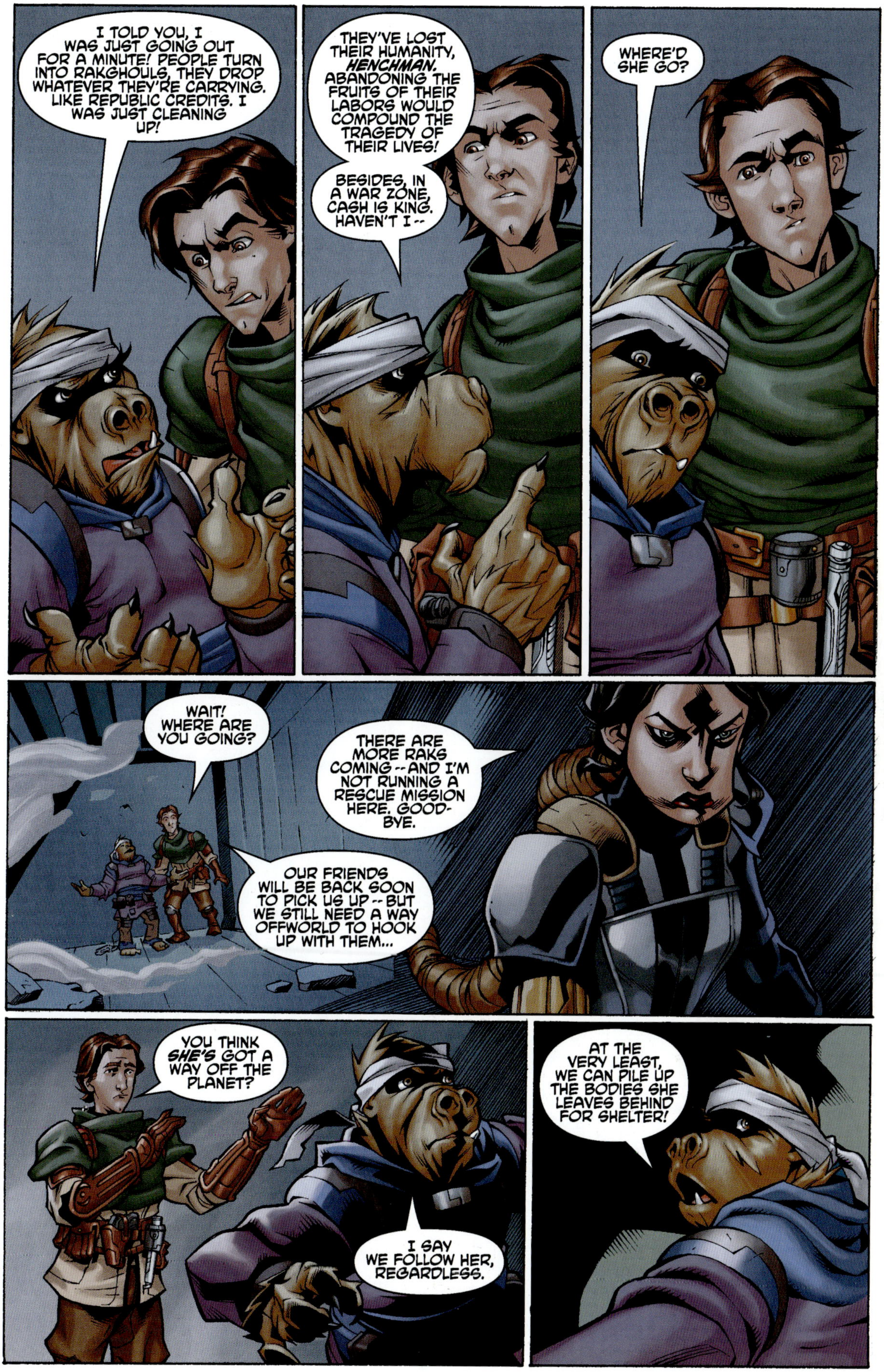
I TOLD YOU, I WAS JUST GOING OUT FOR A MINUTE! PEOPLE TURN INTO RAKGHOULS, THEY DROP WHATEVER THEY'RE CARRYING. LIKE REPUBLIC CREDITS. I WAS JUST CLEANING UP!
THEY'VE LOST THEIR HUMANITY, *HENCHMAN*. ABANDONING THE FRUITS OF THEIR LABORS WOULD COMPOUND THE TRAGEDY OF THEIR LIVES!
BESIDES, IN A WAR ZONE, CASH IS KING. HAVEN'T I --
WHERE'D SHE GO?
WAIT! WHERE ARE YOU GOING?
THERE ARE MORE RAKS COMING -- AND I'M NOT RUNNING A RESCUE MISSION HERE. GOOD-BYE.
OUR FRIENDS WILL BE BACK SOON TO PICK US UP -- BUT WE STILL NEED A WAY OFFWORLD TO HOOK UP WITH THEM...
YOU THINK *SHE'S* GOT A WAY OFF THE PLANET?
I SAY WE FOLLOW HER, REGARDLESS.
AT THE VERY LEAST, WE CAN PILE UP THE BODIES SHE LEAVES BEHIND FOR SHELTER!

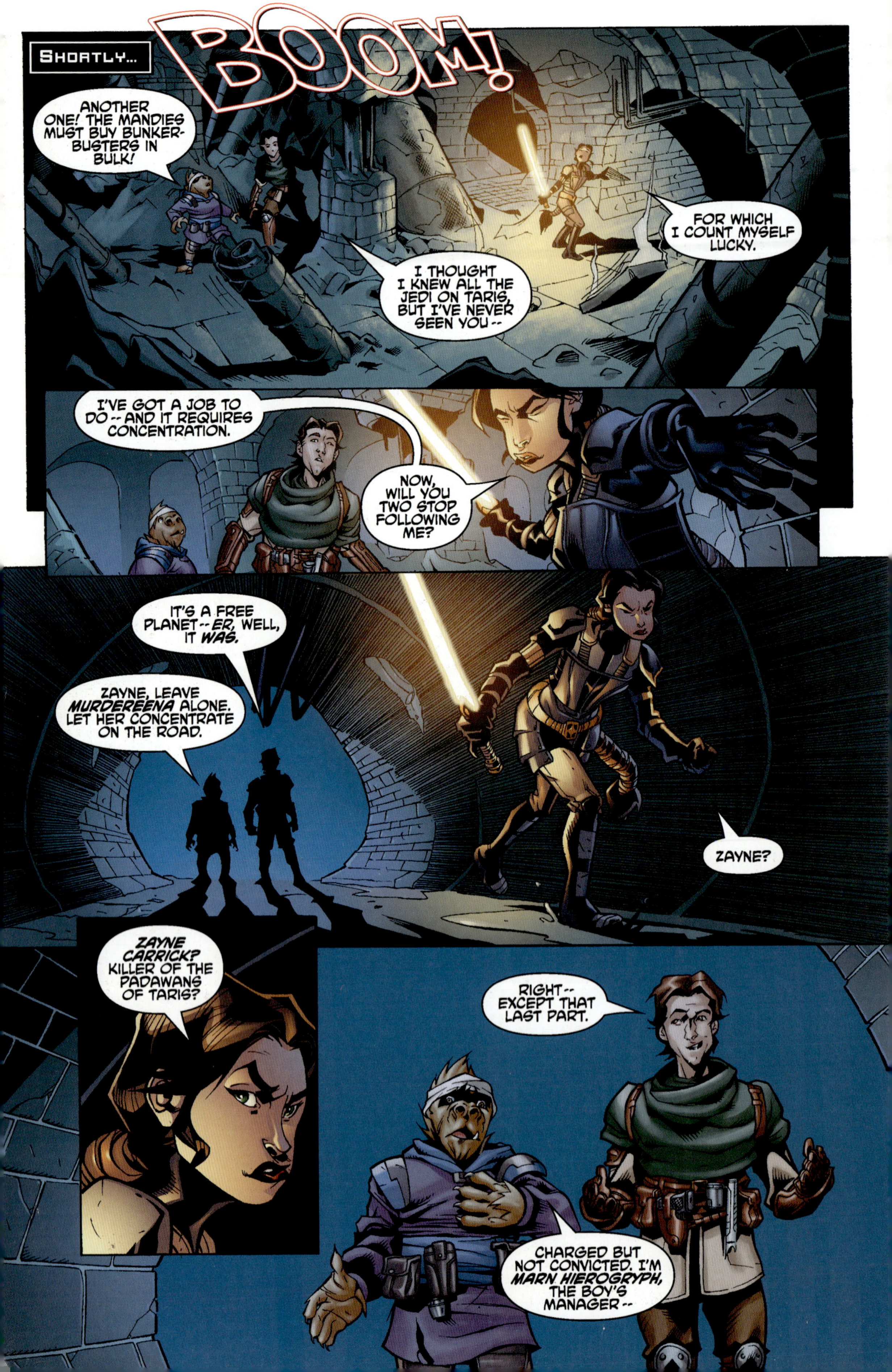
SHORTLY...
BOOM!
ANOTHER ONE! THE MANDIES MUST BUY BUNKER-BUSTERS IN BULK!
I THOUGHT I KNEW ALL THE JEDI ON TARIS, BUT I'VE NEVER SEEN YOU --
FOR WHICH I COUNT MYSELF LUCKY.
I'VE GOT A JOB TO DO -- AND IT REQUIRES CONCENTRATION.
NOW, WILL YOU TWO STOP FOLLOWING ME?
IT'S A FREE PLANET -- *ER*, WELL, IT *WAS*.
ZAYNE, LEAVE *MURDEREENA* ALONE. LET HER CONCENTRATE ON THE ROAD.
ZAYNE?
ZAYNE CARRICK? KILLER OF THE PADAWANS OF TARIS?
RIGHT -- EXCEPT THAT LAST PART.
CHARGED BUT NOT CONVICTED. I'M *MARN HIEROGRYPH*, THE BOY'S MANAGER --

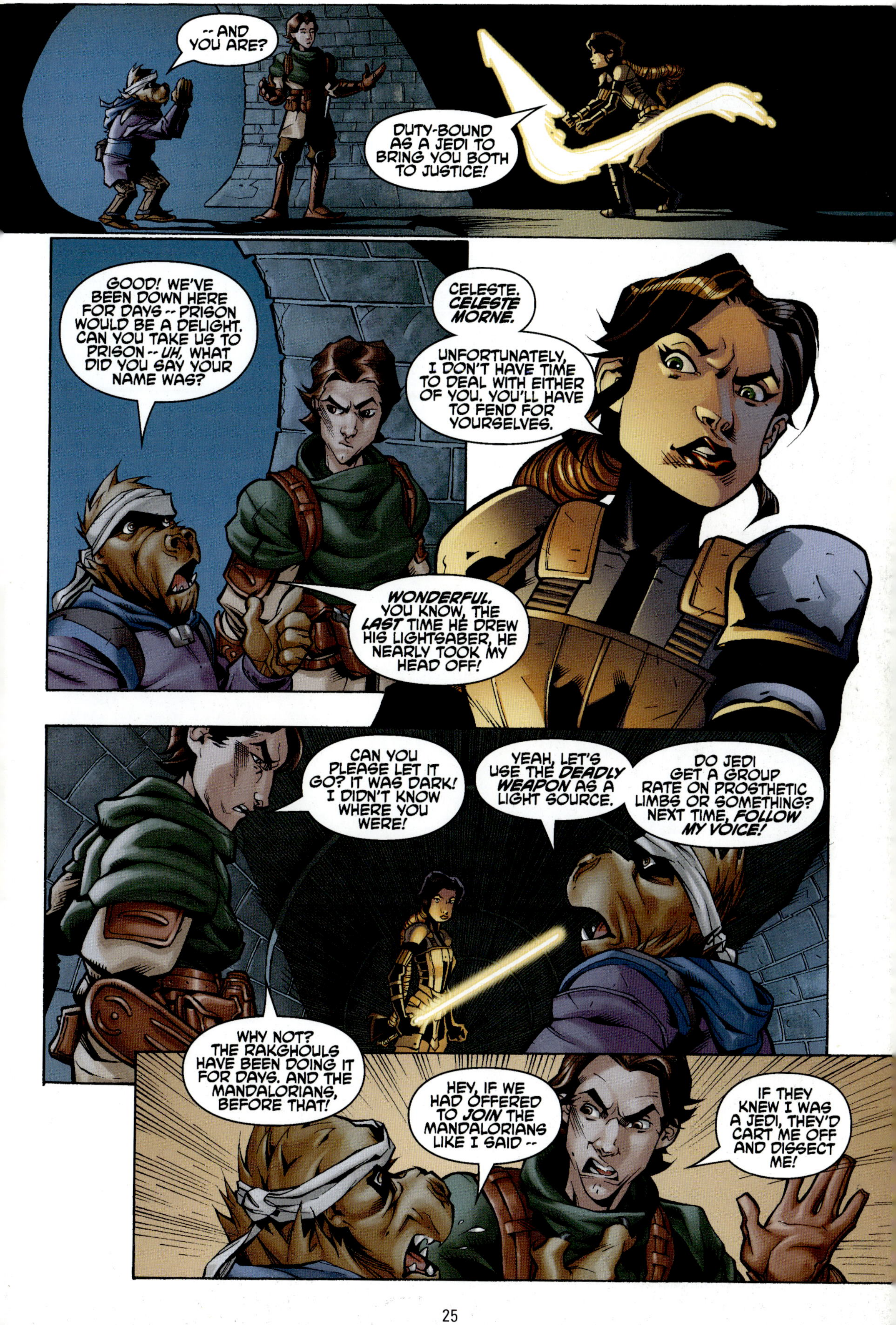
-- AND YOU ARE?
DUTY-BOUND AS A JEDI TO BRING YOU BOTH TO JUSTICE!
GOOD! WE'VE BEEN DOWN HERE FOR DAYS -- PRISON WOULD BE A DELIGHT. CAN YOU TAKE US TO PRISON -- *UH,* WHAT DID YOU SAY YOUR NAME WAS?
CELESTE. *CELESTE MORNE.*
UNFORTUNATELY, I DON'T HAVE TIME TO DEAL WITH EITHER OF YOU. YOU'LL HAVE TO FEND FOR YOURSELVES.
WONDERFUL. YOU KNOW, THE *LAST* TIME HE DREW HIS LIGHTSABER, HE NEARLY TOOK MY HEAD OFF!
CAN YOU PLEASE LET IT GO? IT WAS DARK! I DIDN'T KNOW WHERE YOU WERE!
YEAH, LET'S USE THE *DEADLY WEAPON* AS A LIGHT SOURCE.
DO JEDI GET A GROUP RATE ON PROSTHETIC LIMBS OR SOMETHING? NEXT TIME, *FOLLOW MY VOICE!*
WHY NOT? THE RAKGHOULS HAVE BEEN DOING IT FOR DAYS. AND THE MANDALORIANS, BEFORE THAT!
HEY, IF WE HAD OFFERED TO *JOIN* THE MANDALORIANS LIKE I SAID --
IF THEY KNEW I WAS A JEDI, THEY'D CART ME OFF AND DISSECT ME!

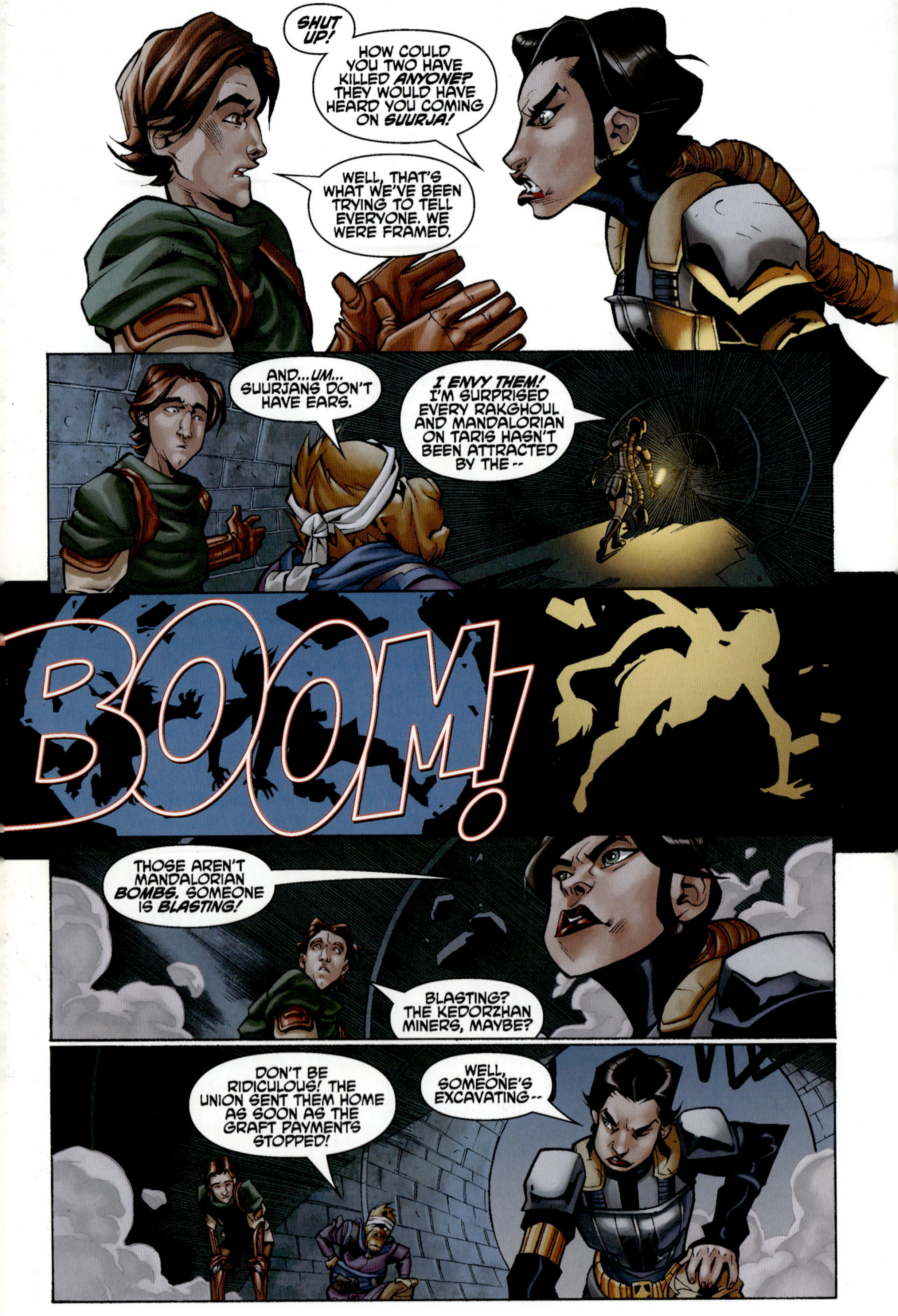
SHUT UP!
HOW COULD YOU TWO HAVE KILLED ANYONE? THEY WOULD HAVE HEARD YOU COMING ON SUURJA!
WELL, THAT'S WHAT WE'VE BEEN TRYING TO TELL EVERYONE. WE WERE FRAMED.
AND...UM... SUURJANS DON'T HAVE EARS.
I ENVY THEM! I'M SURPRISED EVERY RAKGHOUL AND MANDALORIAN ON TARIS HASN'T BEEN ATTRACTED BY THE--
BOOM!
THOSE AREN'T MANDALORIAN BOMBS. SOMEONE IS BLASTING!
BLASTING? THE KEDORZHAN MINERS, MAYBE?
DON'T BE RIDICULOUS! THE UNION SENT THEM HOME AS SOON AS THE GRAFT PAYMENTS STOPPED!
WELL, SOMEONE'S EXCAVATING--

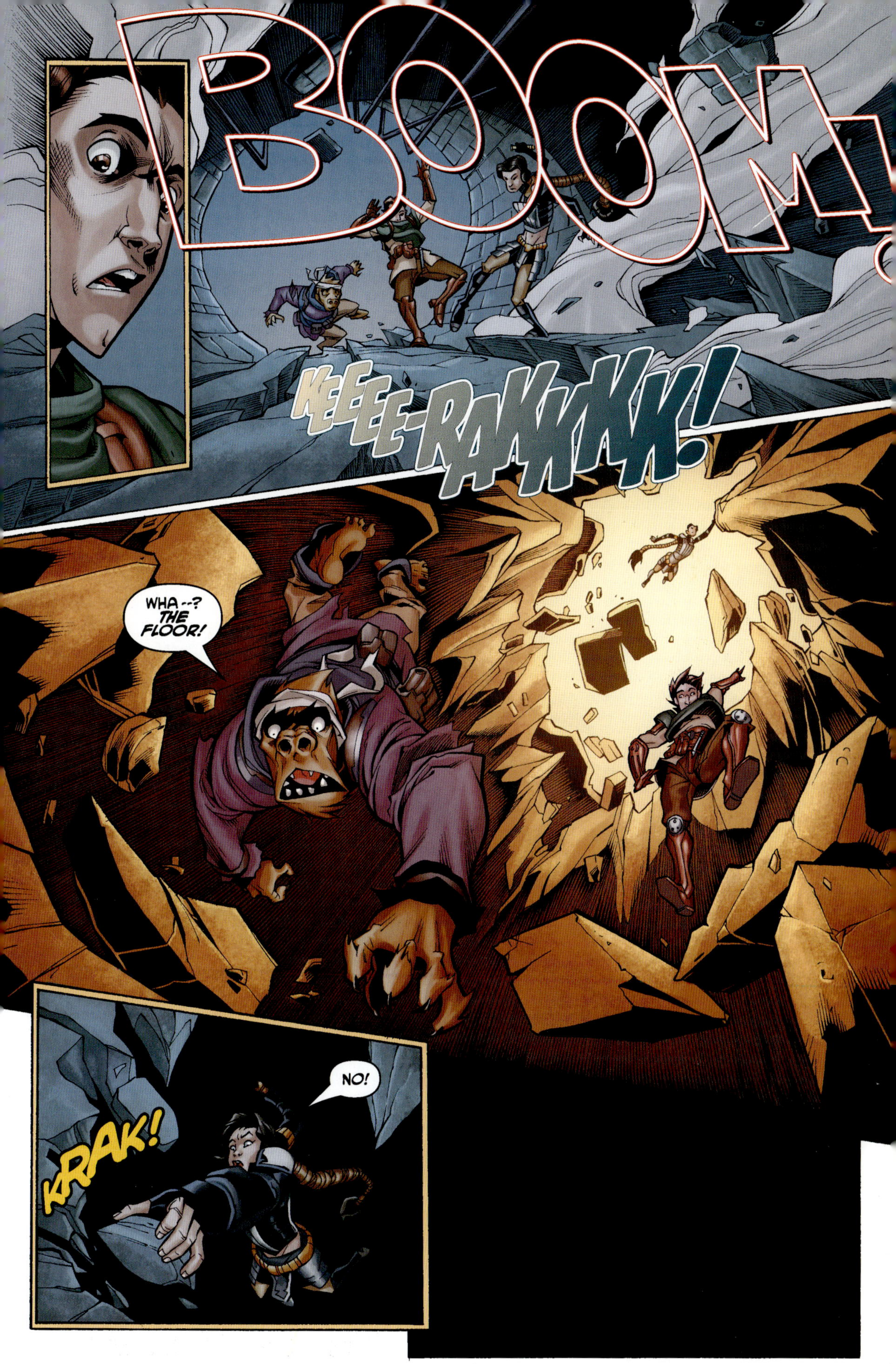
BOOM!
KEEEE-RAKKKKK!
WHA--? THE FLOOR!
KRAK!
NO!

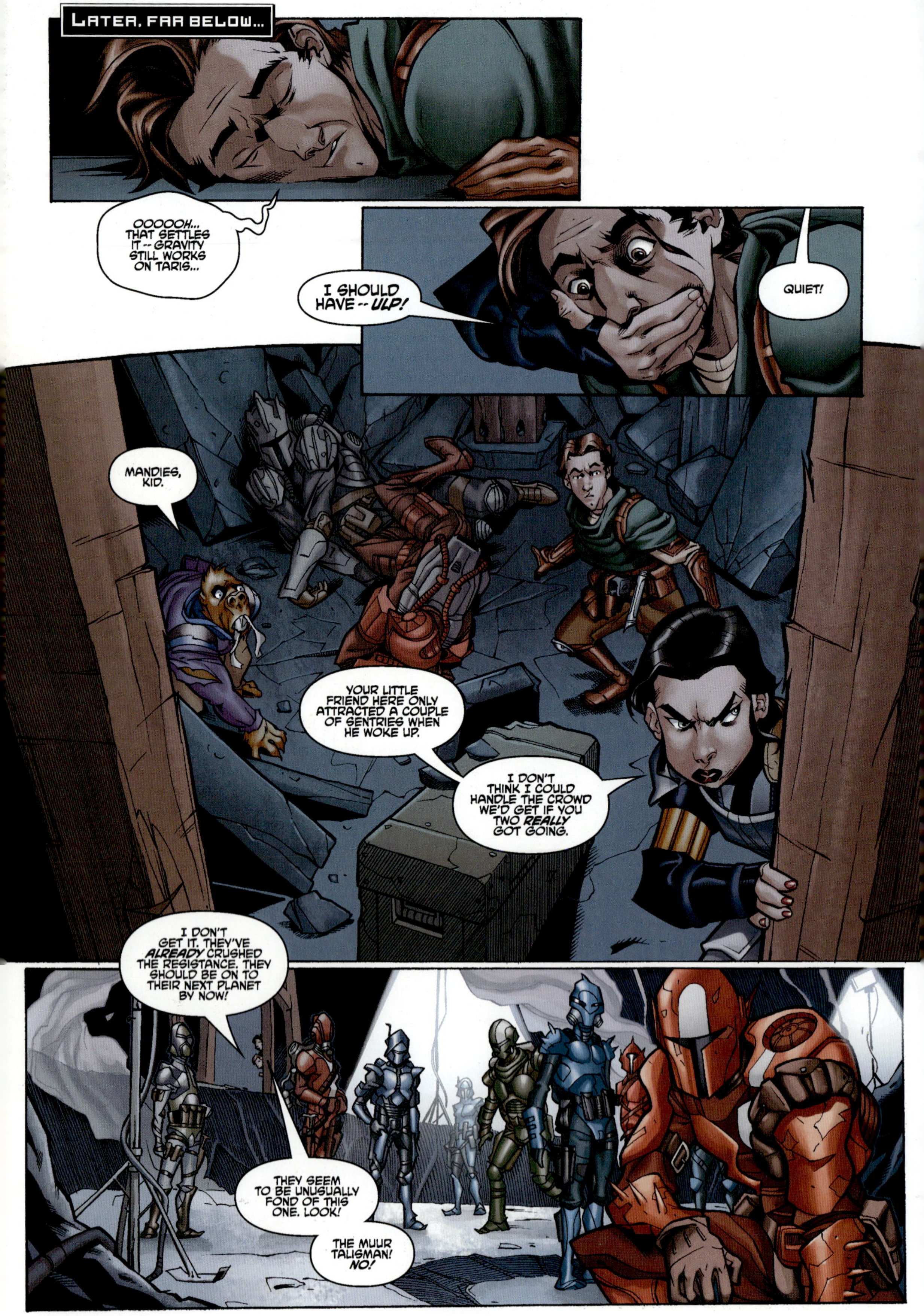
LATER, FAR BELOW...
OOOOOH... THAT SETTLES IT -- GRAVITY STILL WORKS ON TARIS...
I SHOULD HAVE -- ULP!
QUIET!
MANDIES, KID.
YOUR LITTLE FRIEND HERE ONLY ATTRACTED A COUPLE OF SENTRIES WHEN HE WOKE UP.
I DON'T THINK I COULD HANDLE THE CROWD WE'D GET IF YOU TWO REALLY GOT GOING.
I DON'T GET IT. THEY'VE ALREADY CRUSHED THE RESISTANCE. THEY SHOULD BE ON TO THEIR NEXT PLANET BY NOW!
THEY SEEM TO BE UNUSUALLY FOND OF THIS ONE. LOOK!
THE MUUR TALISMAN! NO!

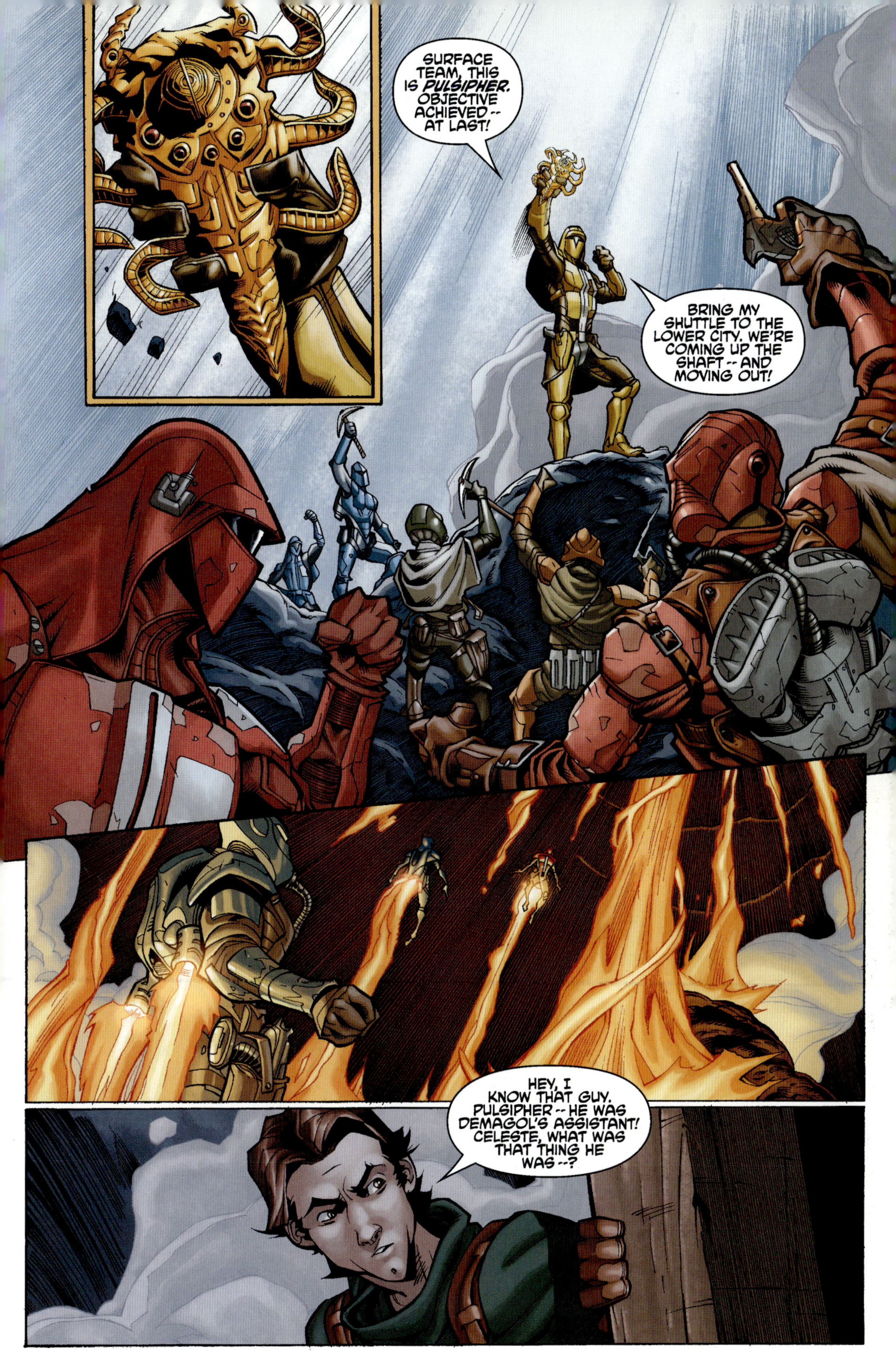
SURFACE TEAM, THIS IS PULSIPHER. OBJECTIVE ACHIEVED -- AT LAST!
BRING MY SHUTTLE TO THE LOWER CITY. WE'RE COMING UP THE SHAFT -- AND MOVING OUT!
HEY, I KNOW THAT GUY. PULSIPHER -- HE WAS DEMAGOL'S ASSISTANT! CELESTE, WHAT WAS THAT THING HE WAS --?

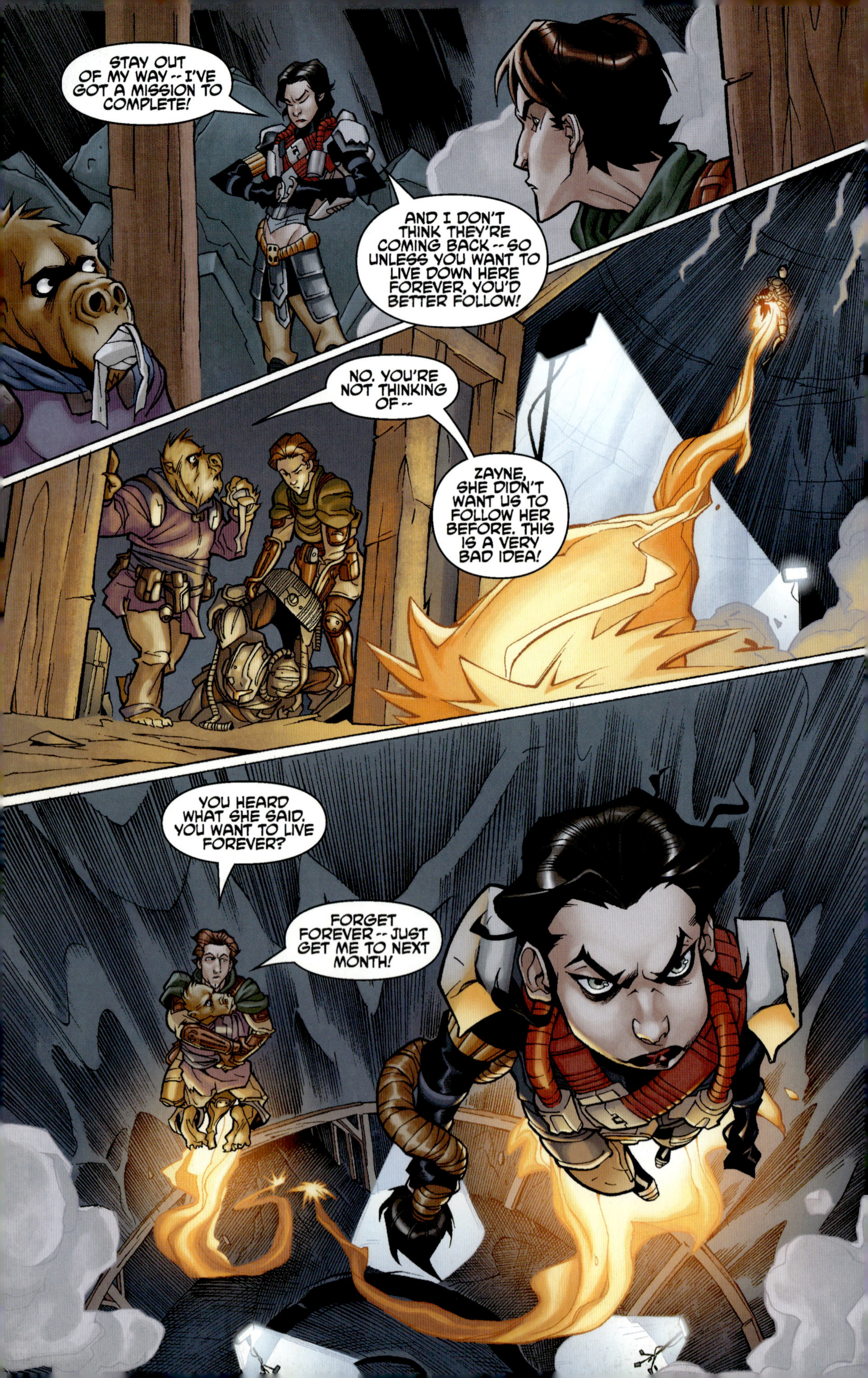
STAY OUT OF MY WAY -- I'VE GOT A MISSION TO COMPLETE!
AND I DON'T THINK THEY'RE COMING BACK -- SO UNLESS YOU WANT TO LIVE DOWN HERE FOREVER, YOU'D BETTER FOLLOW!
NO. YOU'RE NOT THINKING OF --
ZAYNE, SHE DIDN'T WANT US TO FOLLOW HER BEFORE. THIS IS A VERY BAD IDEA!
YOU HEARD WHAT SHE SAID. YOU WANT TO LIVE FOREVER?
FORGET FOREVER -- JUST GET ME TO NEXT MONTH!

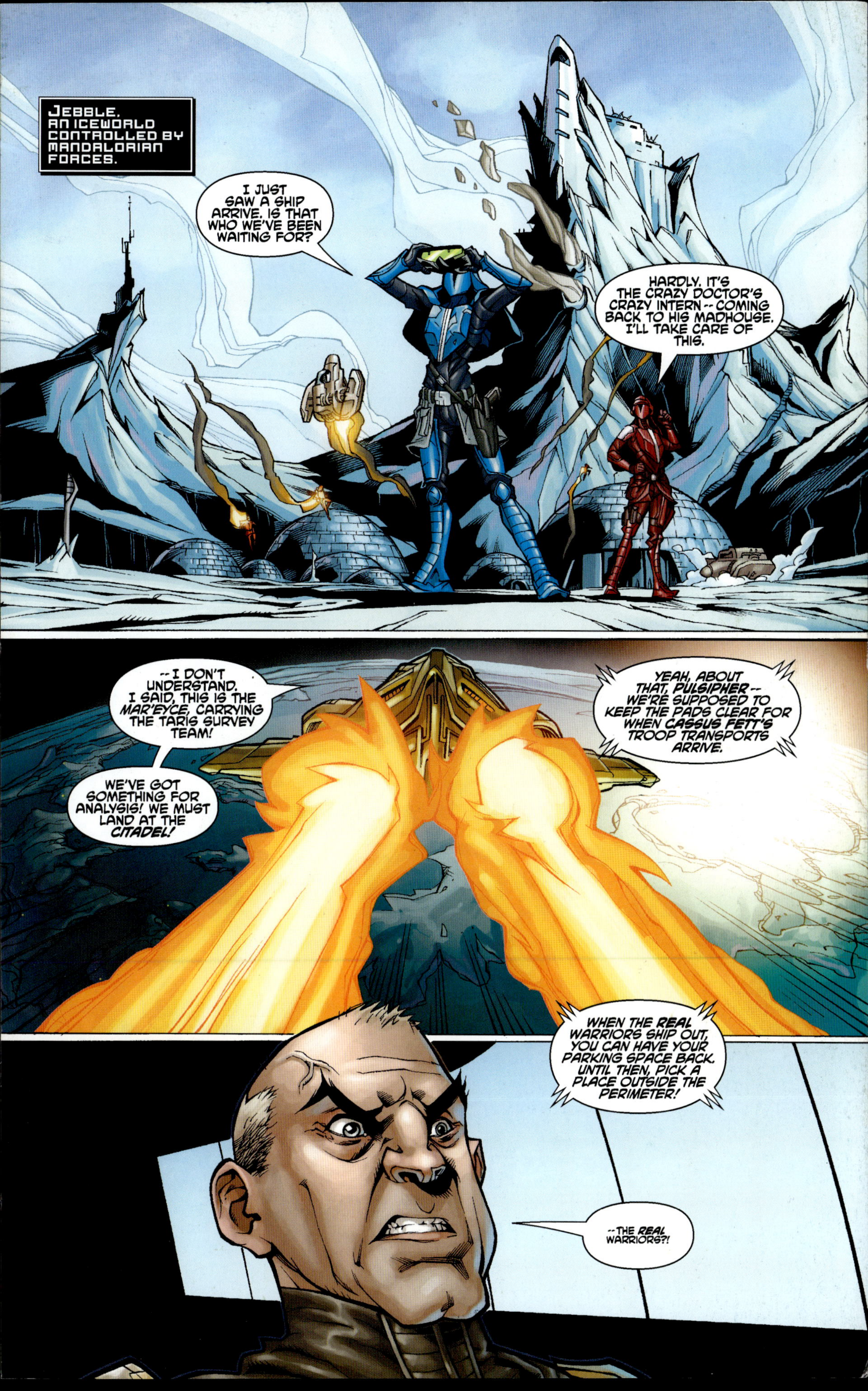
JEBBLE. AN ICEWORLD CONTROLLED BY MANDALORIAN FORCES.
I JUST SAW A SHIP ARRIVE. IS THAT WHO WE'VE BEEN WAITING FOR?
HARDLY. IT'S THE CRAZY DOCTOR'S CRAZY INTERN -- COMING BACK TO HIS MADHOUSE. I'LL TAKE CARE OF THIS.
-- I DON'T UNDERSTAND. I SAID, THIS IS THE MAR'EYCE, CARRYING THE TARIS SURVEY TEAM!
WE'VE GOT SOMETHING FOR ANALYSIS! WE MUST LAND AT THE CITADEL!
YEAH, ABOUT THAT, PULSIPHER -- WE'RE SUPPOSED TO KEEP THE PADS CLEAR FOR WHEN CASSUS FETT'S TROOP TRANSPORTS ARRIVE.
WHEN THE REAL WARRIORS SHIP OUT, YOU CAN HAVE YOUR PARKING SPACE BACK. UNTIL THEN, PICK A PLACE OUTSIDE THE PERIMETER!
-- THE REAL WARRIORS?!

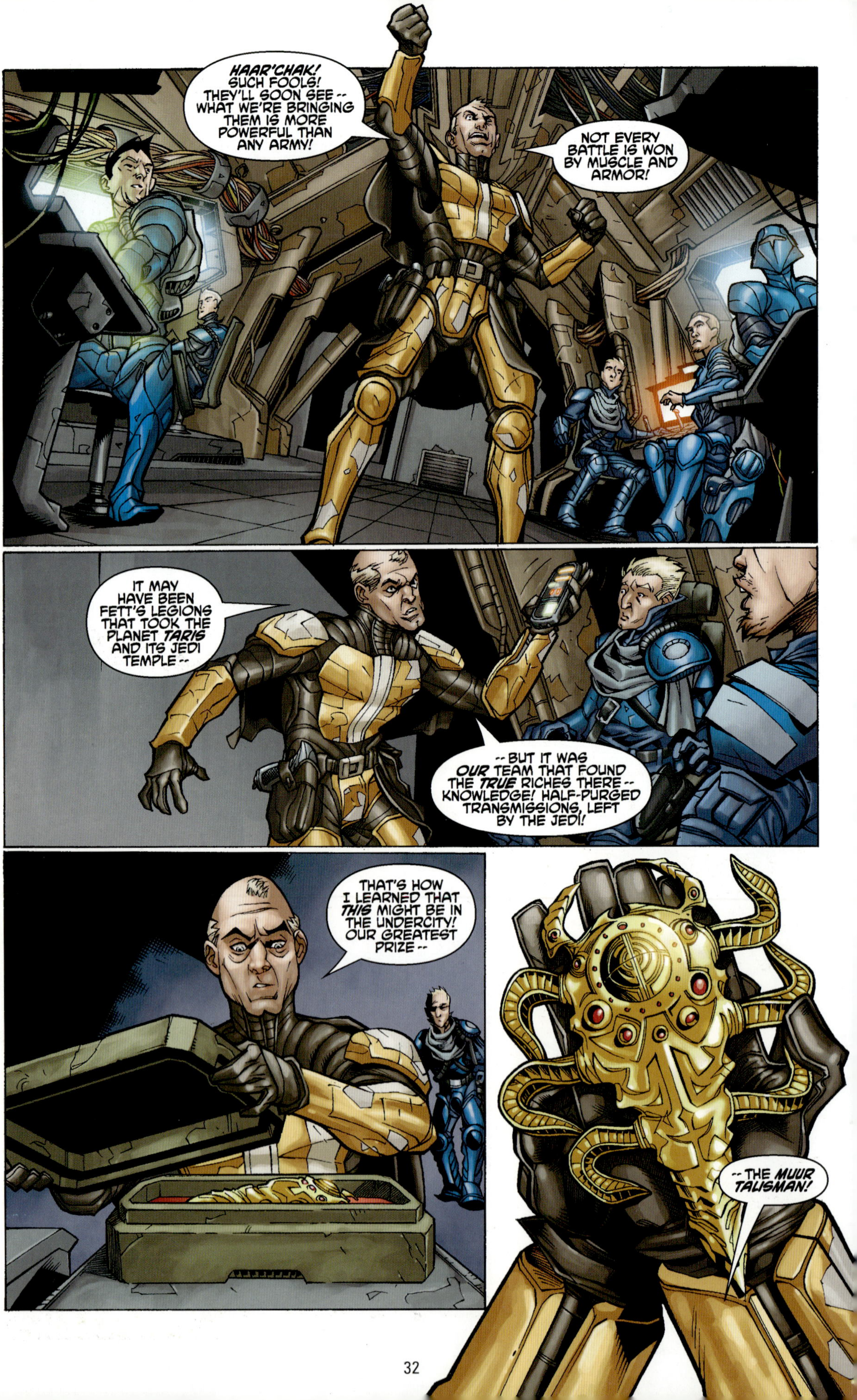

HAAR'CHAK! SUCH FOOLS! THEY'LL SOON SEE -- WHAT WE'RE BRINGING THEM IS MORE POWERFUL THAN ANY ARMY!
NOT EVERY BATTLE IS WON BY MUSCLE AND ARMOR!
IT MAY HAVE BEEN FETT'S LEGIONS THAT TOOK THE PLANET TARIS AND ITS JEDI TEMPLE --
-- BUT IT WAS OUR TEAM THAT FOUND THE TRUE RICHES THERE -- KNOWLEDGE! HALF-PURGED TRANSMISSIONS, LEFT BY THE JEDI!
THAT'S HOW I LEARNED THAT THIS MIGHT BE IN THE UNDERCITY! OUR GREATEST PRIZE --
-- THE MUUR TALISMAN!

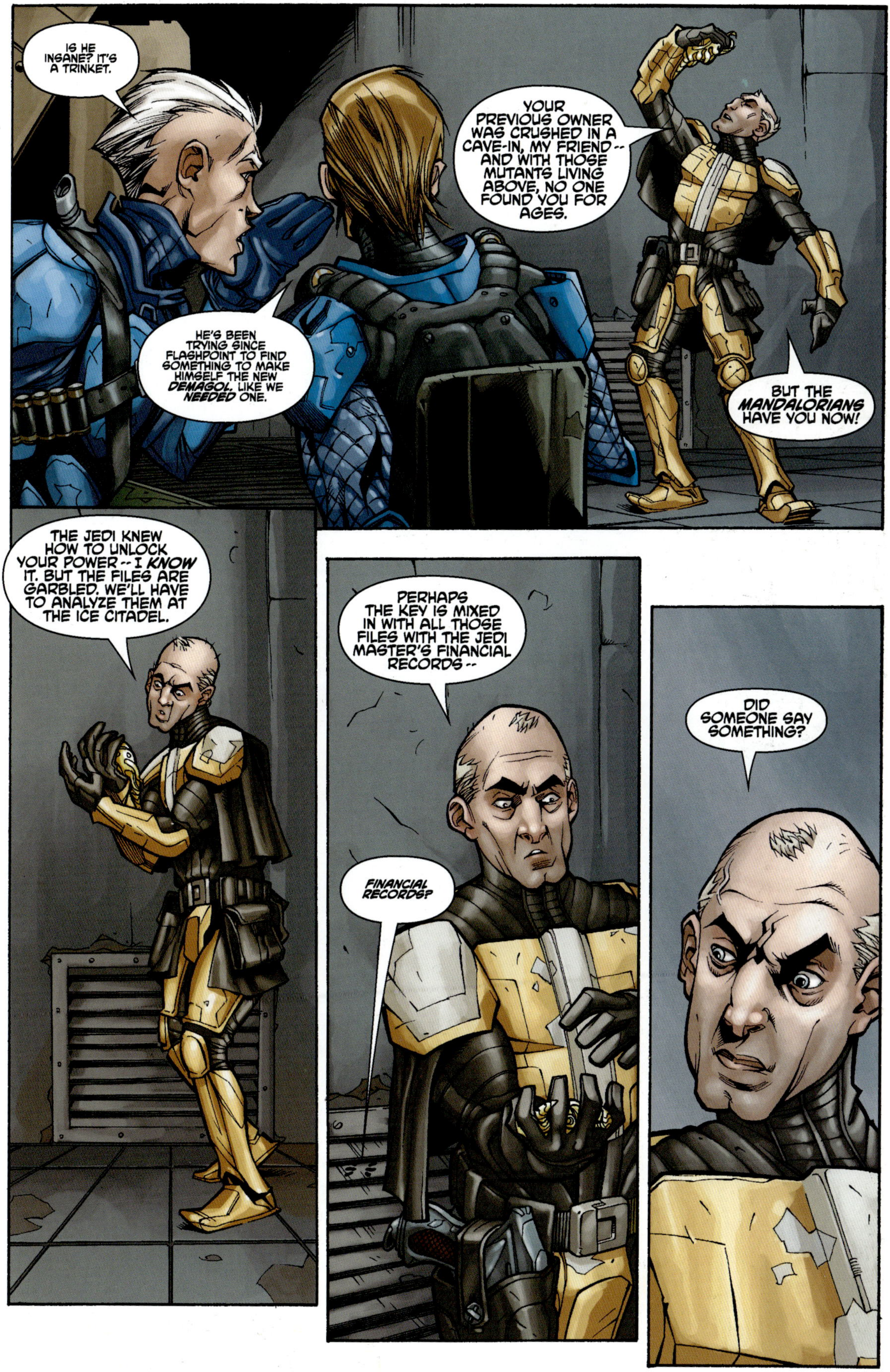
IS HE INSANE? IT'S A TRINKET.
HE'S BEEN TRYING SINCE FLASHPOINT TO FIND SOMETHING TO MAKE HIMSELF THE NEW *DEMAGOL*, LIKE WE *NEEDED* ONE.
YOUR PREVIOUS OWNER WAS CRUSHED IN A CAVE-IN, MY FRIEND-- AND WITH THOSE MUTANTS LIVING ABOVE, NO ONE FOUND YOU FOR AGES.
BUT THE *MANDALORIANS* HAVE YOU NOW!
THE JEDI KNEW HOW TO UNLOCK YOUR POWER-- I *KNOW* IT. BUT THE FILES ARE GARBLED. WE'LL HAVE TO ANALYZE THEM AT THE ICE CITADEL.
PERHAPS THE KEY IS MIXED IN WITH ALL THOSE FILES WITH THE JEDI MASTER'S FINANCIAL RECORDS--
FINANCIAL RECORDS?
DID SOMEONE SAY SOMETHING?

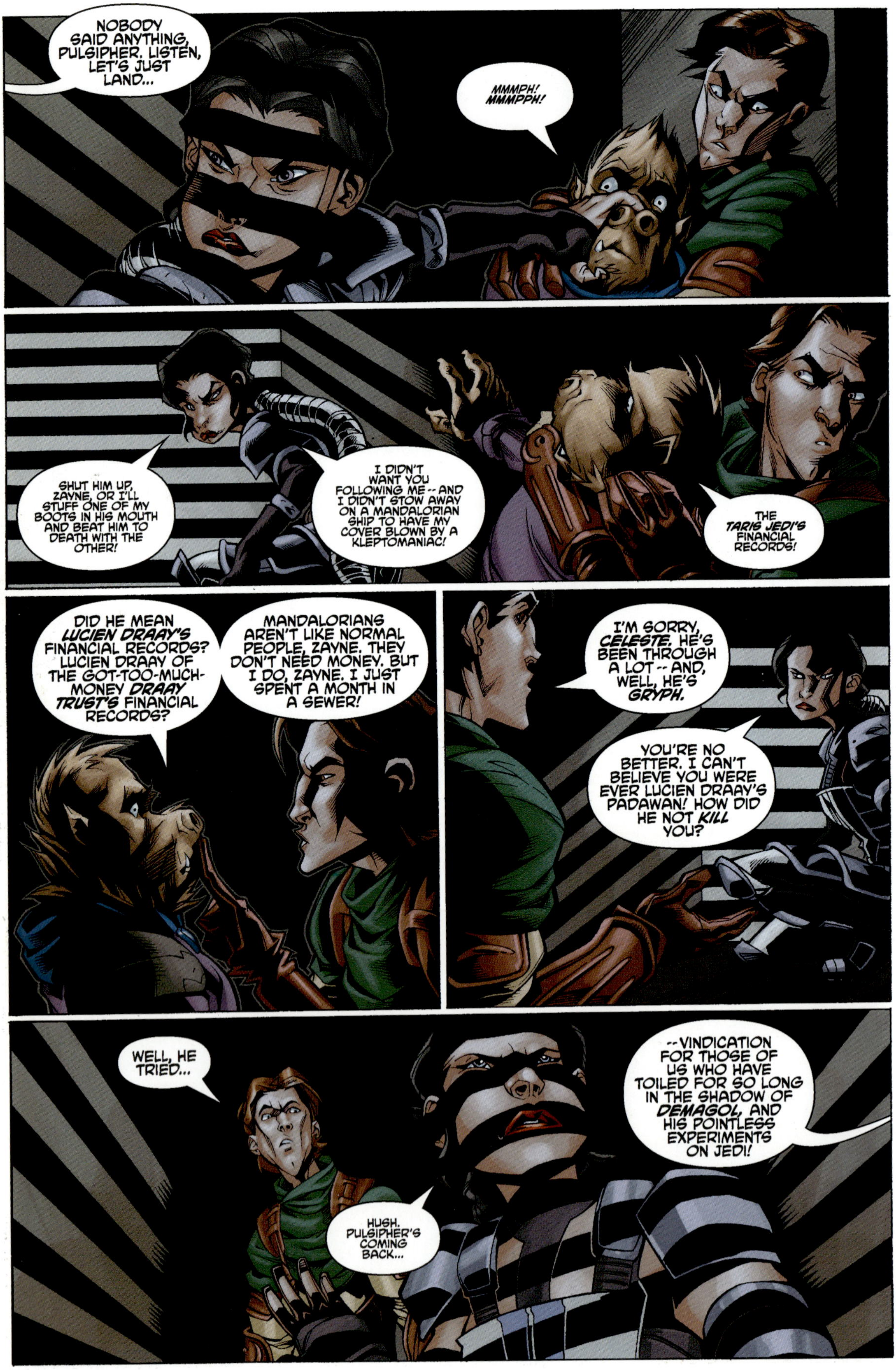
NOBODY SAID ANYTHING, PULSIPHER. LISTEN, LET'S JUST LAND...
MMMPH! MMMPPH!
SHUT HIM UP, ZAYNE, OR I'LL STUFF ONE OF MY BOOTS IN HIS MOUTH AND BEAT HIM TO DEATH WITH THE OTHER!
I DIDN'T WANT YOU FOLLOWING ME-- AND I DIDN'T STOW AWAY ON A MANDALORIAN SHIP TO HAVE MY COVER BLOWN BY A KLEPTOMANIAC!
THE TARIS JEDI'S FINANCIAL RECORDS!
DID HE MEAN LUCIEN DRAAY'S FINANCIAL RECORDS? LUCIEN DRAAY OF THE GOT-TOO-MUCH-MONEY DRAAY TRUST'S FINANCIAL RECORDS?
MANDALORIANS AREN'T LIKE NORMAL PEOPLE, ZAYNE. THEY DON'T NEED MONEY. BUT I DO, ZAYNE. I JUST SPENT A MONTH IN A SEWER!
I'M SORRY, CELESTE. HE'S BEEN THROUGH A LOT-- AND, WELL, HE'S GRYPH.
YOU'RE NO BETTER. I CAN'T BELIEVE YOU WERE EVER LUCIEN DRAAY'S PADAWAN! HOW DID HE NOT KILL YOU?
WELL, HE TRIED...
--VINDICATION FOR THOSE OF US WHO HAVE TOILED FOR SO LONG IN THE SHADOW OF DEMAGOL, AND HIS POINTLESS EXPERIMENTS ON JEDI!
HUSH. PULSIPHER'S COMING BACK...

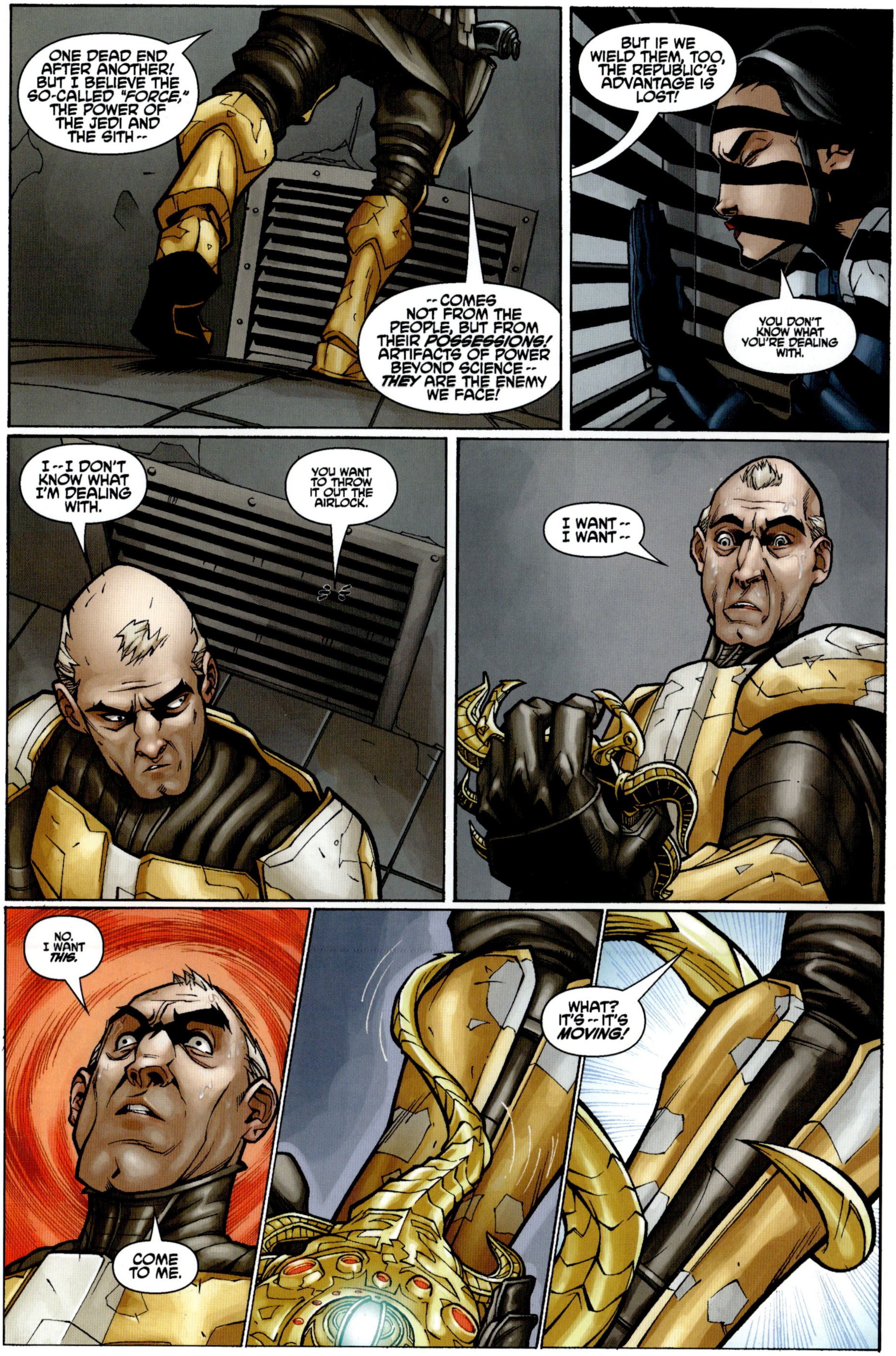
ONE DEAD END AFTER ANOTHER! BUT I BELIEVE THE SO-CALLED "FORCE," THE POWER OF THE JEDI AND THE SITH --
-- COMES NOT FROM THE PEOPLE, BUT FROM THEIR POSSESSIONS! ARTIFACTS OF POWER BEYOND SCIENCE -- THEY ARE THE ENEMY WE FACE!
BUT IF WE WIELD THEM, TOO, THE REPUBLIC'S ADVANTAGE IS LOST!
YOU DON'T KNOW WHAT YOU'RE DEALING WITH.
I -- I DON'T KNOW WHAT I'M DEALING WITH.
YOU WANT TO THROW IT OUT THE AIRLOCK.
I WANT -- I WANT --
NO. I WANT THIS.
COME TO ME.
WHAT? IT'S -- IT'S MOVING!

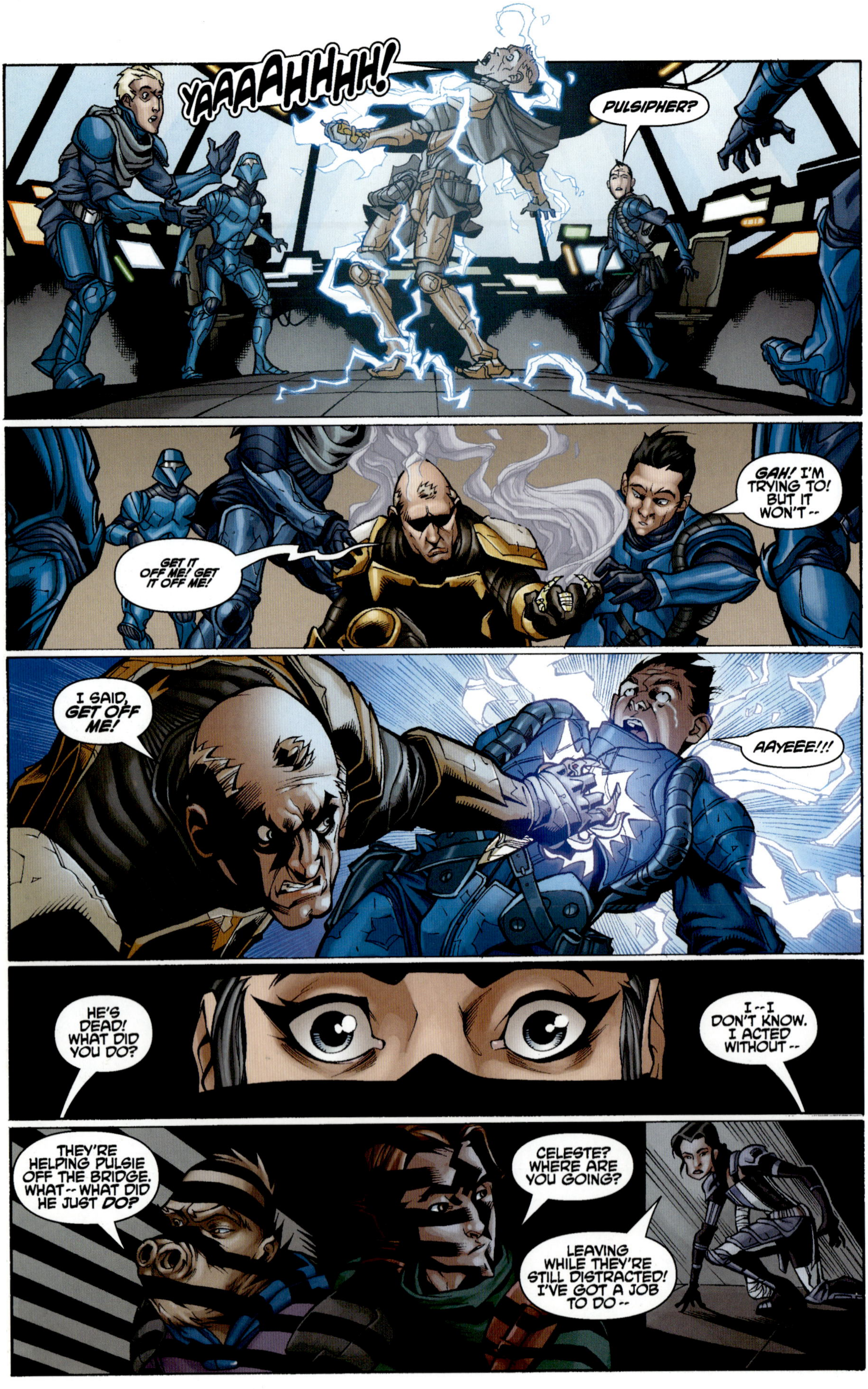
YAAAAHHHH!
PULSIPHER?
GAH! I'M TRYING TO! BUT IT WON'T --
GET IT OFF ME! GET IT OFF ME!
I SAID, GET OFF ME!
AAYEEE!!!
HE'S DEAD! WHAT DID YOU DO?
I -- I DON'T KNOW. I ACTED WITHOUT --
THEY'RE HELPING PULSIE OFF THE BRIDGE. WHAT -- WHAT DID HE JUST DO?
CELESTE? WHERE ARE YOU GOING?
LEAVING WHILE THEY'RE STILL DISTRACTED! I'VE GOT A JOB TO DO --

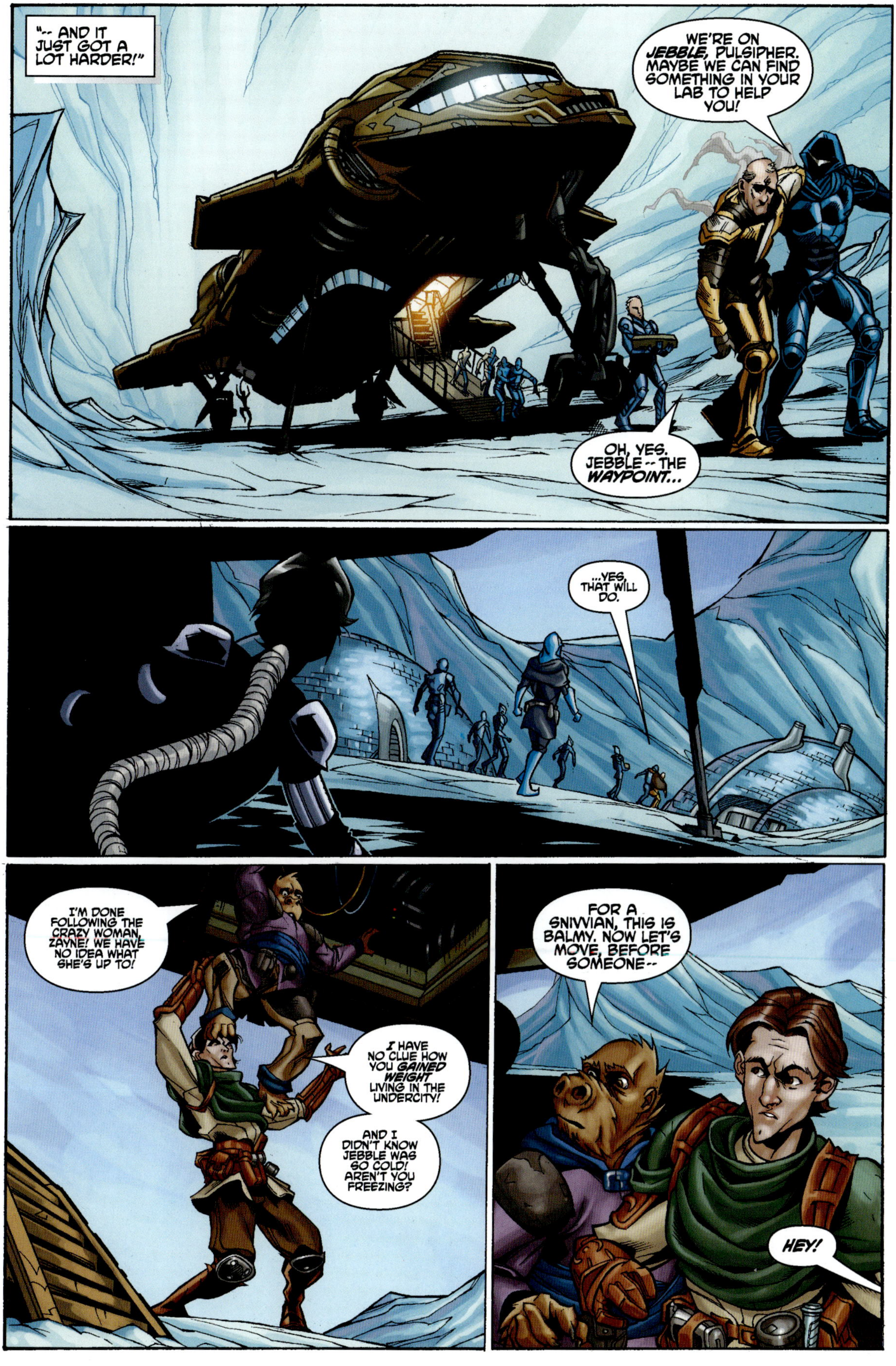
"-- AND IT JUST GOT A LOT HARDER!"
WE'RE ON *JEBBLE,* PULSIPHER. MAYBE WE CAN FIND SOMETHING IN YOUR LAB TO HELP YOU!
OH, YES. JEBBLE -- THE *WAYPOINT...*
...YES, THAT WILL DO.
I'M DONE FOLLOWING THE CRAZY WOMAN, ZAYNE! WE HAVE NO IDEA WHAT SHE'S UP TO!
I HAVE NO CLUE HOW YOU *GAINED WEIGHT* LIVING IN THE UNDERCITY!
AND I DIDN'T KNOW JEBBLE WAS SO COLD! AREN'T YOU FREEZING?
FOR A SNIVVIAN, THIS IS BALMY. NOW LET'S MOVE, BEFORE SOMEONE--
HEY!

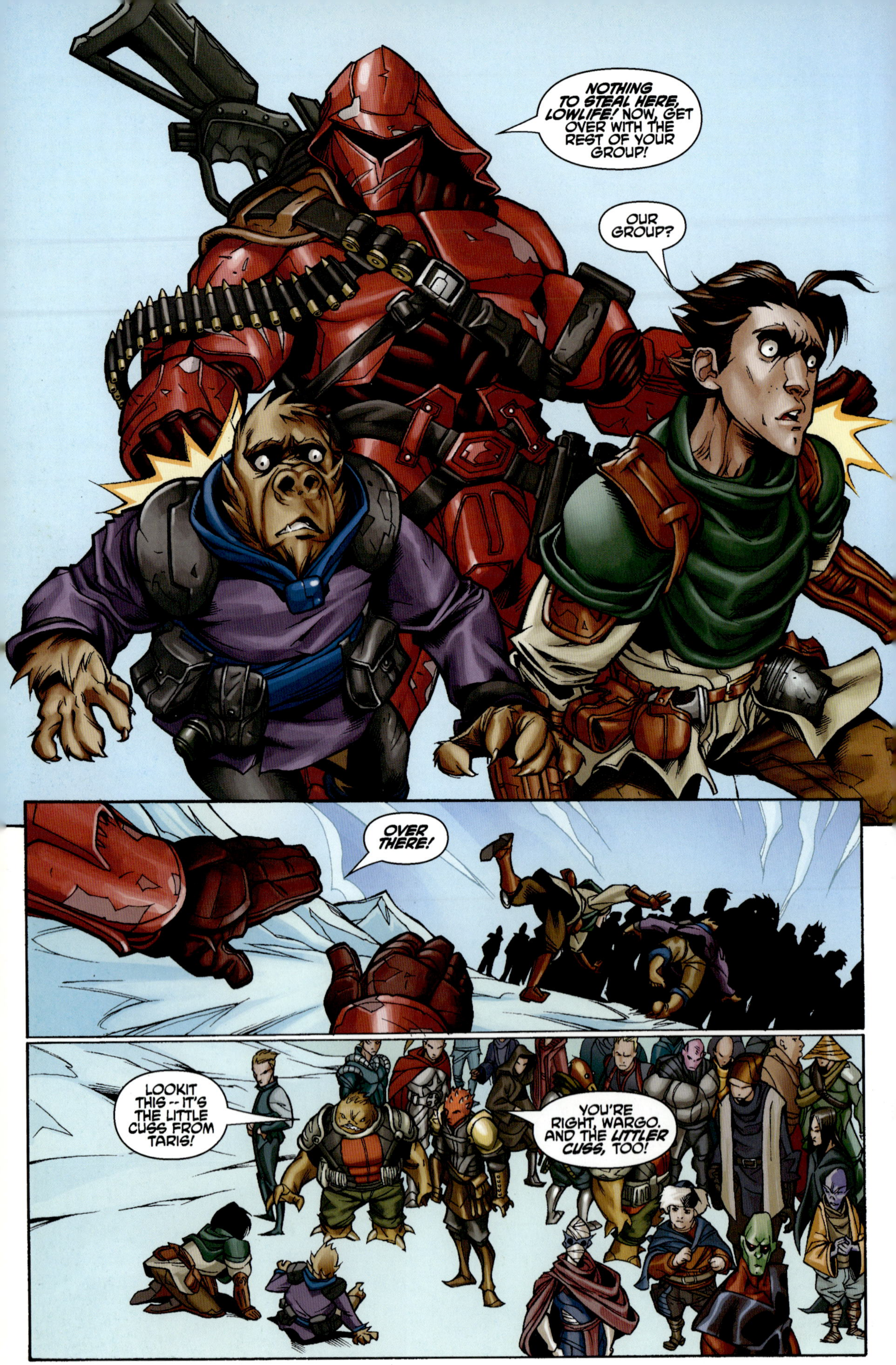
NOTHING TO STEAL HERE, LOWLIFE! NOW, GET OVER WITH THE REST OF YOUR GROUP!
OUR GROUP?
OVER THERE!
LOOKIT THIS -- IT'S THE LITTLE CUSS FROM TARIS!
YOU'RE RIGHT, WARGO. AND THE LITTLER CUSS, TOO!

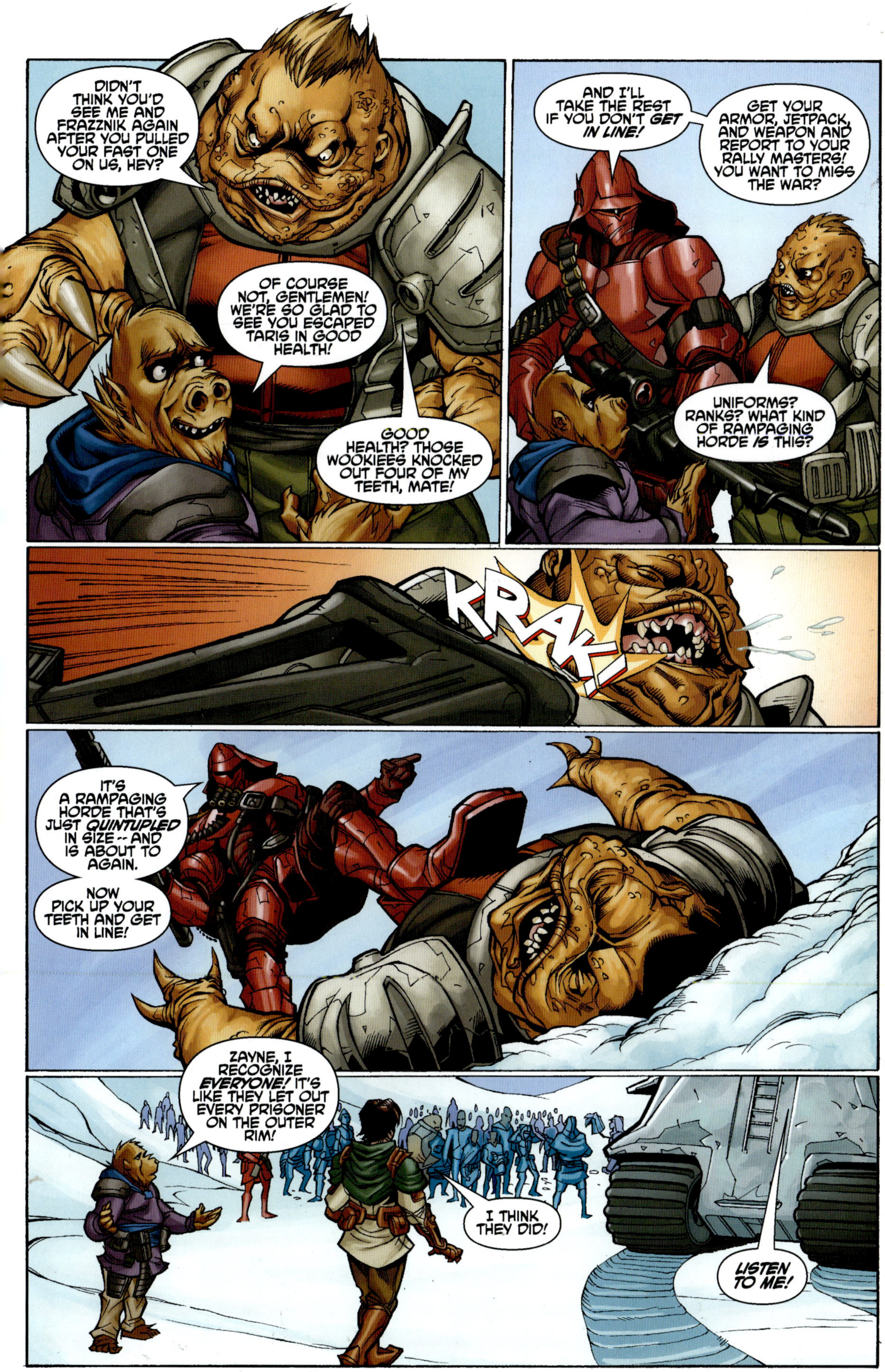
DIDN'T THINK YOU'D SEE ME AND FRAZZNIK AGAIN AFTER YOU PULLED YOUR FAST ONE ON US, HEY?
OF COURSE NOT, GENTLEMEN! WE'RE SO GLAD TO SEE YOU ESCAPED TARIS IN GOOD HEALTH!
GOOD HEALTH? THOSE WOOKIEES KNOCKED OUT FOUR OF MY TEETH, MATE!
AND I'LL TAKE THE REST IF YOU DON'T *GET IN LINE!*
GET YOUR ARMOR, JETPACK, AND WEAPON AND REPORT TO YOUR RALLY MASTERS! YOU WANT TO MISS THE WAR?
UNIFORMS? RANKS? WHAT KIND OF RAMPAGING HORDE *IS* THIS?
KRAK!
IT'S A RAMPAGING HORDE THAT'S JUST *QUINTUPLED* IN SIZE -- AND IS ABOUT TO AGAIN.
NOW PICK UP YOUR TEETH AND GET IN LINE!
ZAYNE, I RECOGNIZE *EVERYONE!* IT'S LIKE THEY LET OUT EVERY PRISONER ON THE OUTER RIM!
I THINK THEY DID!
LISTEN TO ME!

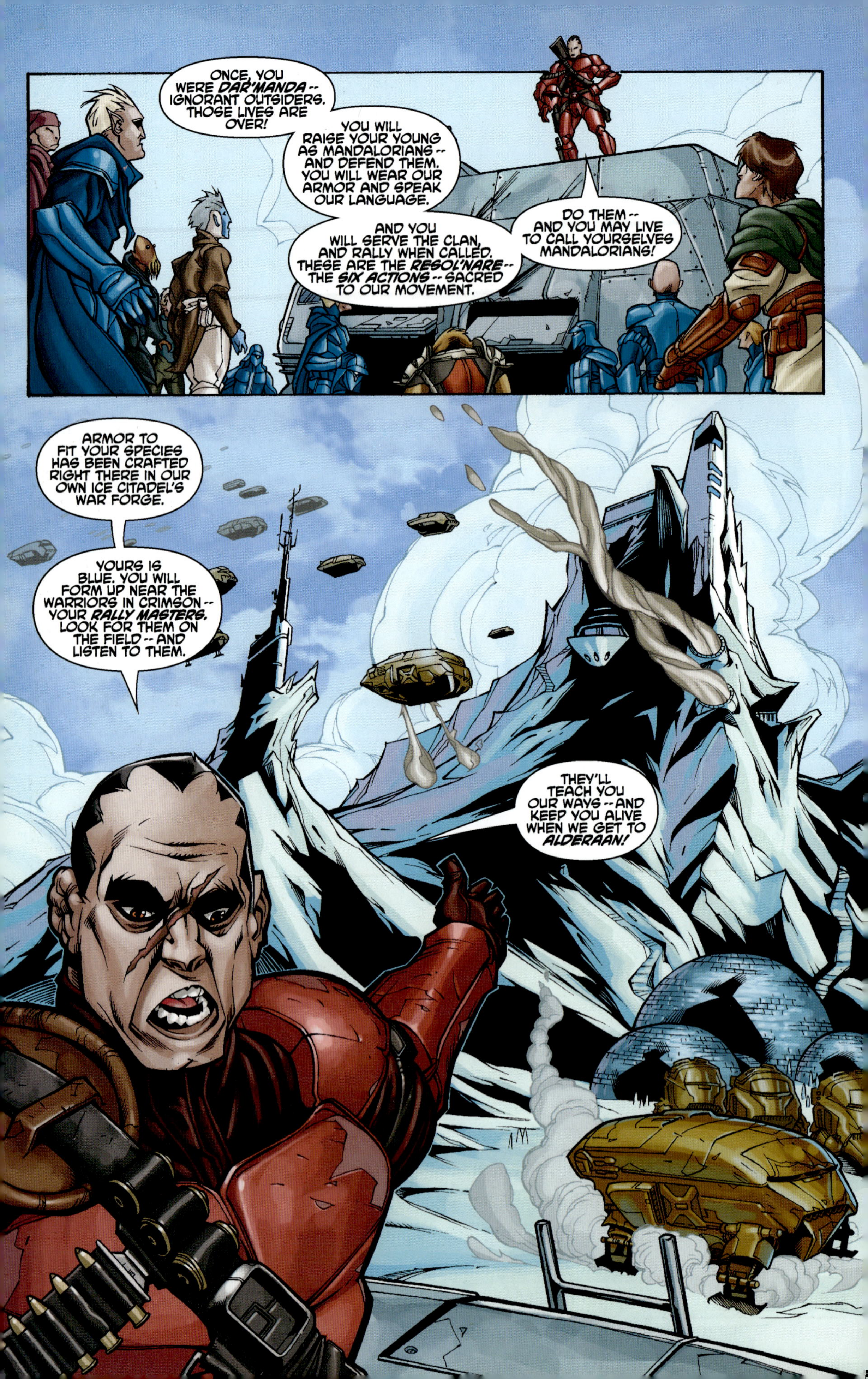
ONCE, YOU WERE DAR'MANDA -- IGNORANT OUTSIDERS. THOSE LIVES ARE OVER!
YOU WILL RAISE YOUR YOUNG AS MANDALORIANS -- AND DEFEND THEM. YOU WILL WEAR OUR ARMOR AND SPEAK OUR LANGUAGE.
AND YOU WILL SERVE THE CLAN, AND RALLY WHEN CALLED. THESE ARE THE RESOL'NARE -- THE SIX ACTIONS -- SACRED TO OUR MOVEMENT.
DO THEM -- AND YOU MAY LIVE TO CALL YOURSELVES MANDALORIANS!
ARMOR TO FIT YOUR SPECIES HAS BEEN CRAFTED RIGHT THERE IN OUR OWN ICE CITADEL'S WAR FORGE.
YOURS IS BLUE. YOU WILL FORM UP NEAR THE WARRIORS IN CRIMSON -- YOUR RALLY MASTERS. LOOK FOR THEM ON THE FIELD -- AND LISTEN TO THEM.
THEY'LL TEACH YOU OUR WAYS -- AND KEEP YOU ALIVE WHEN WE GET TO ALDERAAN!

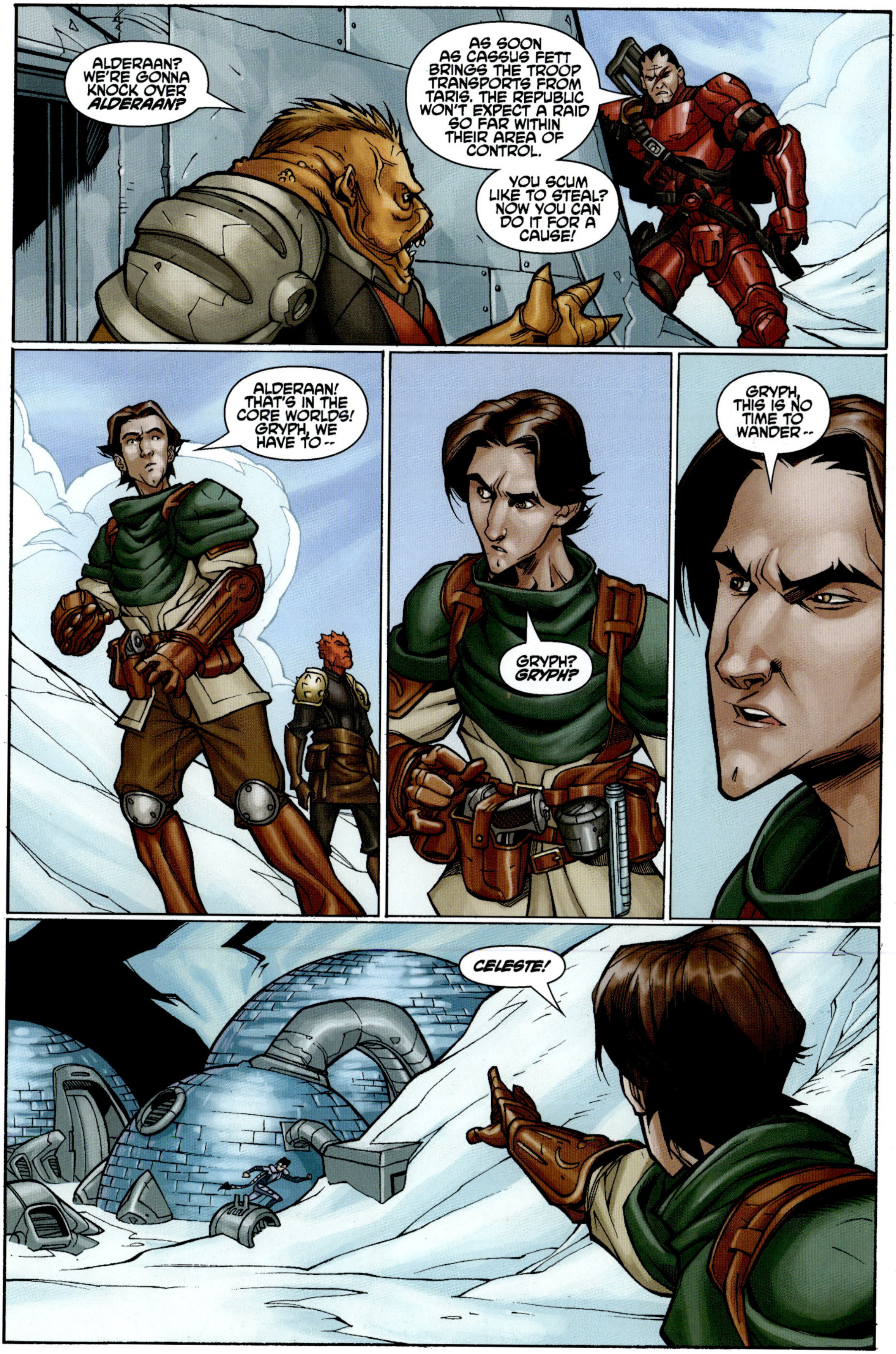
ALDERAAN? WE'RE GONNA KNOCK OVER *ALDERAAN?*
AS SOON AS CASSUS FETT BRINGS THE TROOP TRANSPORTS FROM TARIS. THE REPUBLIC WON'T EXPECT A RAID SO FAR WITHIN THEIR AREA OF CONTROL.
YOU SCUM LIKE TO STEAL? NOW YOU CAN DO IT FOR A CAUSE!
ALDERAAN! THAT'S IN THE CORE WORLDS! GRYPH, WE HAVE TO --
GRYPH? *GRYPH?*
GRYPH, THIS IS NO TIME TO WANDER --
CELESTE!

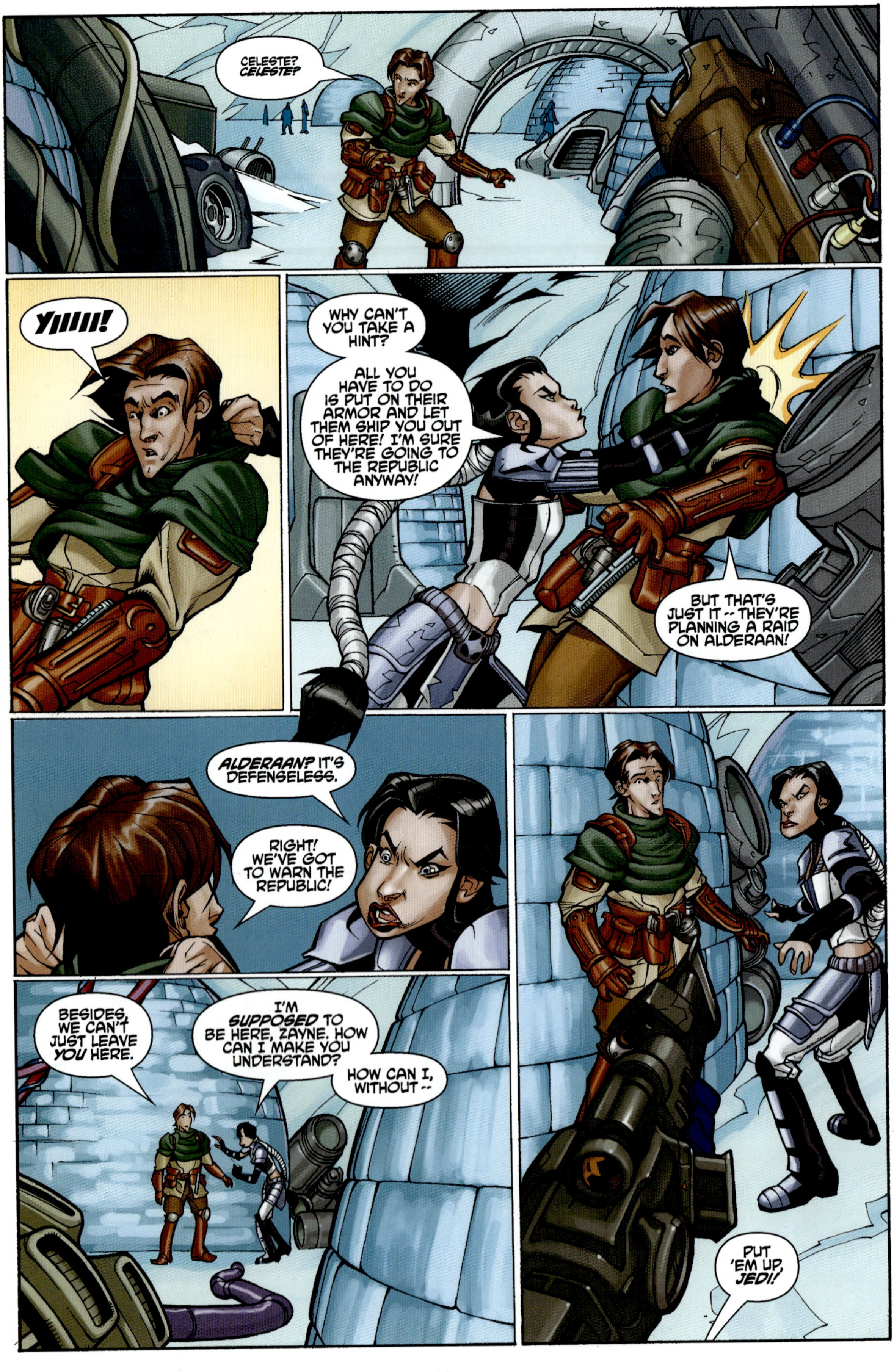
CELESTE? CELESTE?
YIIII!
WHY CAN'T YOU TAKE A HINT?
ALL YOU HAVE TO DO IS PUT ON THEIR ARMOR AND LET THEM SHIP YOU OUT OF HERE! I'M SURE THEY'RE GOING TO THE REPUBLIC ANYWAY!
BUT THAT'S JUST IT -- THEY'RE PLANNING A RAID ON ALDERAAN!
ALDERAAN? IT'S DEFENSELESS.
RIGHT! WE'VE GOT TO WARN THE REPUBLIC!
BESIDES, WE CAN'T JUST LEAVE YOU HERE.
I'M SUPPOSED TO BE HERE, ZAYNE. HOW CAN I MAKE YOU UNDERSTAND?
HOW CAN I, WITHOUT --
PUT 'EM UP, JEDI!

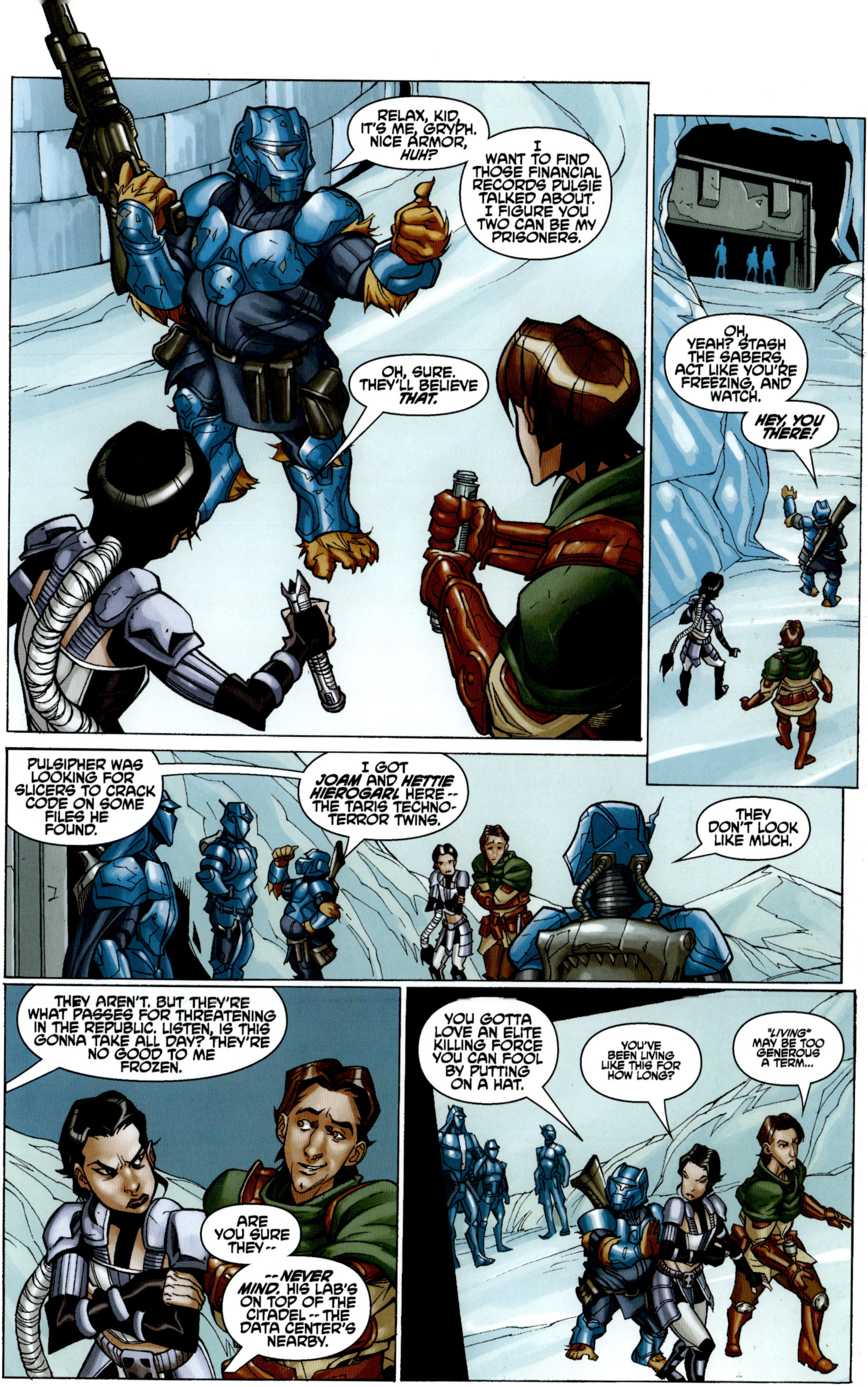

RELAX, KID, IT'S ME, GRYPH. NICE ARMOR, *HUH?*
I WANT TO FIND THOSE FINANCIAL RECORDS PULSIE TALKED ABOUT. I FIGURE YOU TWO CAN BE MY PRISONERS.
OH, SURE. THEY'LL BELIEVE *THAT.*
OH, YEAH? STASH THE SABERS, ACT LIKE YOU'RE FREEZING, AND WATCH.
HEY, YOU THERE!
PULSIPHER WAS LOOKING FOR SLICERS TO CRACK CODE ON SOME FILES HE FOUND.
I GOT *JOAM* AND *HETTIE HIEROGARL* HERE -- THE TARIS TECHNO-TERROR TWINS.
THEY DON'T LOOK LIKE MUCH.
THEY AREN'T. BUT THEY'RE WHAT PASSES FOR THREATENING IN THE REPUBLIC. LISTEN, IS THIS GONNA TAKE ALL DAY? THEY'RE NO GOOD TO ME FROZEN.
ARE YOU SURE THEY --
-- *NEVER MIND.* HIS LAB'S ON TOP OF THE CITADEL -- THE DATA CENTER'S NEARBY.
YOU GOTTA LOVE AN ELITE KILLING FORCE YOU CAN FOOL BY PUTTING ON A HAT.
YOU'VE BEEN LIVING LIKE THIS FOR HOW LONG?
"LIVING" MAY BE TOO GENEROUS A TERM...

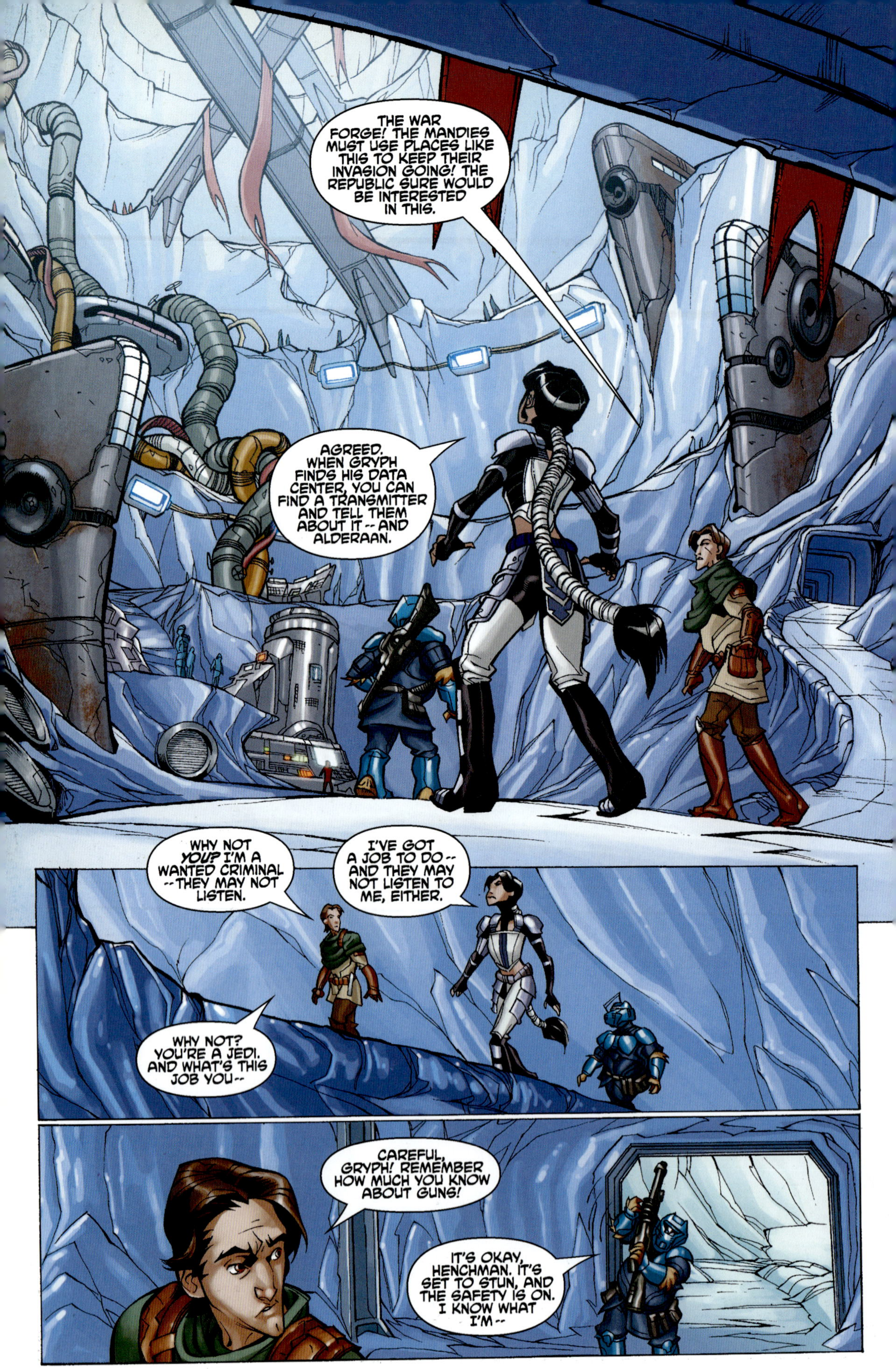

THE WAR FORGE! THE MANDIES MUST USE PLACES LIKE THIS TO KEEP THEIR INVASION GOING! THE REPUBLIC SURE WOULD BE INTERESTED IN THIS.
AGREED. WHEN GRYPH FINDS HIS DATA CENTER, YOU CAN FIND A TRANSMITTER AND TELL THEM ABOUT IT -- AND ALDERAAN.
WHY NOT *YOU?* I'M A WANTED CRIMINAL -- THEY MAY NOT LISTEN.
I'VE GOT A JOB TO DO -- AND THEY MAY NOT LISTEN TO ME, EITHER.
WHY NOT? YOU'RE A JEDI. AND WHAT'S THIS JOB YOU --
CAREFUL, GRYPH! REMEMBER HOW MUCH YOU KNOW ABOUT GUNS!
IT'S OKAY, HENCHMAN. IT'S SET TO STUN, AND THE SAFETY IS ON. I KNOW WHAT I'M --

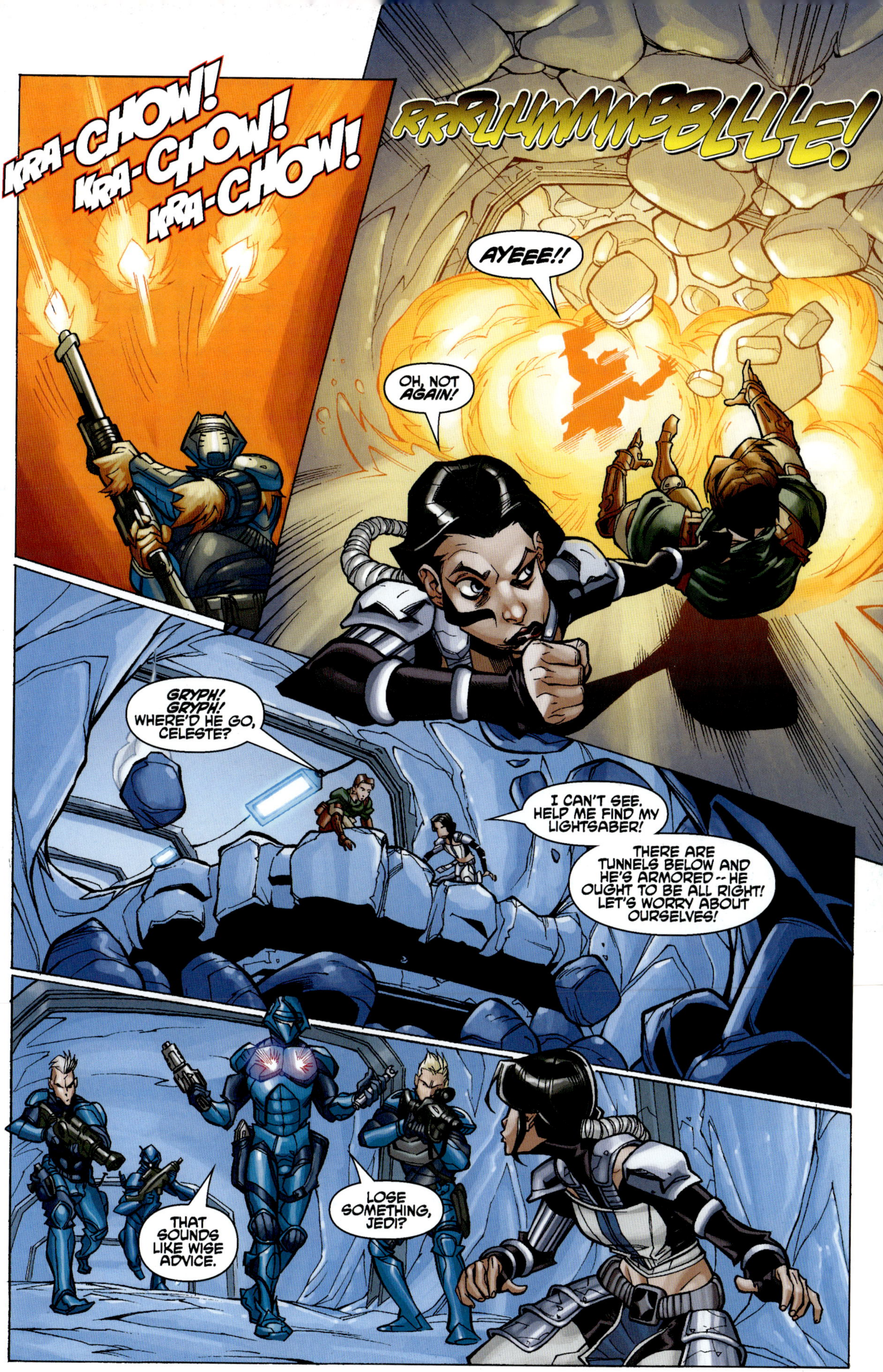
KRA-CHOW! KRA-CHOW! KRA-CHOW!
RRRUUMMMBBLLLE!
AYEEE!!
OH, NOT AGAIN!
GRYPH! GRYPH! WHERE'D HE GO, CELESTE?
I CAN'T SEE. HELP ME FIND MY LIGHTSABER!
THERE ARE TUNNELS BELOW AND HE'S ARMORED -- HE OUGHT TO BE ALL RIGHT! LET'S WORRY ABOUT OURSELVES!
THAT SOUNDS LIKE WISE ADVICE.
LOSE SOMETHING, JEDI?

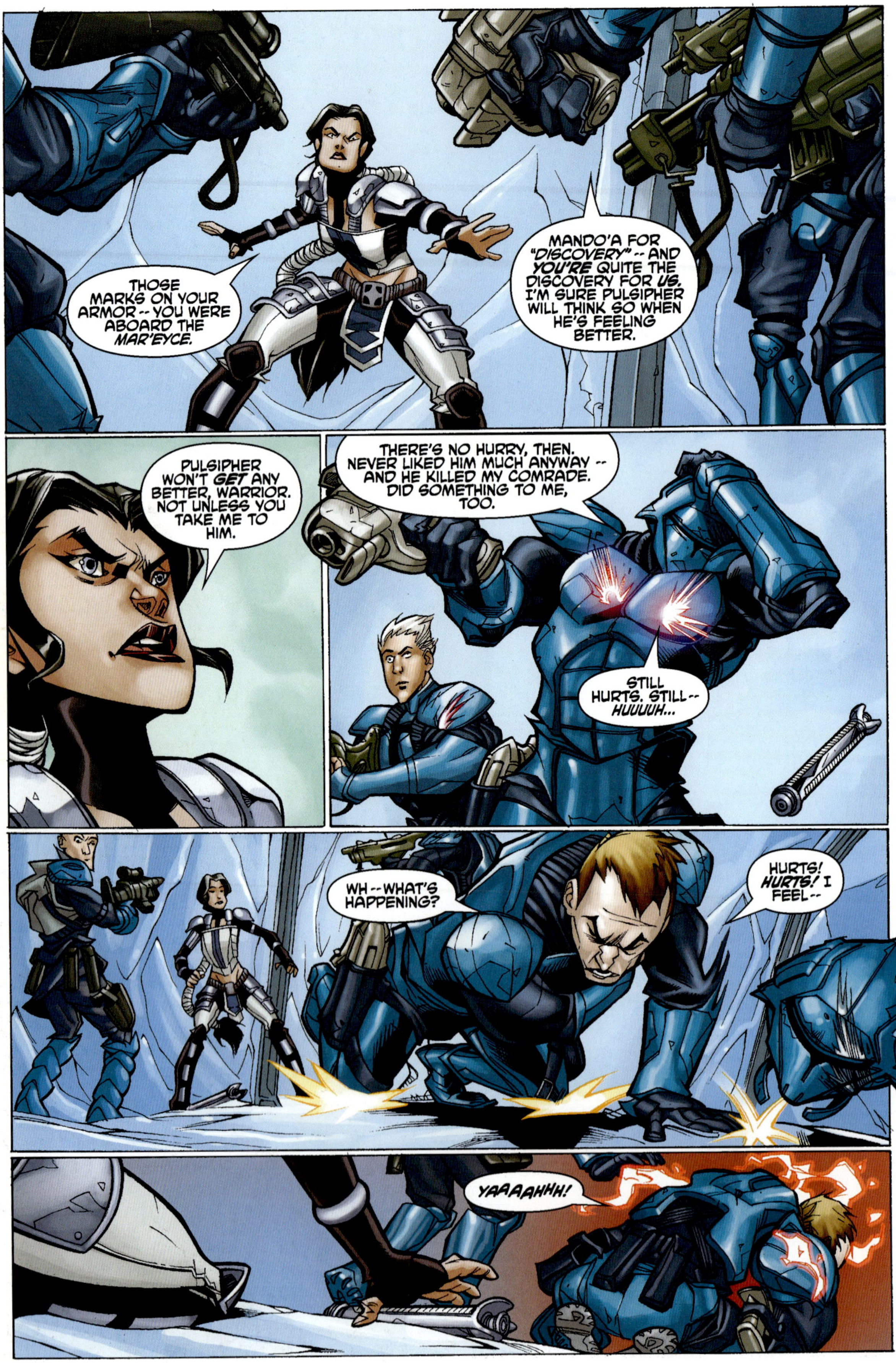
THOSE MARKS ON YOUR ARMOR -- YOU WERE ABOARD THE *MAR'EYCE.*
MANDO'A FOR *"DISCOVERY"* -- AND ***YOU'RE*** QUITE THE DISCOVERY FOR ***US.*** I'M SURE PULSIPHER WILL THINK SO WHEN HE'S FEELING BETTER.
PULSIPHER WON'T ***GET*** ANY BETTER, WARRIOR. NOT UNLESS YOU TAKE ME TO HIM.
THERE'S NO HURRY, THEN. NEVER LIKED HIM MUCH ANYWAY -- AND HE KILLED MY COMRADE. DID SOMETHING TO ME, TOO.
STILL HURTS. STILL -- ***HUUUUH...***
WH -- WHAT'S HAPPENING?
HURTS! ***HURTS!*** I FEEL --
YAAAAHHH!

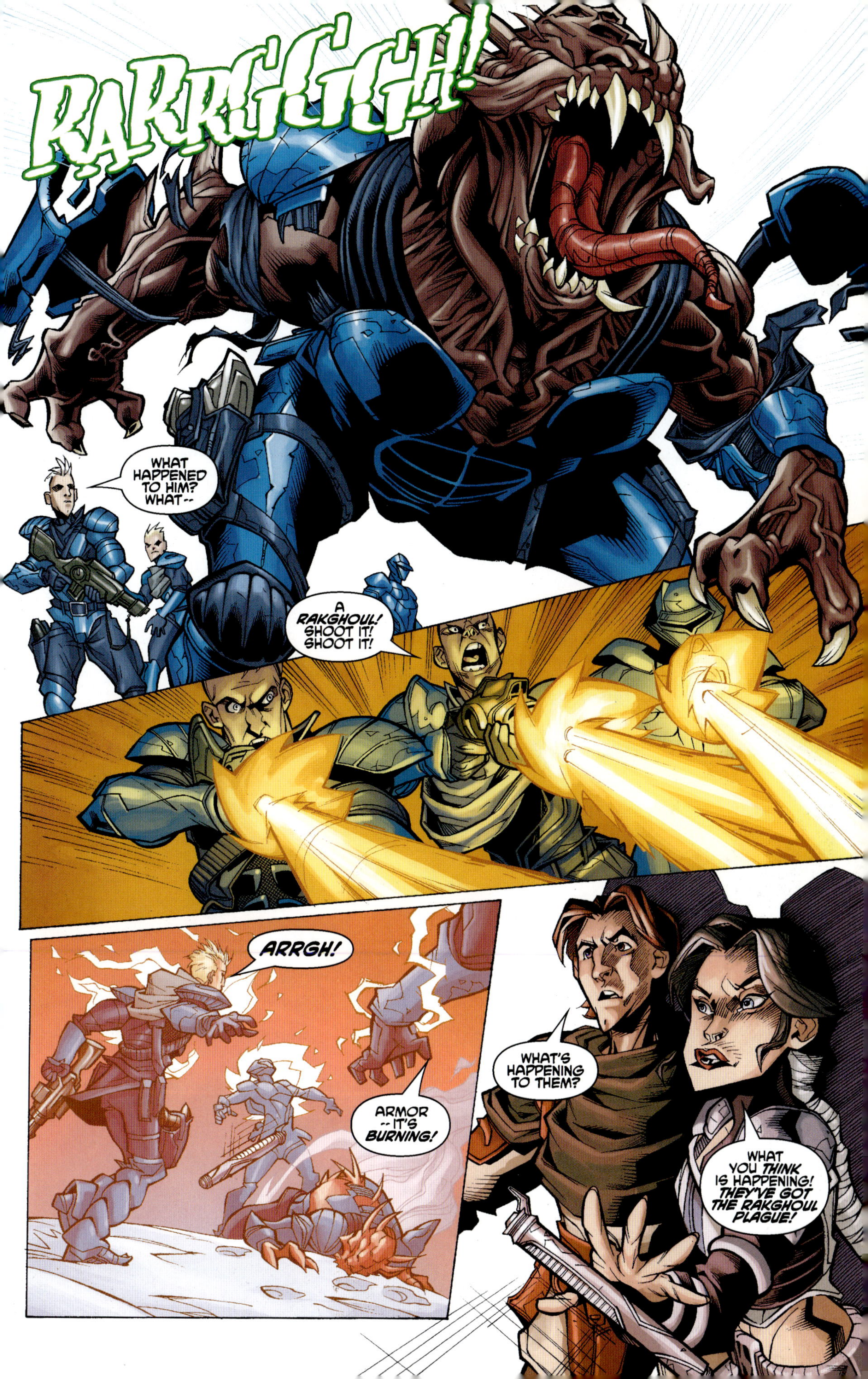
RARRGGGH!
WHAT HAPPENED TO HIM? WHAT--
A RAKGHOUL! SHOOT IT! SHOOT IT!
ARRGH!
ARMOR --IT'S BURNING!
WHAT'S HAPPENING TO THEM?
WHAT YOU THINK IS HAPPENING! THEY'VE GOT THE RAKGHOUL PLAGUE!

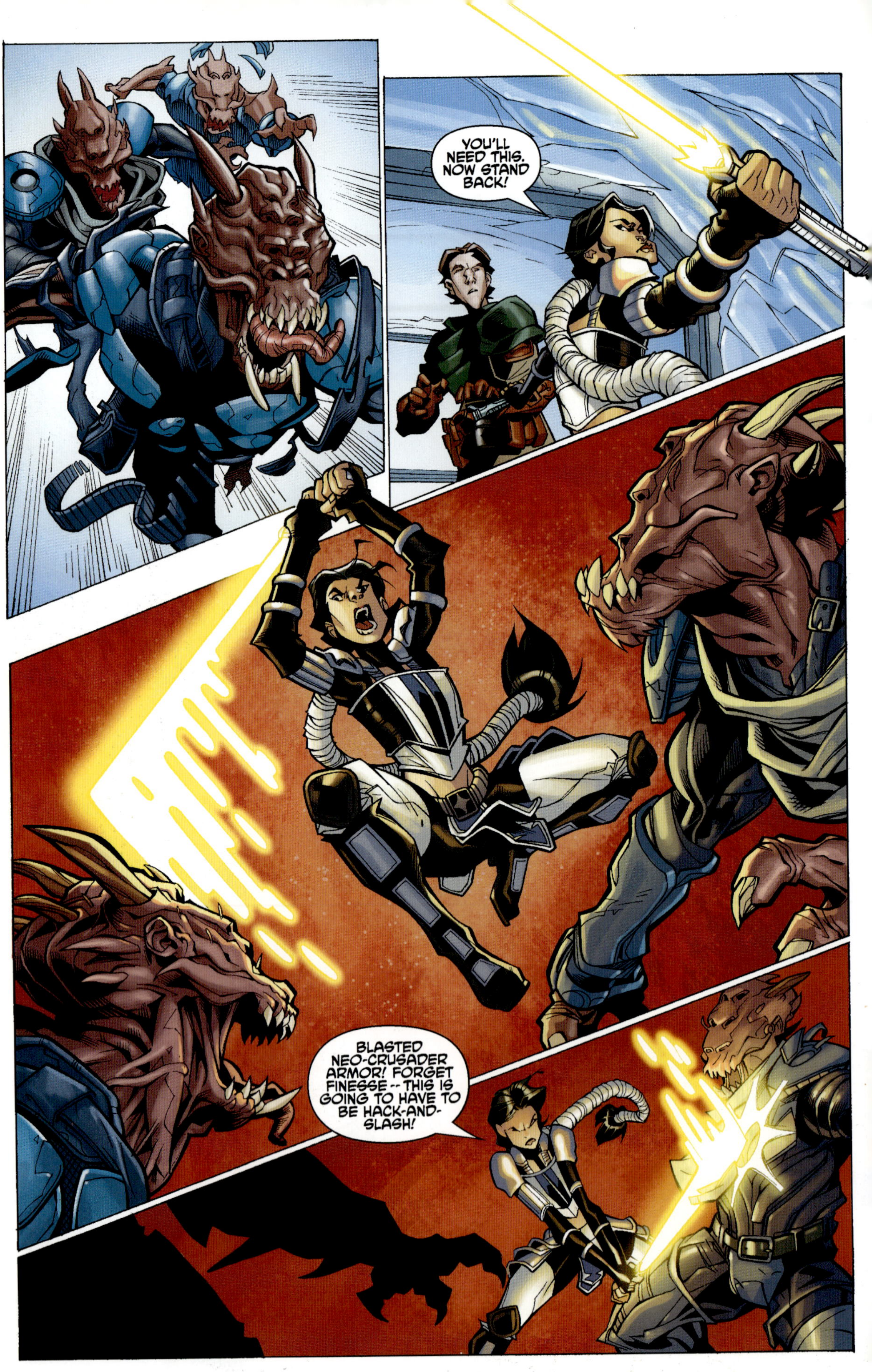
YOU'LL NEED THIS. NOW STAND BACK!
BLASTED NEO-CRUSADER ARMOR! FORGET FINESSE -- THIS IS GOING TO HAVE TO BE HACK-AND-SLASH!

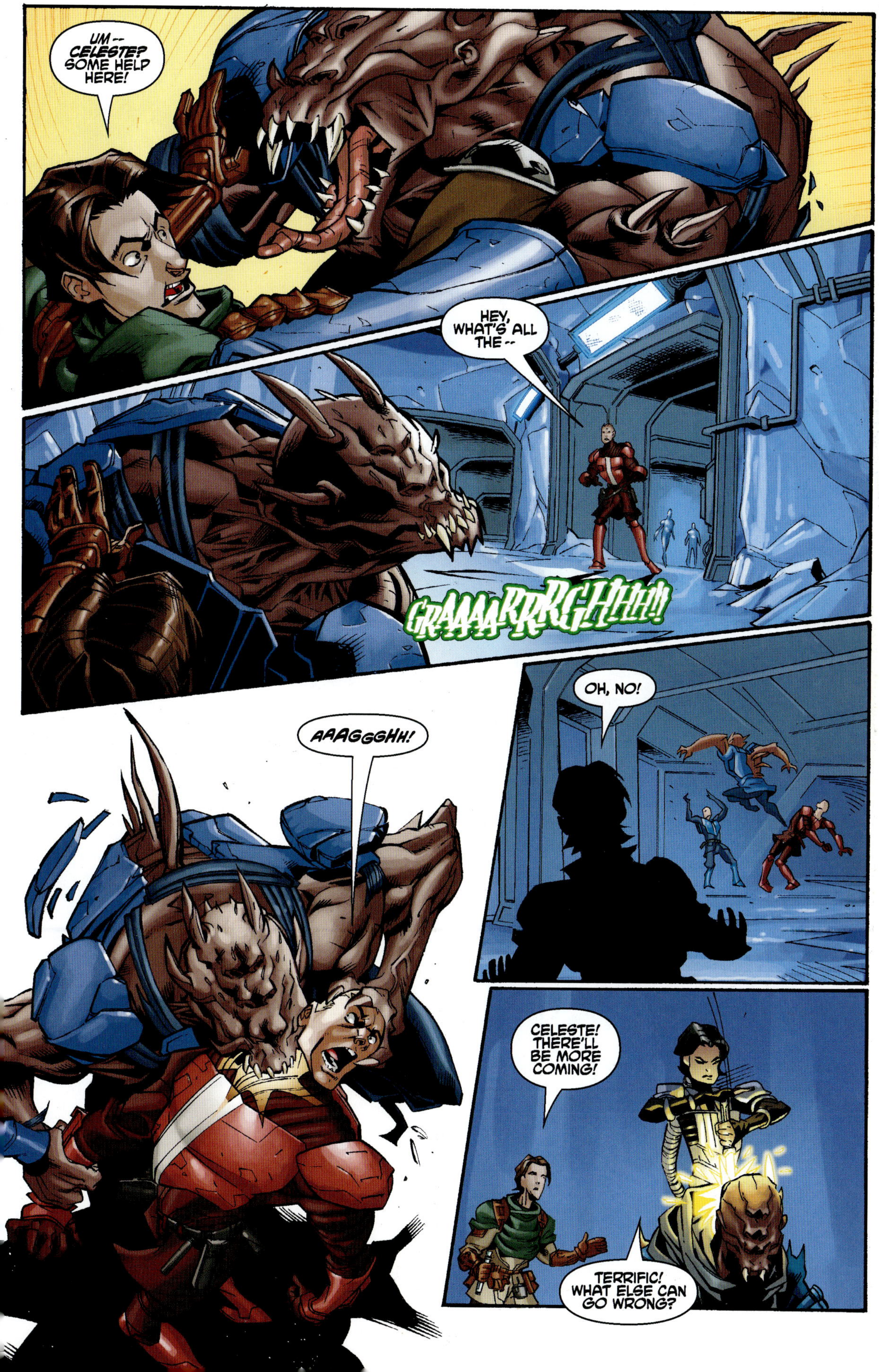
UM -- CELESTE? SOME HELP HERE!
HEY, WHAT'S ALL THE --
GRAAAARRRGHHH!!
OH, NO!
AAAGGGHH!
CELESTE! THERE'LL BE MORE COMING!
TERRIFIC! WHAT ELSE CAN GO WRONG?

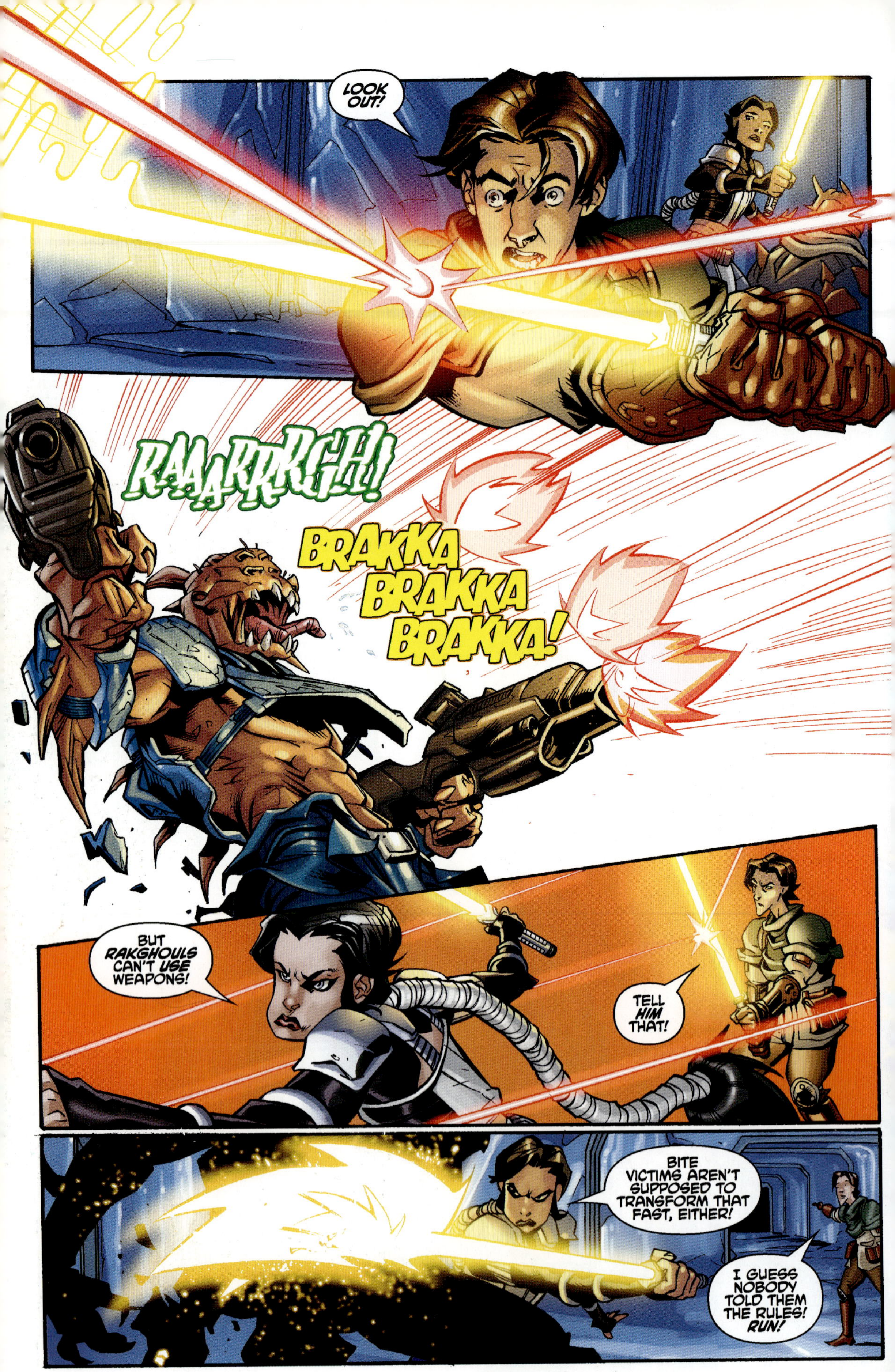

LOOK OUT!
RAAARRRGH!
BRAKKA BRAKKA BRAKKA!
BUT RAKGHOULS CAN'T USE WEAPONS!
TELL HIM THAT!
BITE VICTIMS AREN'T SUPPOSED TO TRANSFORM THAT FAST, EITHER!
I GUESS NOBODY TOLD THEM THE RULES! RUN!

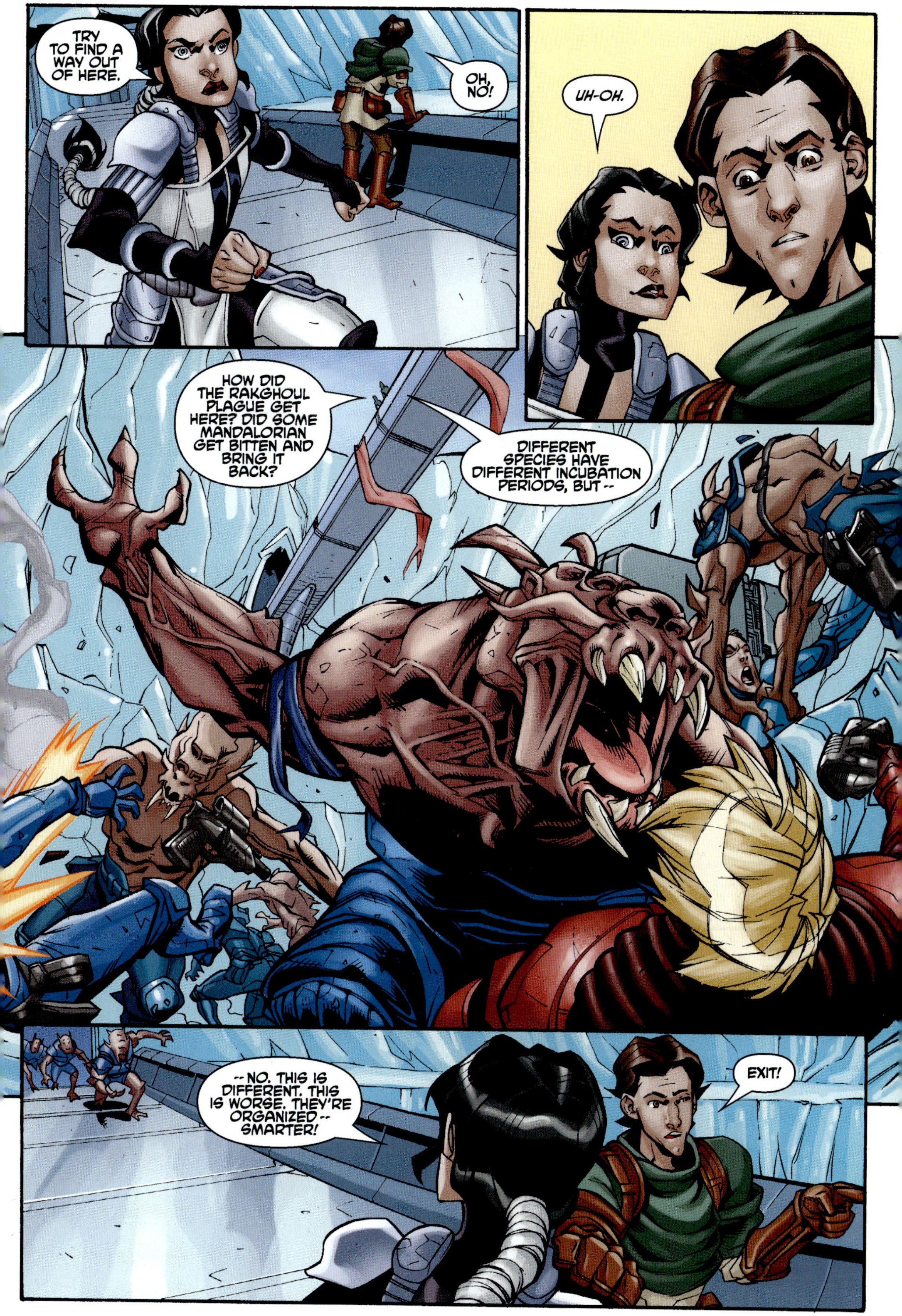
TRY TO FIND A WAY OUT OF HERE.
OH, NO!
UH-OH.
HOW DID THE RAKGHOUL PLAGUE GET HERE? DID SOME MANDALORIAN GET BITTEN AND BRING IT BACK?
DIFFERENT SPECIES HAVE DIFFERENT INCUBATION PERIODS, BUT --
-- NO. THIS IS DIFFERENT. THIS IS WORSE. THEY'RE ORGANIZED -- SMARTER!
EXIT!

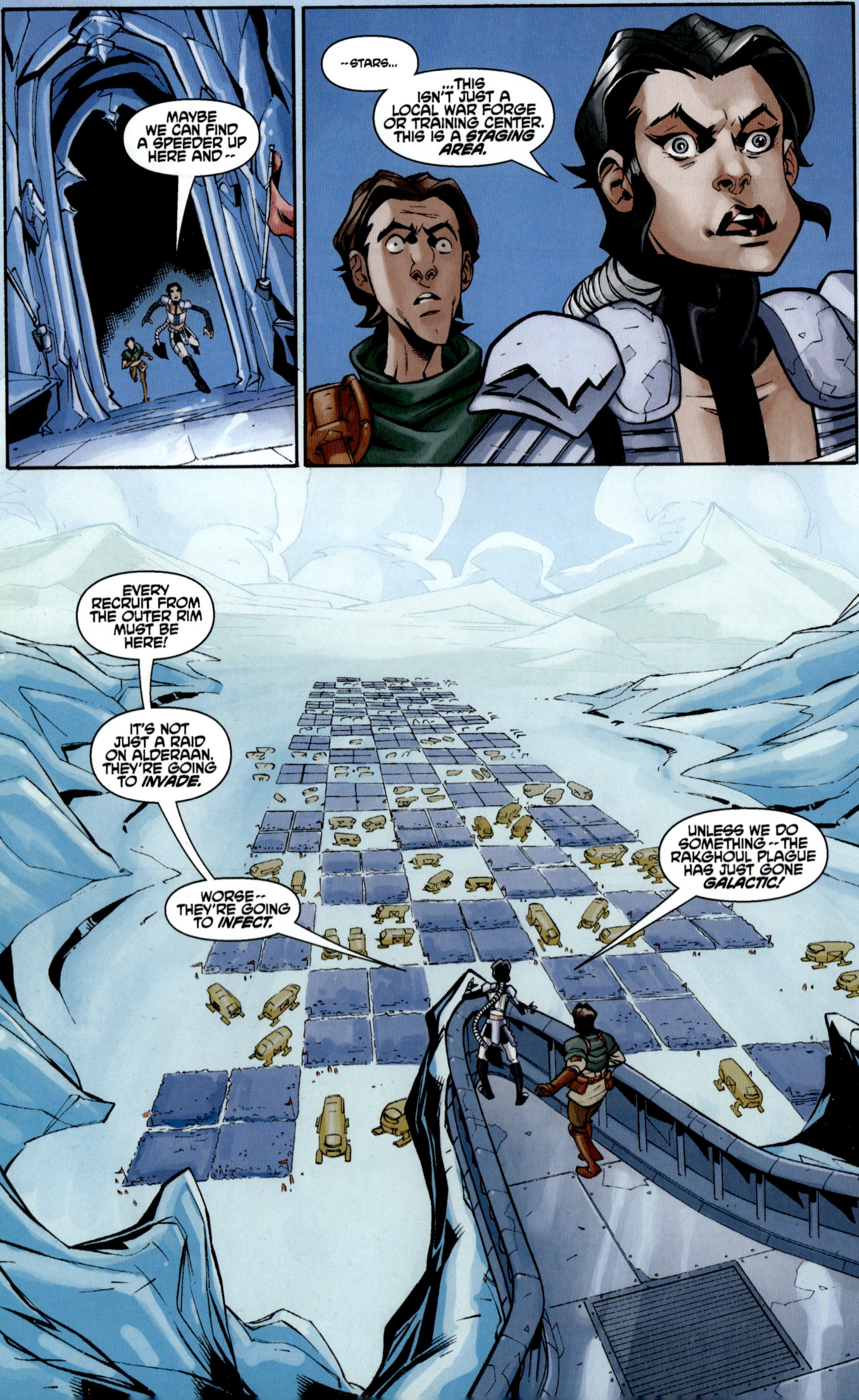
MAYBE WE CAN FIND A SPEEDER UP HERE AND --
--STARS...
...THIS ISN'T JUST A LOCAL WAR FORGE OR TRAINING CENTER. THIS IS A *STAGING AREA.*
EVERY RECRUIT FROM THE OUTER RIM MUST BE HERE!
IT'S NOT JUST A RAID ON ALDERAAN. THEY'RE GOING TO *INVADE.*
WORSE-- THEY'RE GOING TO *INFECT.*
UNLESS WE DO SOMETHING -- THE RAKGHOUL PLAGUE HAS JUST GONE *GALACTIC!*

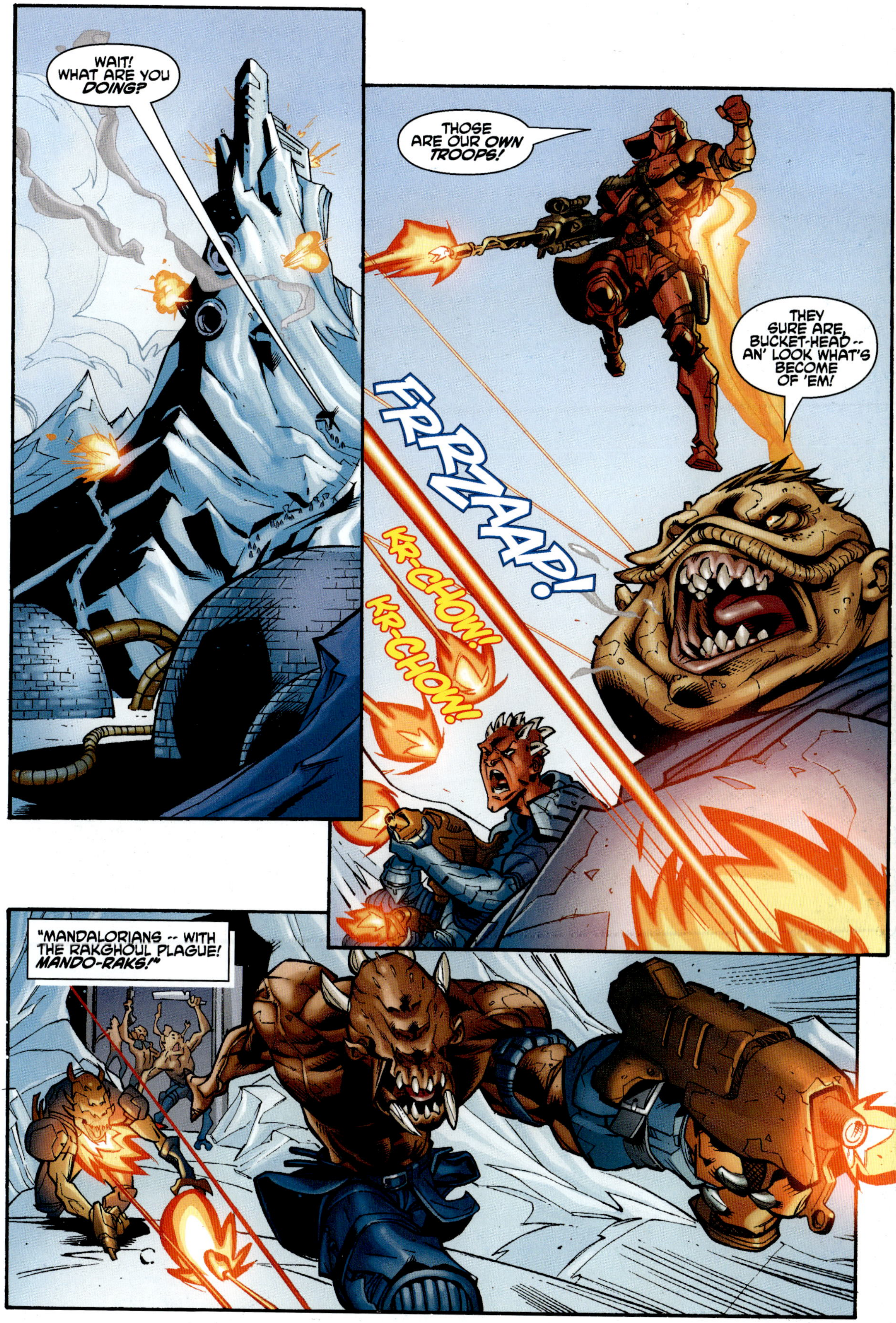
WAIT! WHAT ARE YOU DOING?
THOSE ARE OUR OWN TROOPS!
THEY SURE ARE, BUCKET-HEAD -- AN' LOOK WHAT'S BECOME OF 'EM!
FRRZAAP!
KR-CHOW! KR-CHOW!
"MANDALORIANS -- WITH THE RAKGHOUL PLAGUE! MANDO-RAKS!"

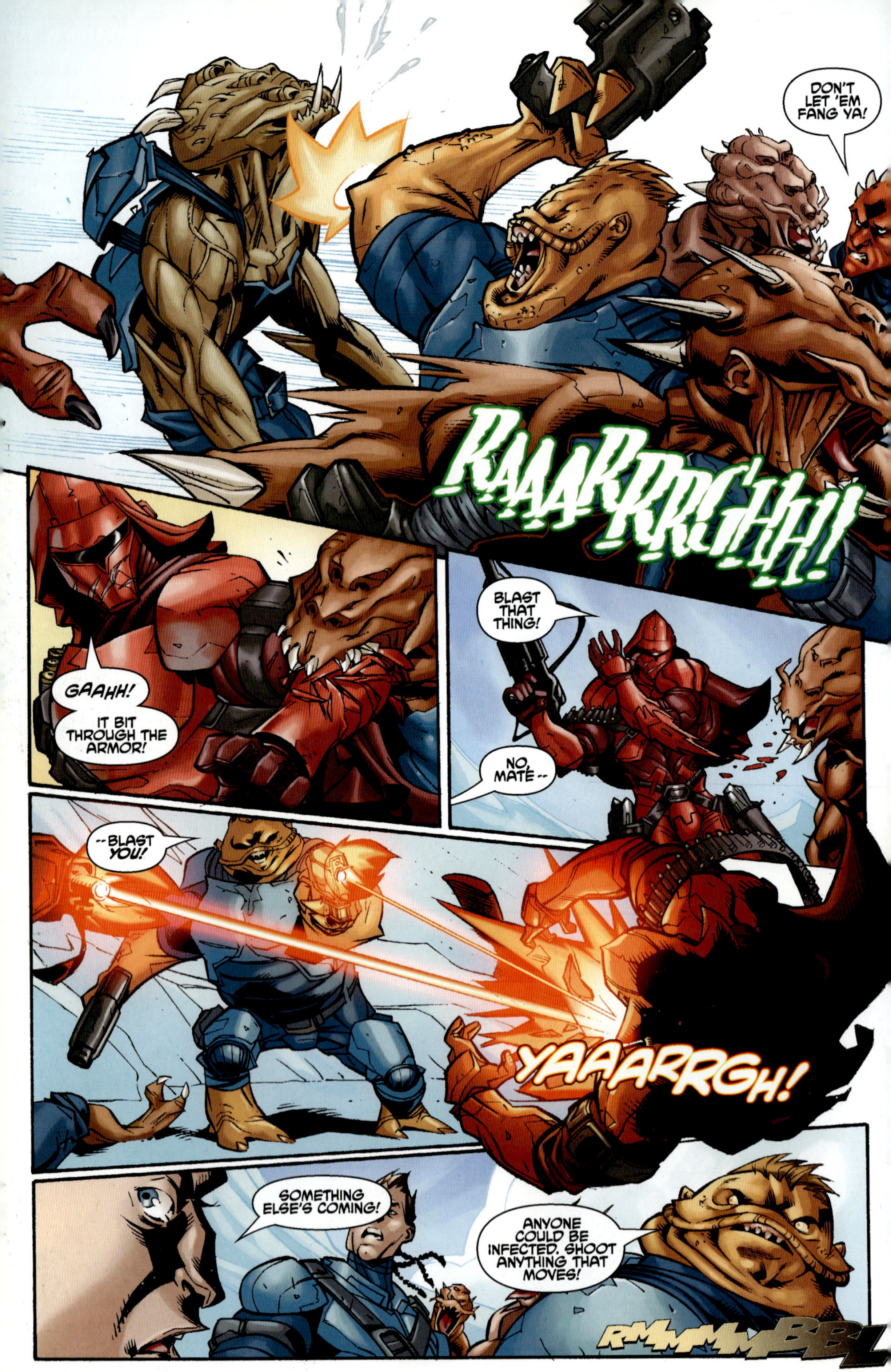
DON'T LET 'EM FANG YA!
KAAAKRRRGHH!
GAAHH!
IT BIT THROUGH THE ARMOR!
BLAST THAT THING!
NO, MATE --
--BLAST YOU!
YAAARRGH!
SOMETHING ELSE'S COMING!
ANYONE COULD BE INFECTED. SHOOT ANYTHING THAT MOVES!
RMMMMMBBL

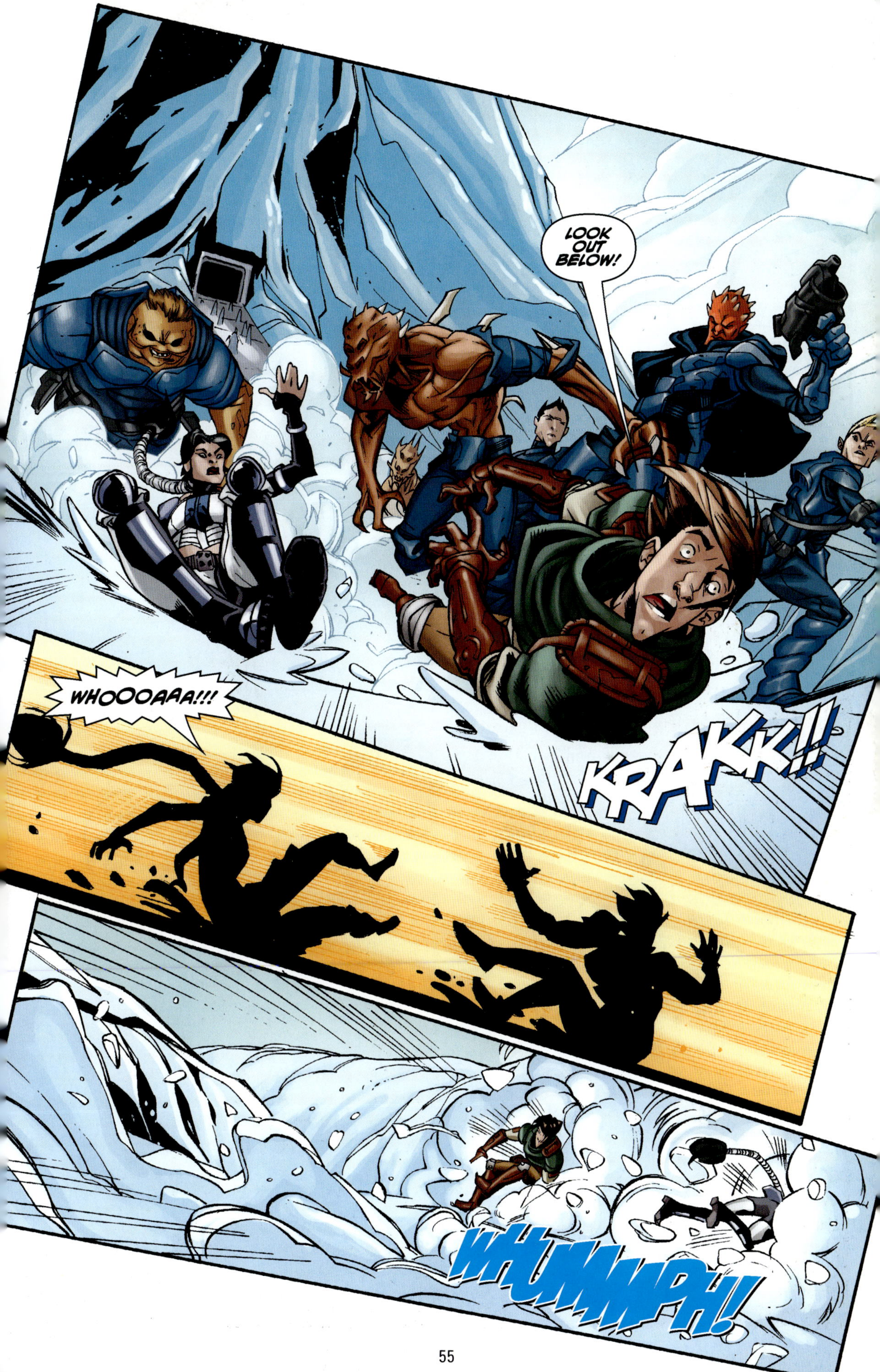
LOOK OUT BELOW!
KRAKK!!
WHOOOAAA!!!
WHUMMPH!

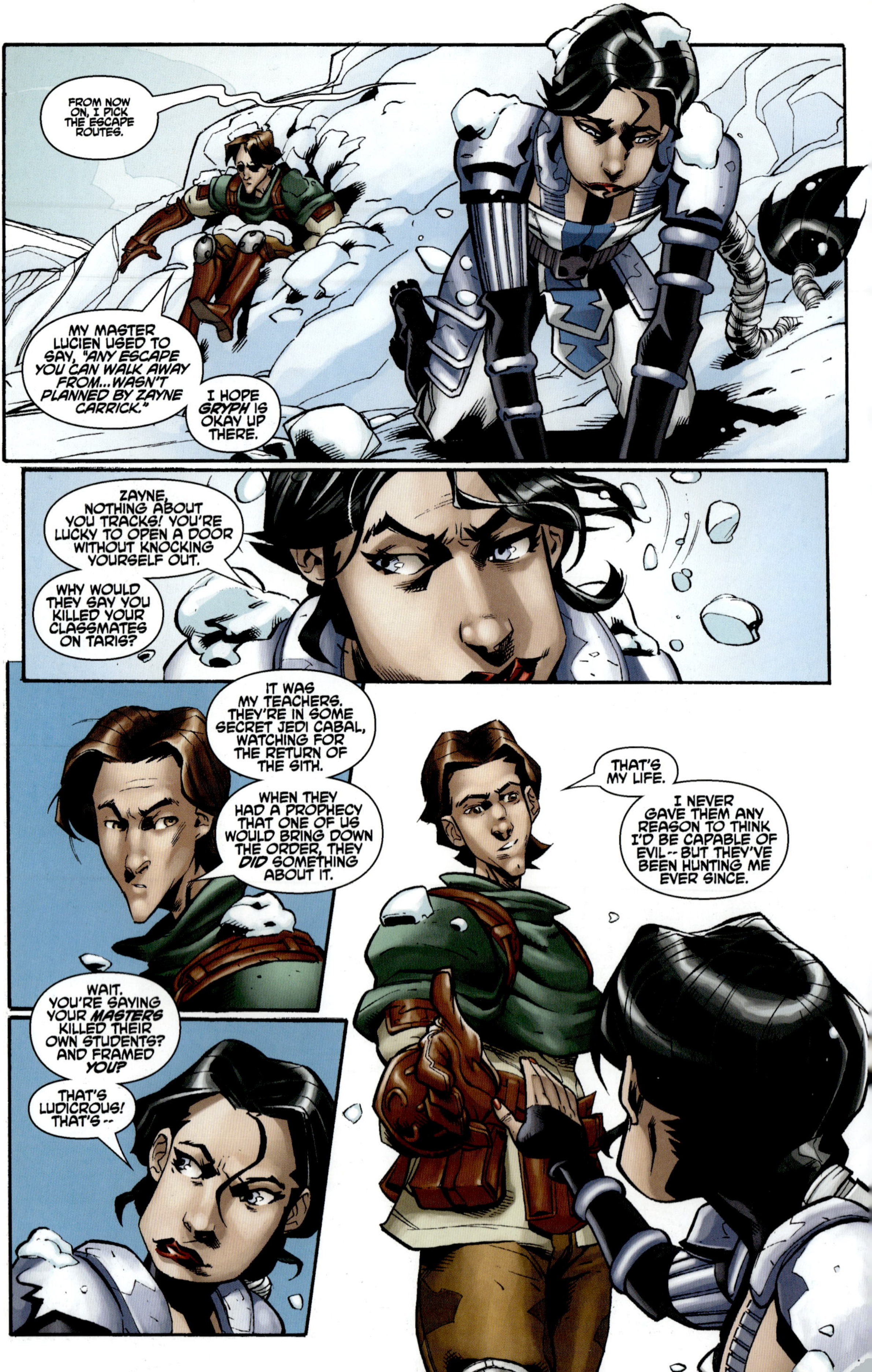
FROM NOW ON, I PICK THE ESCAPE ROUTES.
MY MASTER LUCIEN USED TO SAY, "ANY ESCAPE YOU CAN WALK AWAY FROM...WASN'T PLANNED BY ZAYNE CARRICK."
I HOPE GRYPH IS OKAY UP THERE.
ZAYNE, NOTHING ABOUT YOU TRACKS! YOU'RE LUCKY TO OPEN A DOOR WITHOUT KNOCKING YOURSELF OUT.
WHY WOULD THEY SAY YOU KILLED YOUR CLASSMATES ON TARIS?
IT WAS MY TEACHERS. THEY'RE IN SOME SECRET JEDI CABAL, WATCHING FOR THE RETURN OF THE SITH.
WHEN THEY HAD A PROPHECY THAT ONE OF US WOULD BRING DOWN THE ORDER, THEY DID SOMETHING ABOUT IT.
WAIT. YOU'RE SAYING YOUR MASTERS KILLED THEIR OWN STUDENTS? AND FRAMED YOU?
THAT'S LUDICROUS! THAT'S --
THAT'S MY LIFE.
I NEVER GAVE THEM ANY REASON TO THINK I'D BE CAPABLE OF EVIL-- BUT THEY'VE BEEN HUNTING ME EVER SINCE.

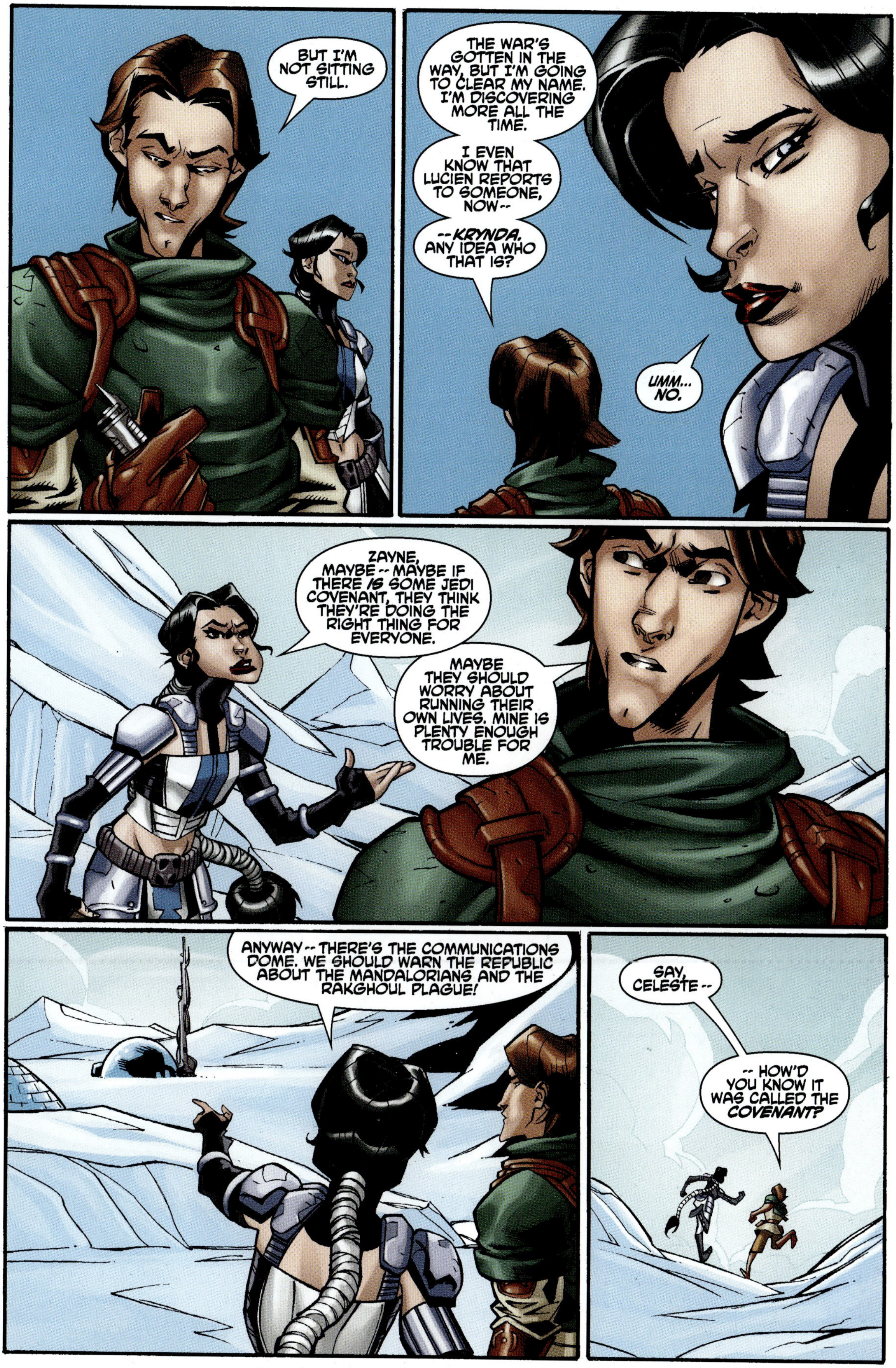

BUT I'M NOT SITTING STILL.
THE WAR'S GOTTEN IN THE WAY, BUT I'M GOING TO CLEAR MY NAME. I'M DISCOVERING MORE ALL THE TIME.
I EVEN KNOW THAT LUCIEN REPORTS TO SOMEONE, NOW--
--*KRYNDA*. ANY IDEA WHO THAT IS?
UMM... NO.
ZAYNE, MAYBE--MAYBE IF THERE *IS* SOME JEDI COVENANT, THEY THINK THEY'RE DOING THE RIGHT THING FOR EVERYONE.
MAYBE THEY SHOULD WORRY ABOUT RUNNING THEIR OWN LIVES. MINE IS PLENTY ENOUGH TROUBLE FOR ME.
ANYWAY--THERE'S THE COMMUNICATIONS DOME. WE SHOULD WARN THE REPUBLIC ABOUT THE MANDALORIANS AND THE RAKGHOUL PLAGUE!
SAY, CELESTE--
--HOW'D YOU KNOW IT WAS CALLED THE *COVENANT*?

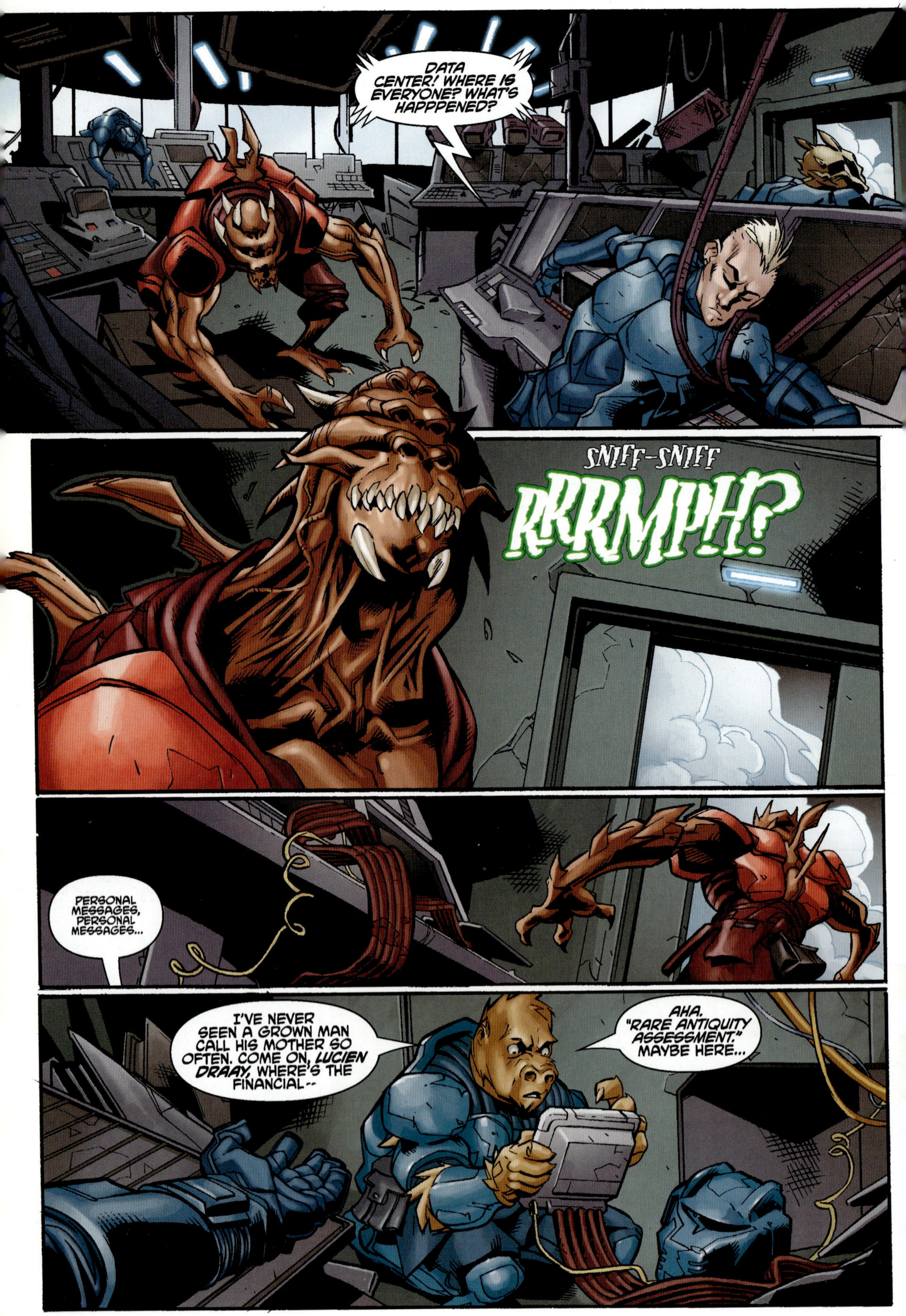
DATA CENTER! WHERE IS EVERYONE? WHAT'S HAPPPENED?
SNIFF-SNIFF
RRRMPH?
PERSONAL MESSAGES, PERSONAL MESSAGES...
I'VE NEVER SEEN A GROWN MAN CALL HIS MOTHER SO OFTEN. COME ON, LUCIEN DRAAY, WHERE'S THE FINANCIAL--
AHA. "RARE ANTIQUITY ASSESSMENT." MAYBE HERE...

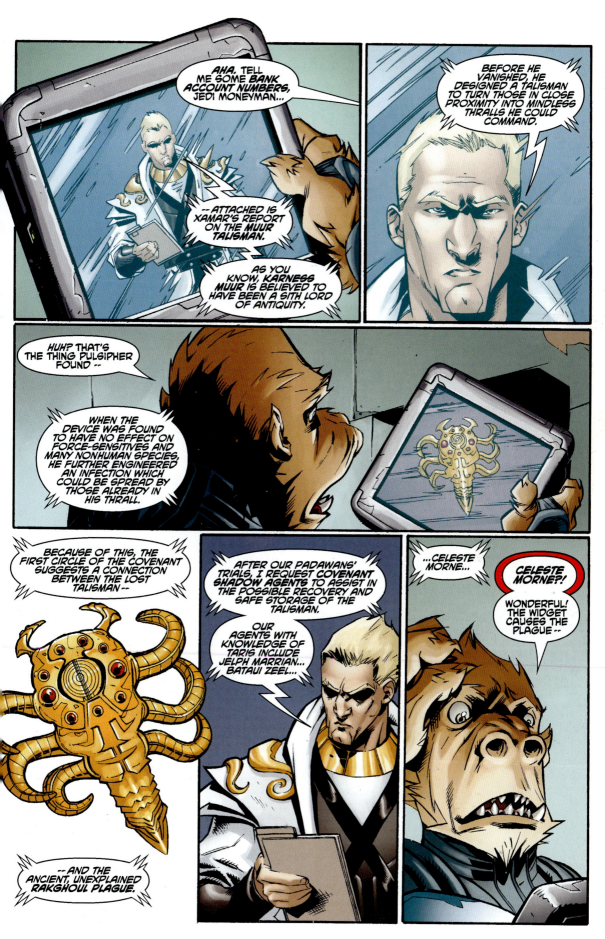

AHA, TELL ME SOME *BANK ACCOUNT NUMBERS,* JEDI MONEYMAN...

-- ATTACHED IS XAMAR'S REPORT ON THE MUUR TALISMAN.

AS YOU KNOW, *KARNESS MUUR* IS BELIEVED TO HAVE BEEN A SITH LORD OF ANTIQUITY.

BEFORE HE VANISHED, HE DESIGNED A TALISMAN TO TURN THOSE IN CLOSE PROXIMITY INTO *MINDLESS THRALLS* HE COULD COMMAND.

HUH? THAT'S THE THING *PULSIPHER* FOUND --

WHEN THE DEVICE WAS FOUND TO HAVE *NO EFFECT* ON FORCE-SENSITIVES AND MANY NONHUMAN SPECIES, HE FURTHER ENGINEERED AN *INFECTION* WHICH COULD BE SPREAD BY THOSE ALREADY IN HIS THRALL.

BECAUSE OF THIS, THE *FIRST CIRCLE* OF THE COVENANT SUGGESTS A CONNECTION BETWEEN THE LOST TALISMAN --

-- AND THE ANCIENT, UNEXPLAINED *RAKGHOUL PLAGUE.*

AFTER OUR PADAWANS' TRIALS, I REQUEST COVENANT SHADOW AGENTS TO ASSIST IN THE POSSIBLE RECOVERY AND SAFE STORAGE OF THE TALISMAN.

OUR AGENTS WITH KNOWLEDGE OF *TARIS* INCLUDE *JELPH MARRIAN... BATAUI ZEEL...*

...*CELESTE MORNE...*

CELESTE MORNE?!

WONDERFUL! THE WIDGET CAUSES THE PLAGUE --

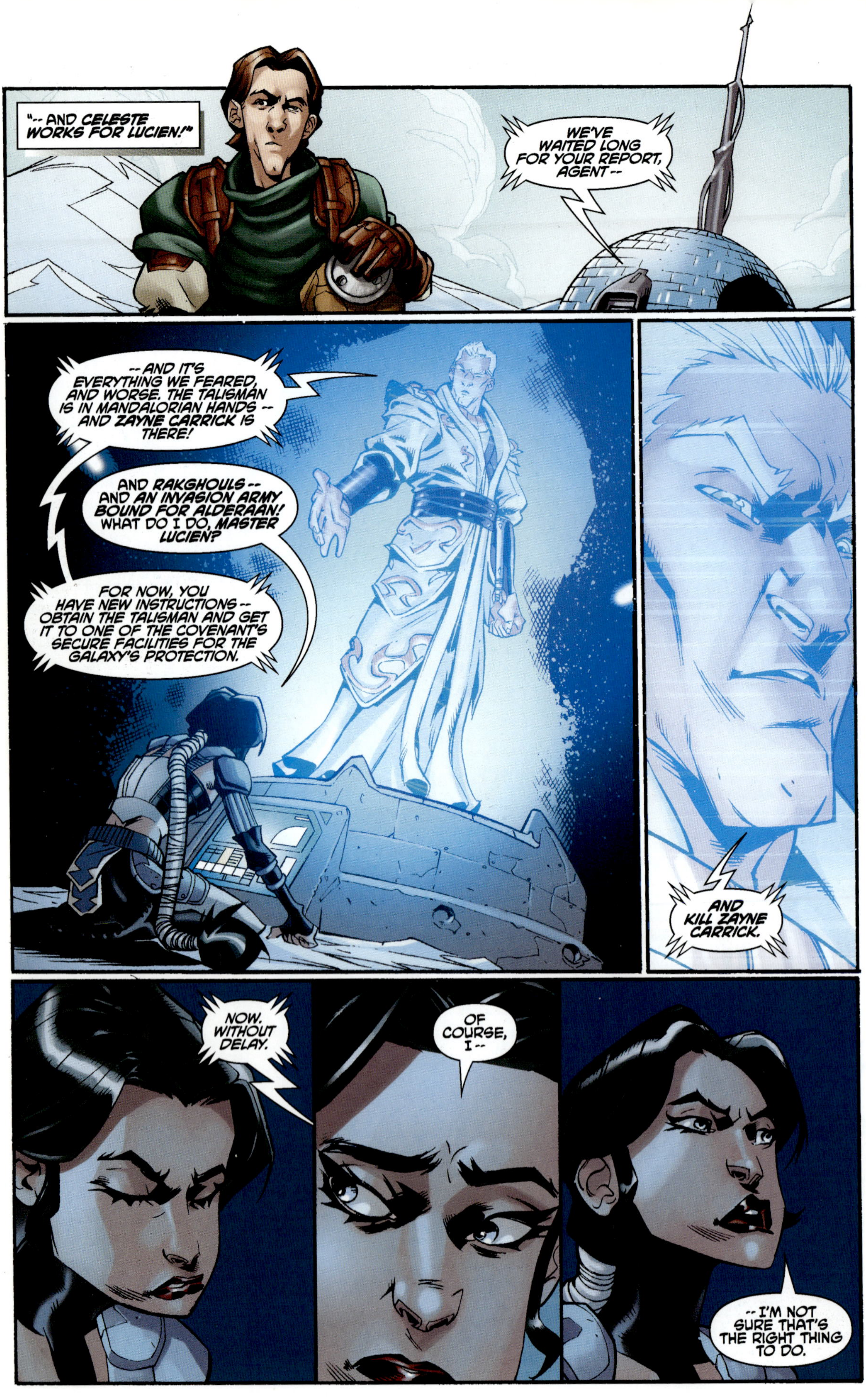
"-- AND CELESTE WORKS FOR LUCIEN!"
WE'VE WAITED LONG FOR YOUR REPORT, AGENT --
-- AND IT'S EVERYTHING WE FEARED, AND WORSE. THE TALISMAN IS IN MANDALORIAN HANDS -- AND ZAYNE CARRICK IS THERE!
AND RAKGHOULS -- AND AN INVASION ARMY BOUND FOR ALDERAAN! WHAT DO I DO, MASTER LUCIEN?
FOR NOW, YOU HAVE NEW INSTRUCTIONS -- OBTAIN THE TALISMAN AND GET IT TO ONE OF THE COVENANT'S SECURE FACILITIES FOR THE GALAXY'S PROTECTION.
AND KILL ZAYNE CARRICK.
NOW. WITHOUT DELAY.
OF COURSE, I --
-- I'M NOT SURE THAT'S THE RIGHT THING TO DO.

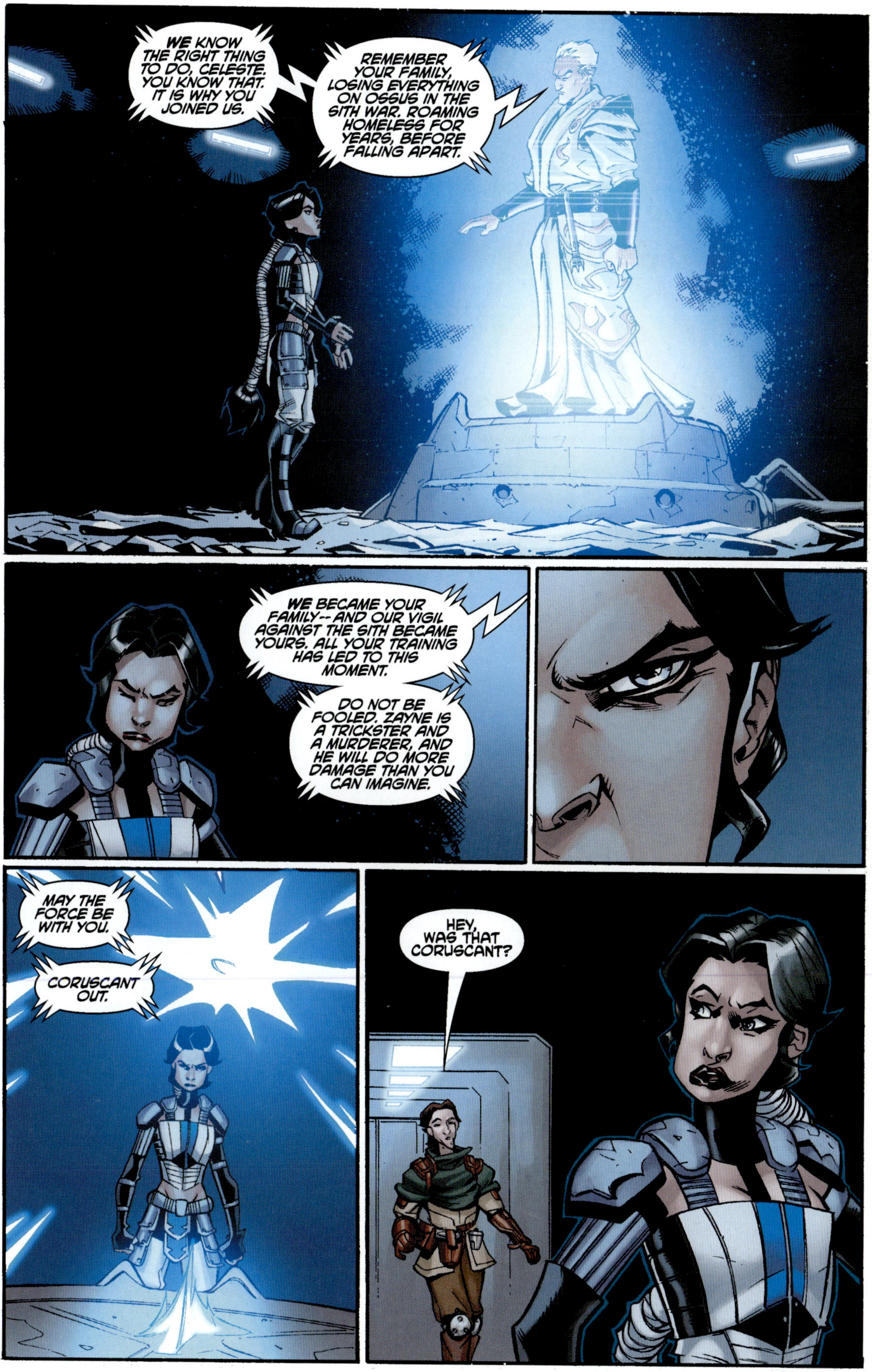
WE KNOW THE RIGHT THING TO DO, CELESTE. YOU KNOW THAT. IT IS WHY YOU JOINED US.
REMEMBER YOUR FAMILY, LOSING EVERYTHING ON OSSUS IN THE SITH WAR. ROAMING HOMELESS FOR YEARS, BEFORE FALLING APART.
WE BECAME YOUR FAMILY-- AND OUR VIGIL AGAINST THE SITH BECAME YOURS. ALL YOUR TRAINING HAS LED TO THIS MOMENT.
DO NOT BE FOOLED. ZAYNE IS A TRICKSTER AND A MURDERER, AND HE WILL DO MORE DAMAGE THAN YOU CAN IMAGINE.
MAY THE FORCE BE WITH YOU.
CORUSCANT OUT.
HEY, WAS THAT CORUSCANT?

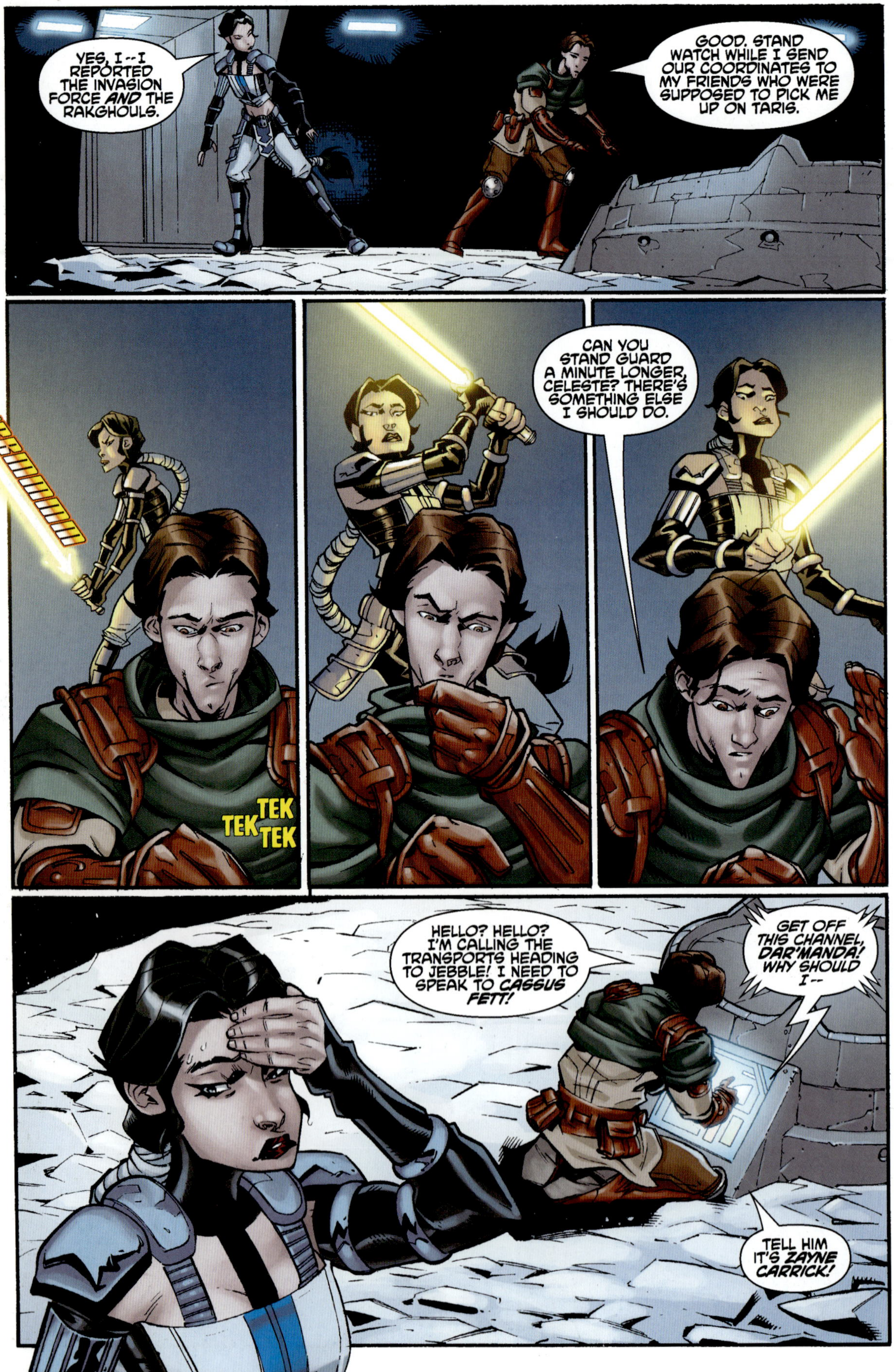
YES, I -- I REPORTED THE INVASION FORCE AND THE RAKGHOULS.
GOOD. STAND WATCH WHILE I SEND OUR COORDINATES TO MY FRIENDS WHO WERE SUPPOSED TO PICK ME UP ON TARIS.
TEK TEK TEK
CAN YOU STAND GUARD A MINUTE LONGER, CELESTE? THERE'S SOMETHING ELSE I SHOULD DO.
HELLO? HELLO? I'M CALLING THE TRANSPORTS HEADING TO JEBBLE! I NEED TO SPEAK TO CASSUS FETT!
GET OFF THIS CHANNEL, DAR'MANDA! WHY SHOULD I --
TELL HIM IT'S ZAYNE CARRICK!

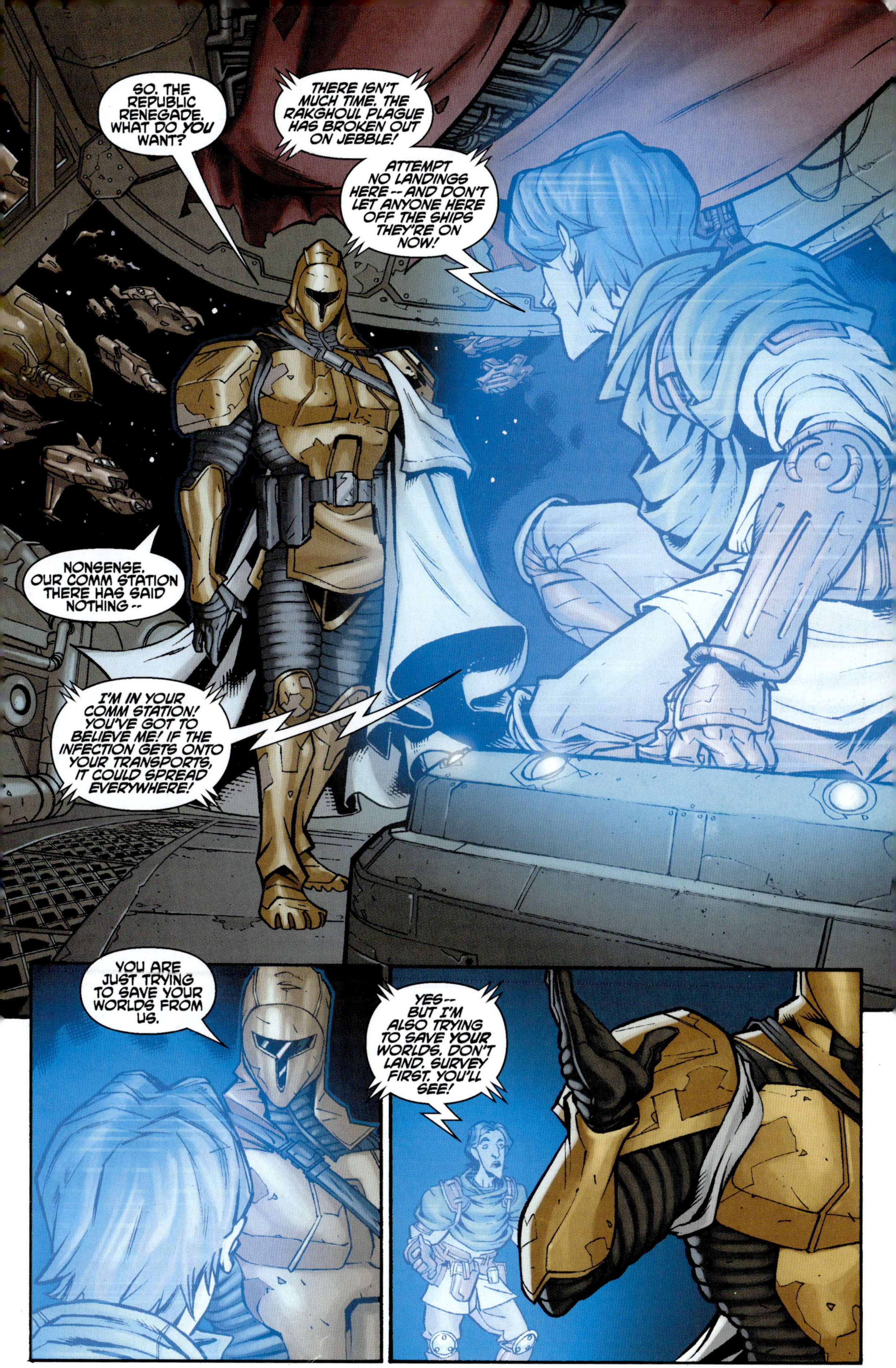
SO, THE REPUBLIC RENEGADE. WHAT DO YOU WANT?
THERE ISN'T MUCH TIME. THE RAKGHOUL PLAGUE HAS BROKEN OUT ON JEBBLE!
ATTEMPT NO LANDINGS HERE -- AND DON'T LET ANYONE HERE OFF THE SHIPS THEY'RE ON NOW!
NONSENSE. OUR COMM STATION THERE HAS SAID NOTHING --
I'M IN YOUR COMM STATION! YOU'VE GOT TO BELIEVE ME! IF THE INFECTION GETS ONTO YOUR TRANSPORTS, IT COULD SPREAD EVERYWHERE!
YOU ARE JUST TRYING TO SAVE YOUR WORLDS FROM US.
YES-- BUT I'M ALSO TRYING TO SAVE YOUR WORLDS. DON'T LAND. SURVEY FIRST. YOU'LL SEE!

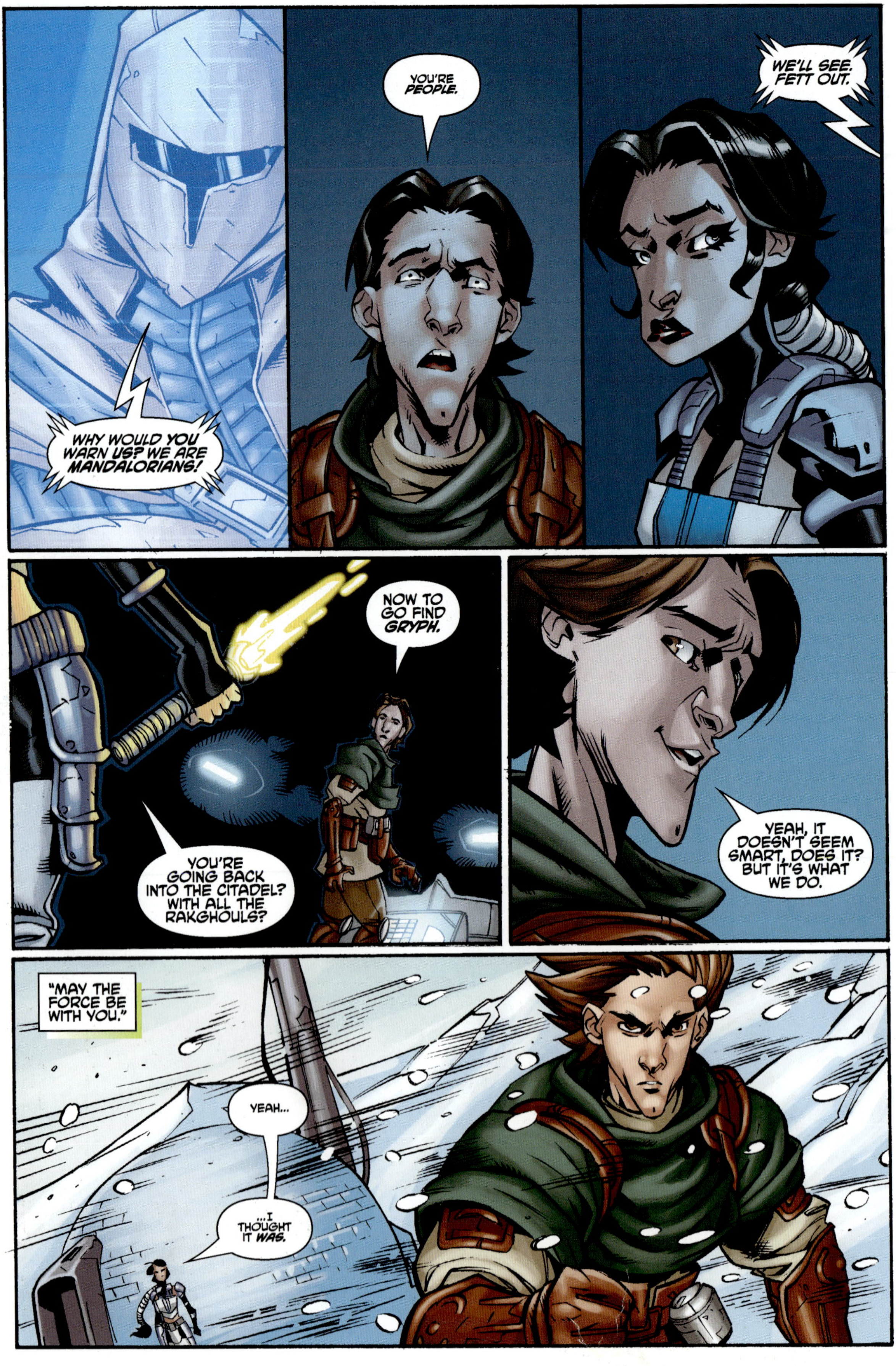
WHY WOULD YOU WARN US? WE ARE MANDALORIANS!
YOU'RE PEOPLE.
WE'LL SEE. FETT OUT.
NOW TO GO FIND GRYPH.
YOU'RE GOING BACK INTO THE CITADEL? WITH ALL THE RAKGHOULS?
YEAH, IT DOESN'T SEEM SMART, DOES IT? BUT IT'S WHAT WE DO.
"MAY THE FORCE BE WITH YOU."
YEAH...
...I THOUGHT IT WAS.

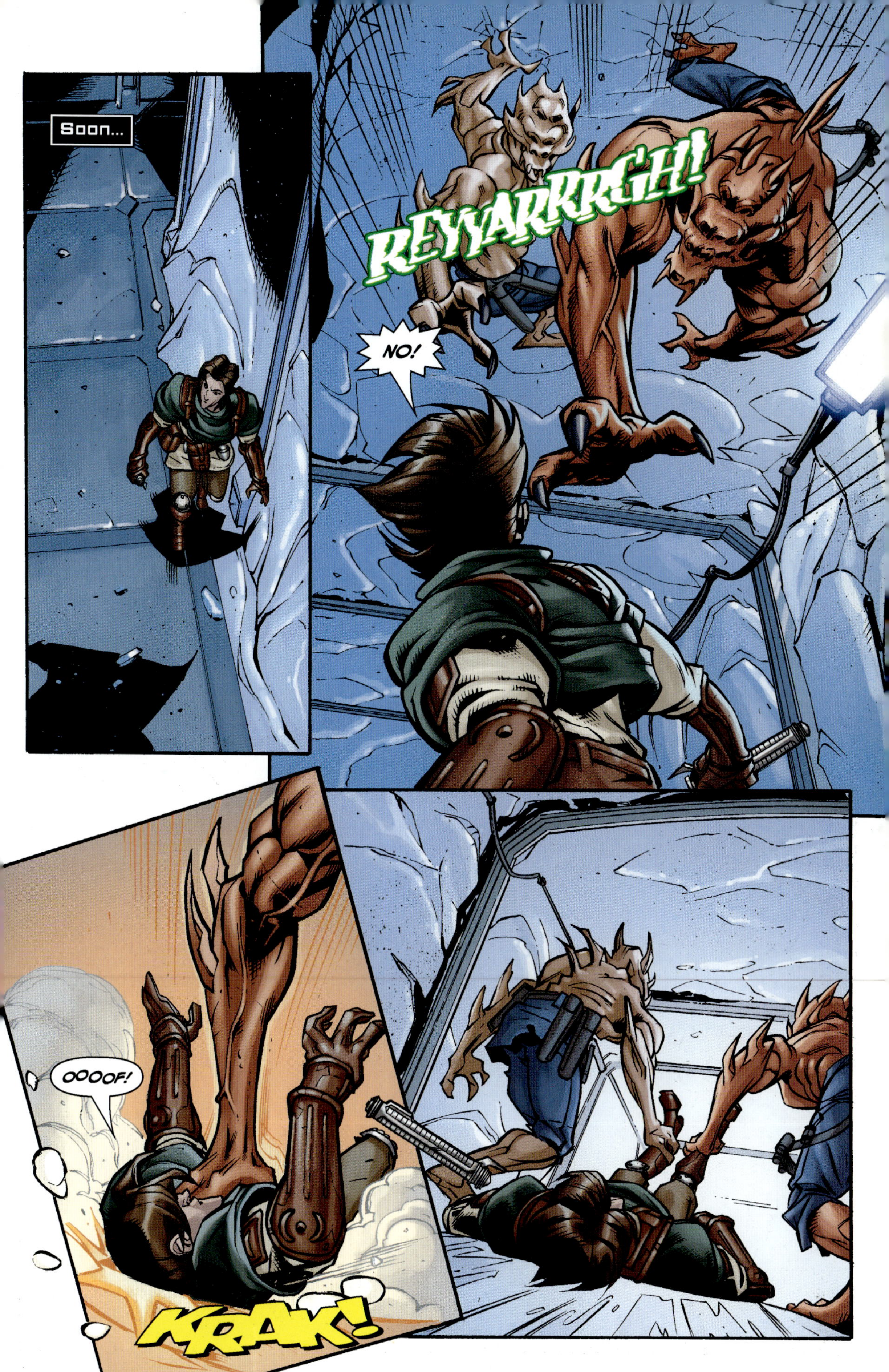
Soon...
REYYARRRGH!
NO!
OOOOF!
KRAK!

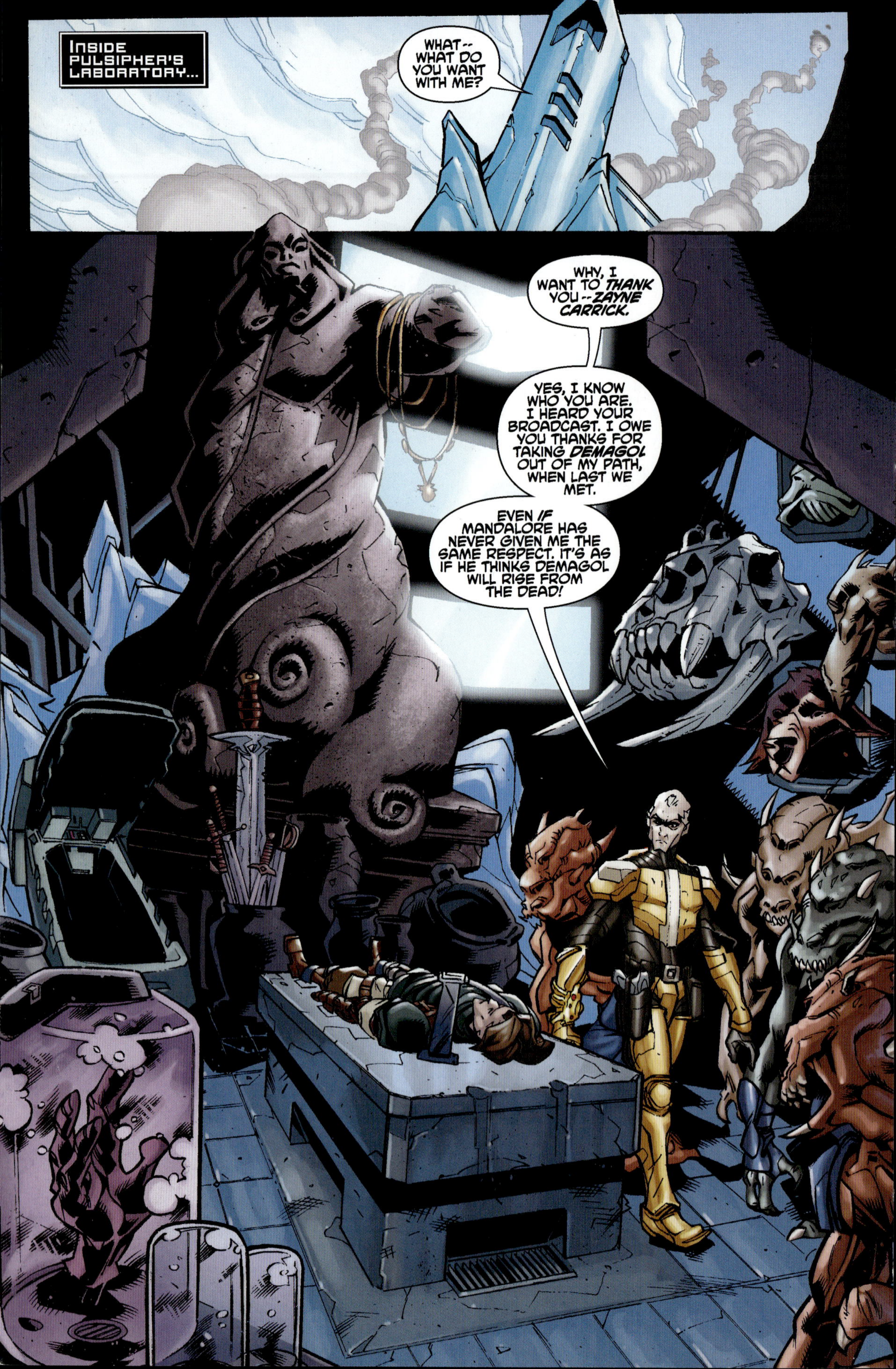
INSIDE PULSIPHER'S LABORATORY...
WHAT-- WHAT DO YOU WANT WITH ME?
WHY, I WANT TO THANK YOU--ZAYNE CARRICK.
YES, I KNOW WHO YOU ARE. I HEARD YOUR BROADCAST. I OWE YOU THANKS FOR TAKING DEMAGOL OUT OF MY PATH, WHEN LAST WE MET.
EVEN IF MANDALORE HAS NEVER GIVEN ME THE SAME RESPECT. IT'S AS IF HE THINKS DEMAGOL WILL RISE FROM THE DEAD!

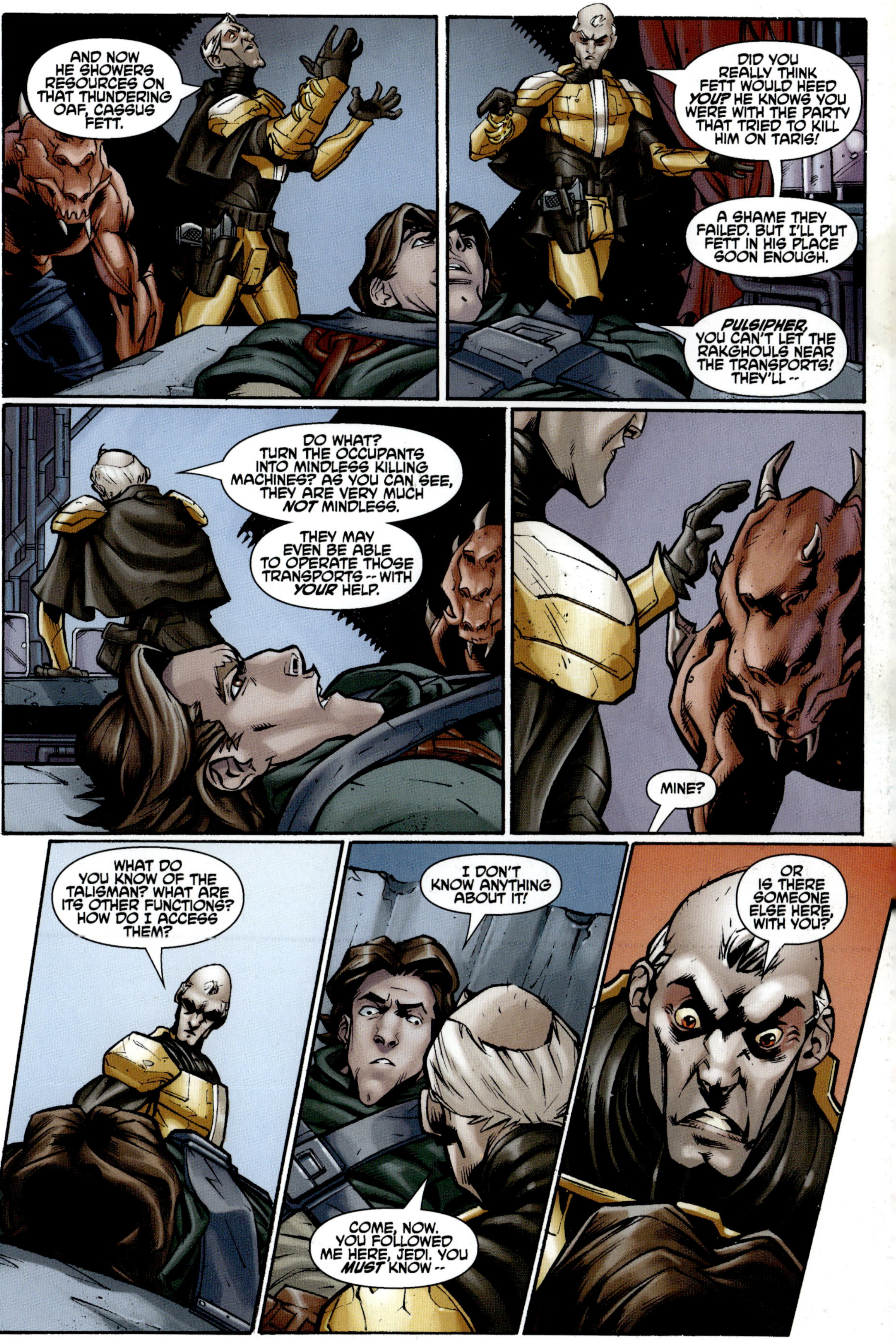
AND NOW HE SHOWERS RESOURCES ON THAT THUNDERING OAF, CASSUS FETT.
DID YOU REALLY THINK FETT WOULD HEED *YOU?* HE KNOWS YOU WERE WITH THE PARTY THAT TRIED TO KILL HIM ON TARIS!
A SHAME THEY FAILED. BUT I'LL PUT FETT IN HIS PLACE SOON ENOUGH.
PULSIPHER, YOU CAN'T LET THE RAKGHOULS NEAR THE TRANSPORTS! THEY'LL --
DO WHAT? TURN THE OCCUPANTS INTO MINDLESS KILLING MACHINES? AS YOU CAN SEE, THEY ARE VERY MUCH *NOT* MINDLESS.
THEY MAY EVEN BE ABLE TO OPERATE THOSE TRANSPORTS -- WITH *YOUR* HELP.
MINE?
WHAT DO YOU KNOW OF THE TALISMAN? WHAT ARE ITS OTHER FUNCTIONS? HOW DO I ACCESS THEM?
I DON'T KNOW ANYTHING ABOUT IT!
COME, NOW. YOU FOLLOWED ME HERE, JEDI. YOU *MUST* KNOW --
OR IS THERE SOMEONE ELSE HERE, WITH YOU?

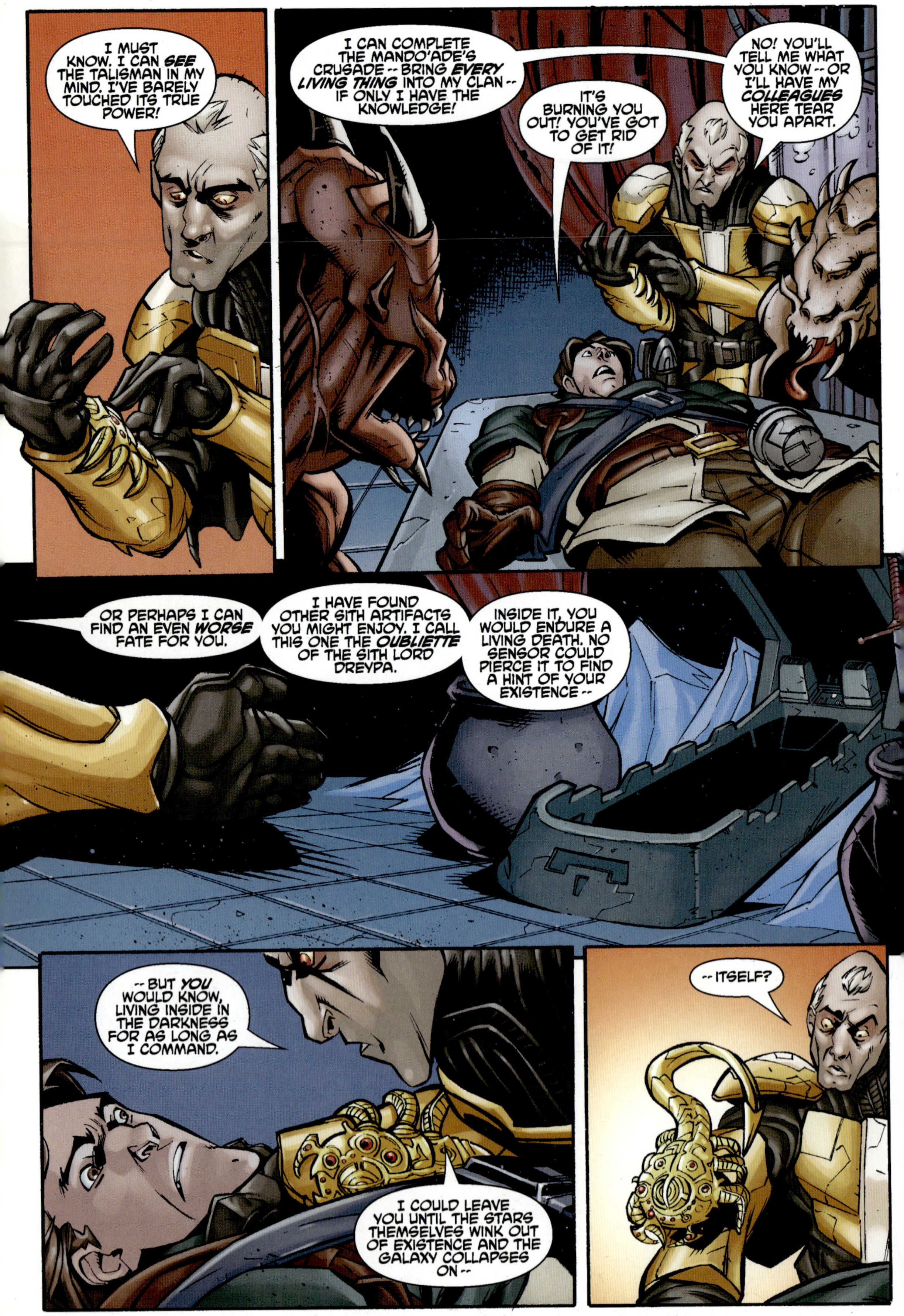
I MUST KNOW. I CAN *SEE* THE TALISMAN IN MY MIND. I'VE BARELY TOUCHED ITS TRUE POWER!
I CAN COMPLETE THE MANDO'ADE'S CRUSADE -- BRING *EVERY LIVING THING* INTO MY CLAN -- IF ONLY I HAVE THE KNOWLEDGE!
IT'S BURNING YOU OUT! YOU'VE GOT TO GET RID OF IT!
NO! YOU'LL TELL ME WHAT YOU KNOW -- OR I'LL HAVE MY *COLLEAGUES* HERE TEAR YOU APART.
OR PERHAPS I CAN FIND AN EVEN *WORSE* FATE FOR YOU.
I HAVE FOUND OTHER SITH ARTIFACTS YOU MIGHT ENJOY. I CALL THIS ONE THE *OUBLIETTE* OF THE SITH LORD DREYPA.
INSIDE IT, YOU WOULD ENDURE A LIVING DEATH. NO SENSOR COULD PIERCE IT TO FIND A HINT OF YOUR EXISTENCE --
-- BUT *YOU* WOULD KNOW, LIVING INSIDE IN THE DARKNESS FOR AS LONG AS I COMMAND.
I COULD LEAVE YOU UNTIL THE STARS THEMSELVES WINK OUT OF EXISTENCE AND THE GALAXY COLLAPSES ON --
-- ITSELF?

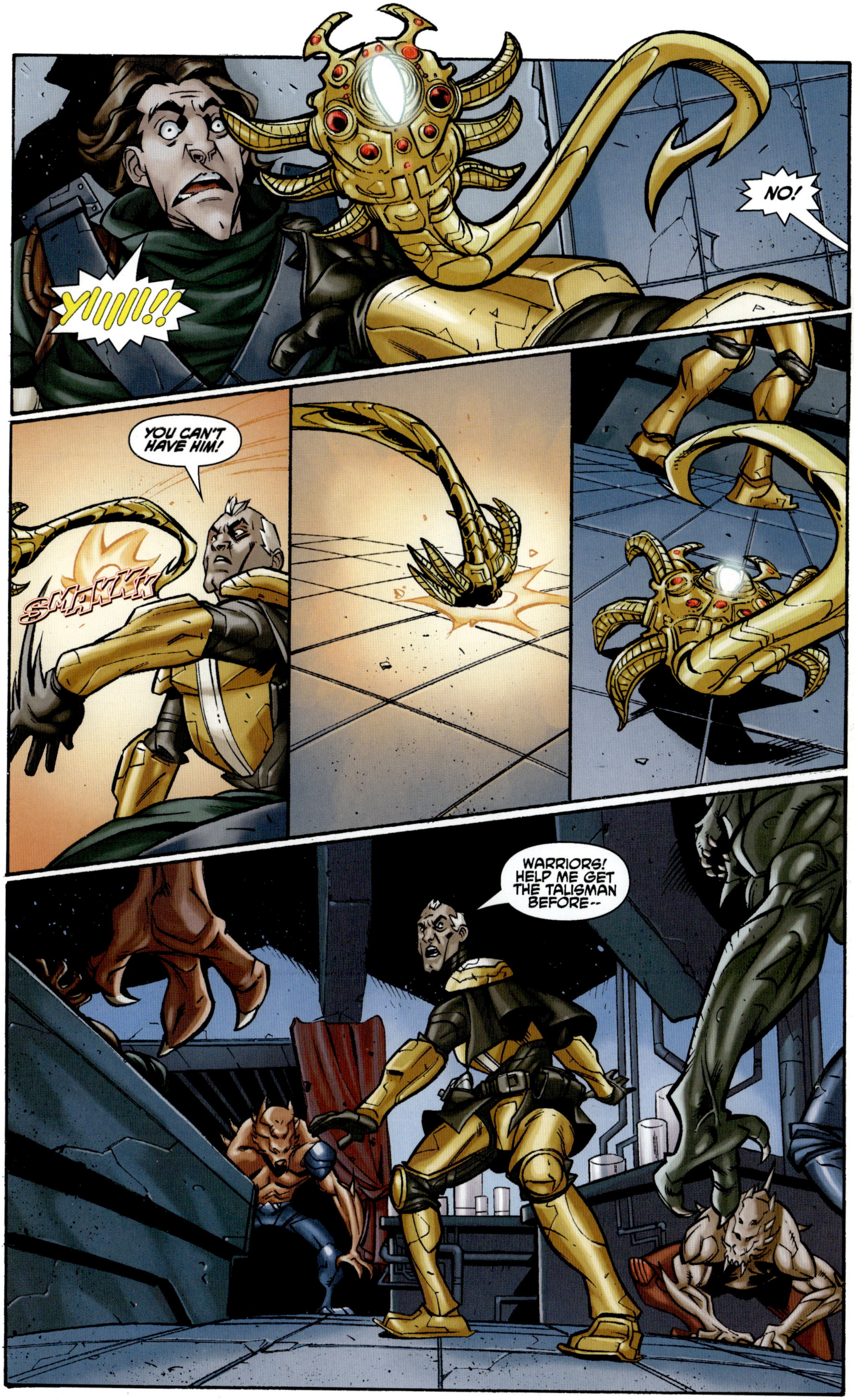
YIIIII!!
NO!
YOU CAN'T HAVE HIM!
SMAKKK
WARRIORS! HELP ME GET THE TALISMAN BEFORE--

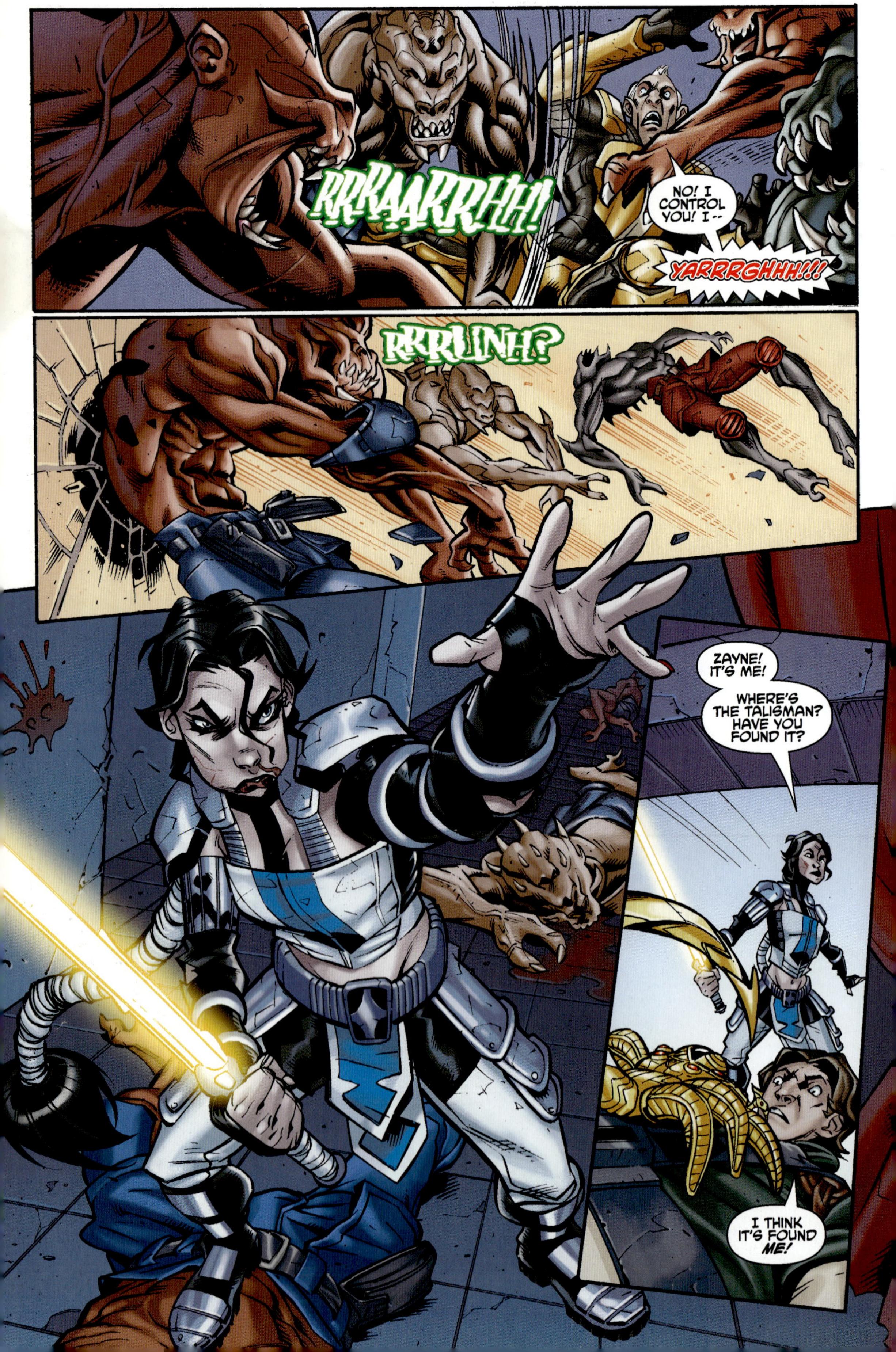
RRRAARRHH!
NO! I CONTROL YOU! I --
YARRRGHHH!!!
RRRUNH?
ZAYNE! IT'S ME!
WHERE'S THE TALISMAN? HAVE YOU FOUND IT?
I THINK IT'S FOUND *ME!*

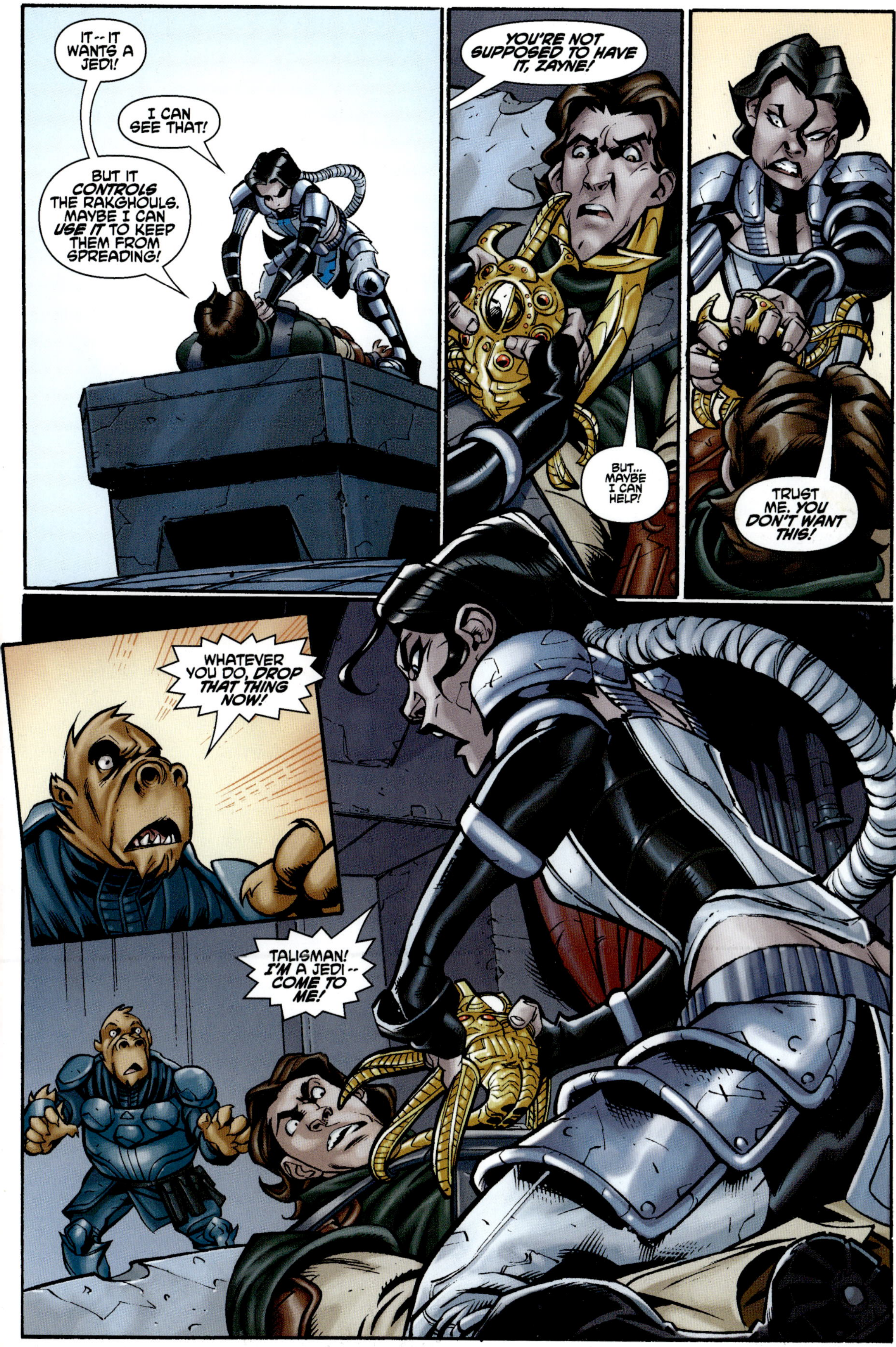
IT--IT WANTS A JEDI!
I CAN SEE THAT!
BUT IT CONTROLS THE RAKGHOULS. MAYBE I CAN USE IT TO KEEP THEM FROM SPREADING!
YOU'RE NOT SUPPOSED TO HAVE IT, ZAYNE!
BUT... MAYBE I CAN HELP!
TRUST ME. YOU DON'T WANT THIS!
WHATEVER YOU DO, DROP THAT THING NOW!
TALISMAN! I'M A JEDI--COME TO ME!

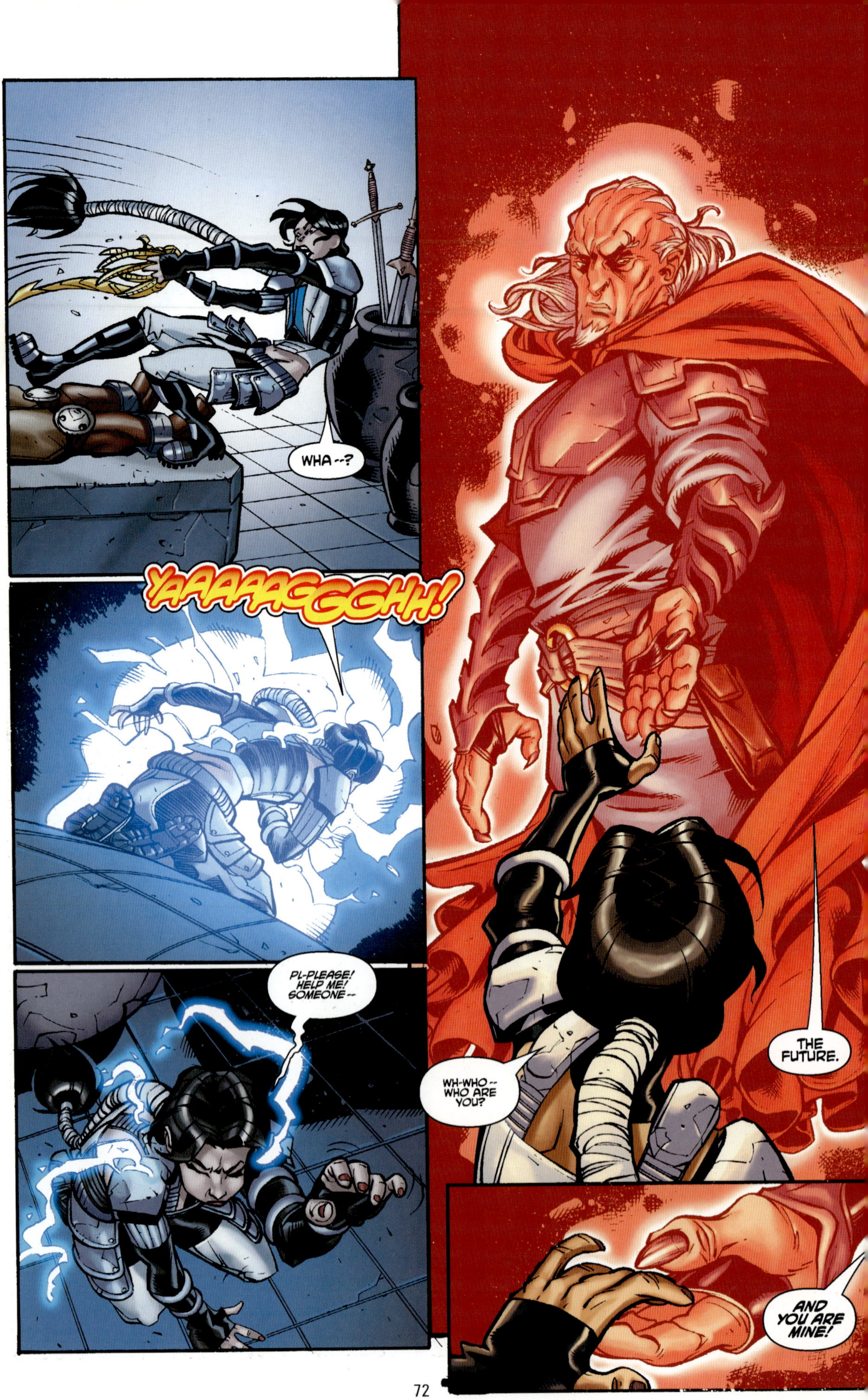

WHA--?
YAAAAAGGGHH!
PL-PLEASE! HELP ME! SOMEONE--
WH-WHO-- WHO ARE YOU?
THE FUTURE.
AND YOU ARE MINE!

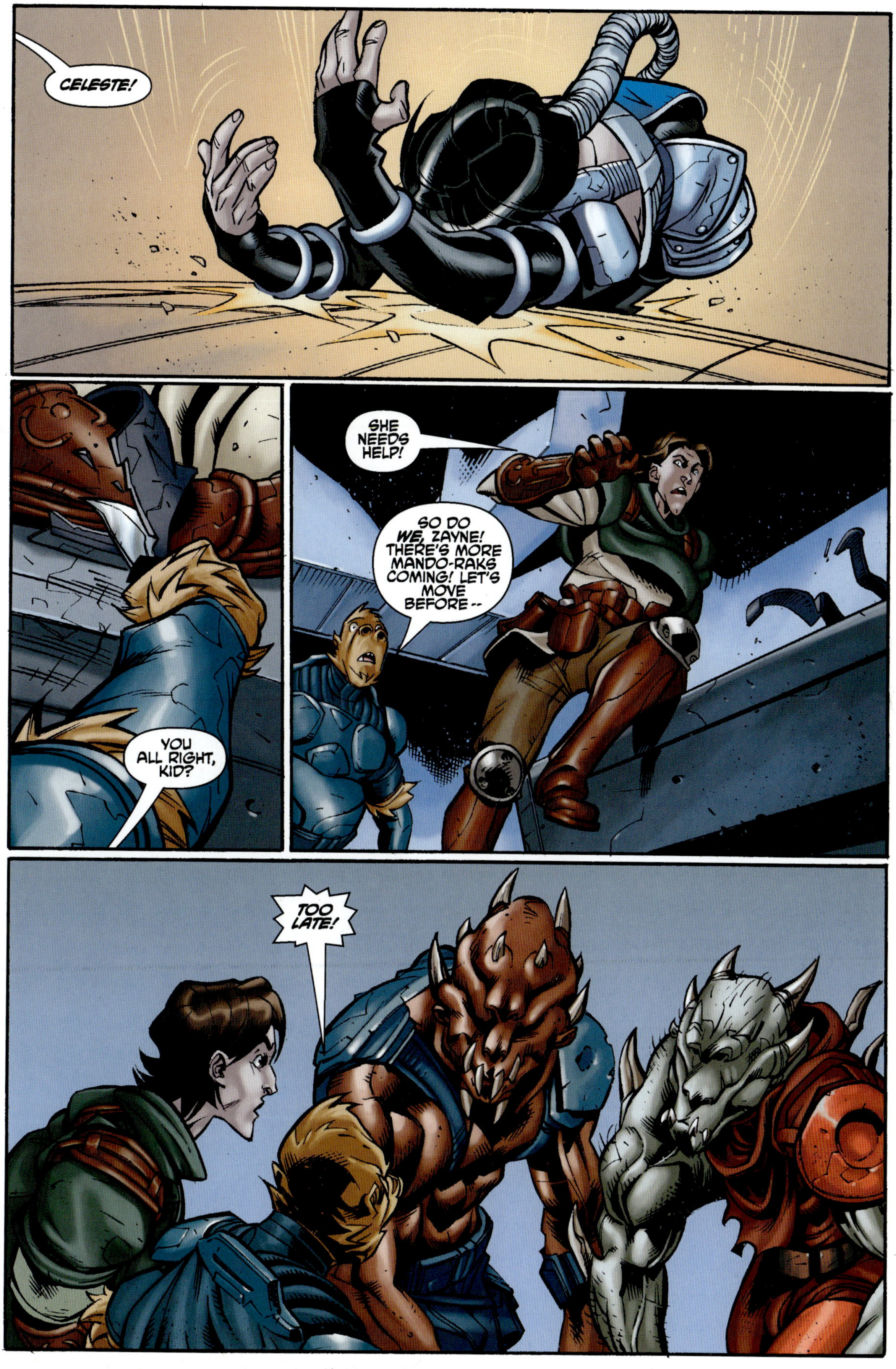
CELESTE!
YOU ALL RIGHT, KID?
SHE NEEDS HELP!
SO DO WE, ZAYNE! THERE'S MORE MANDO-RAKS COMING! LET'S MOVE BEFORE--
TOO LATE!

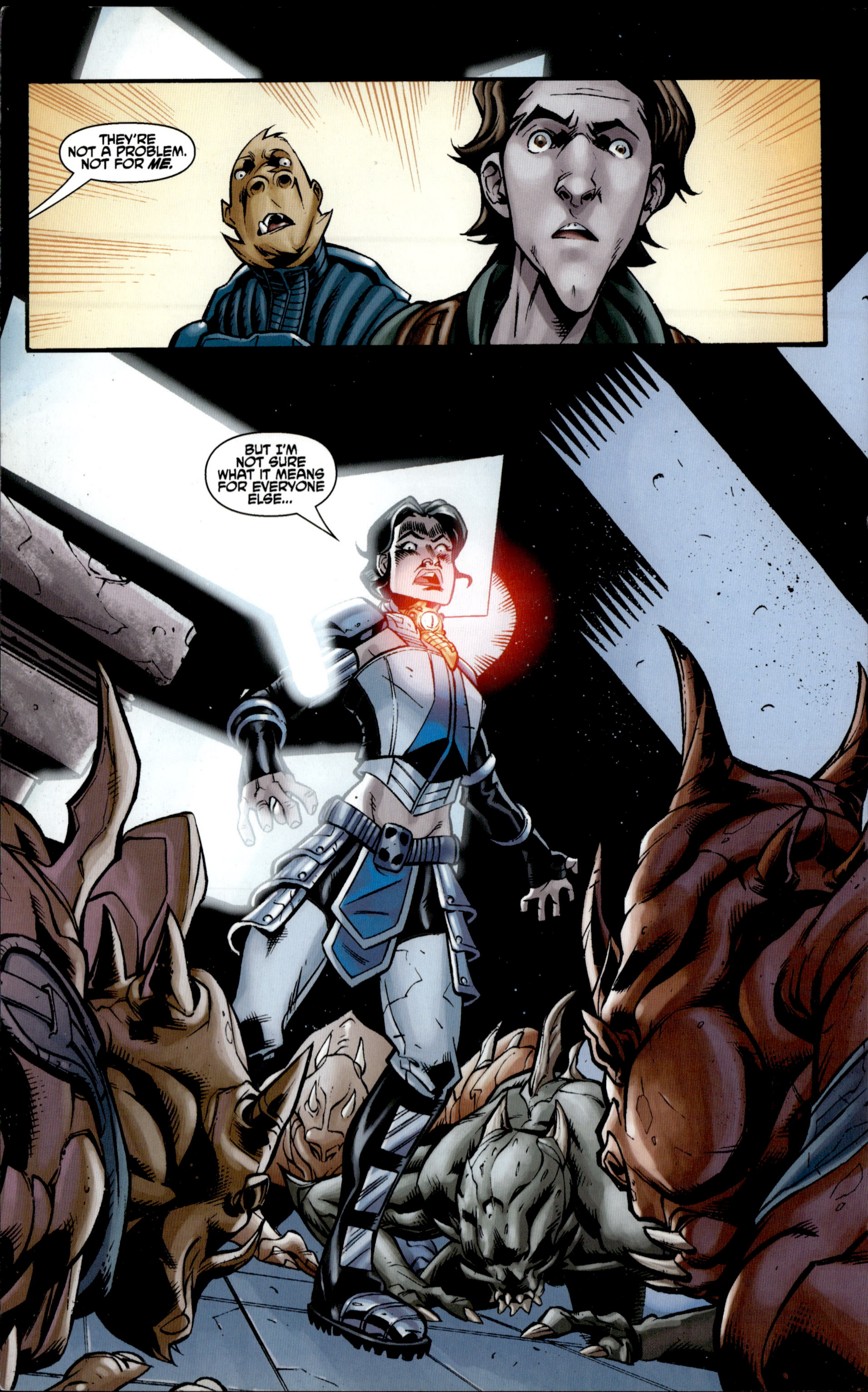
THEY'RE NOT A PROBLEM. NOT FOR *ME.*
BUT I'M NOT SURE WHAT IT MEANS FOR EVERYONE ELSE...

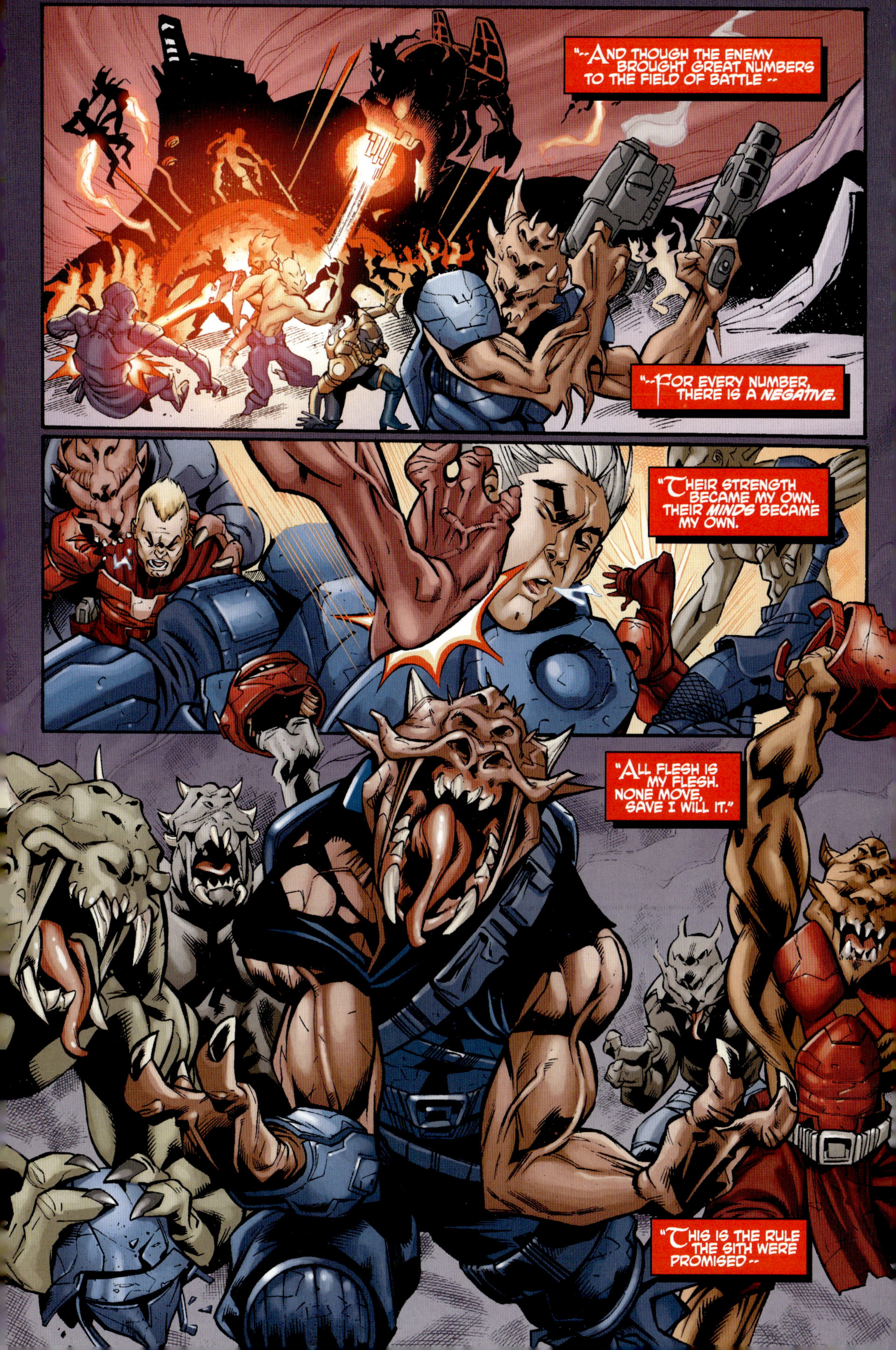
"--And though the enemy brought great numbers to the field of battle --
"--For every number, there is a *negative.*
"Their strength became my own. Their *minds* became my own.
"All flesh is my flesh. None move, save I will it."
"This is the rule the Sith were promised --

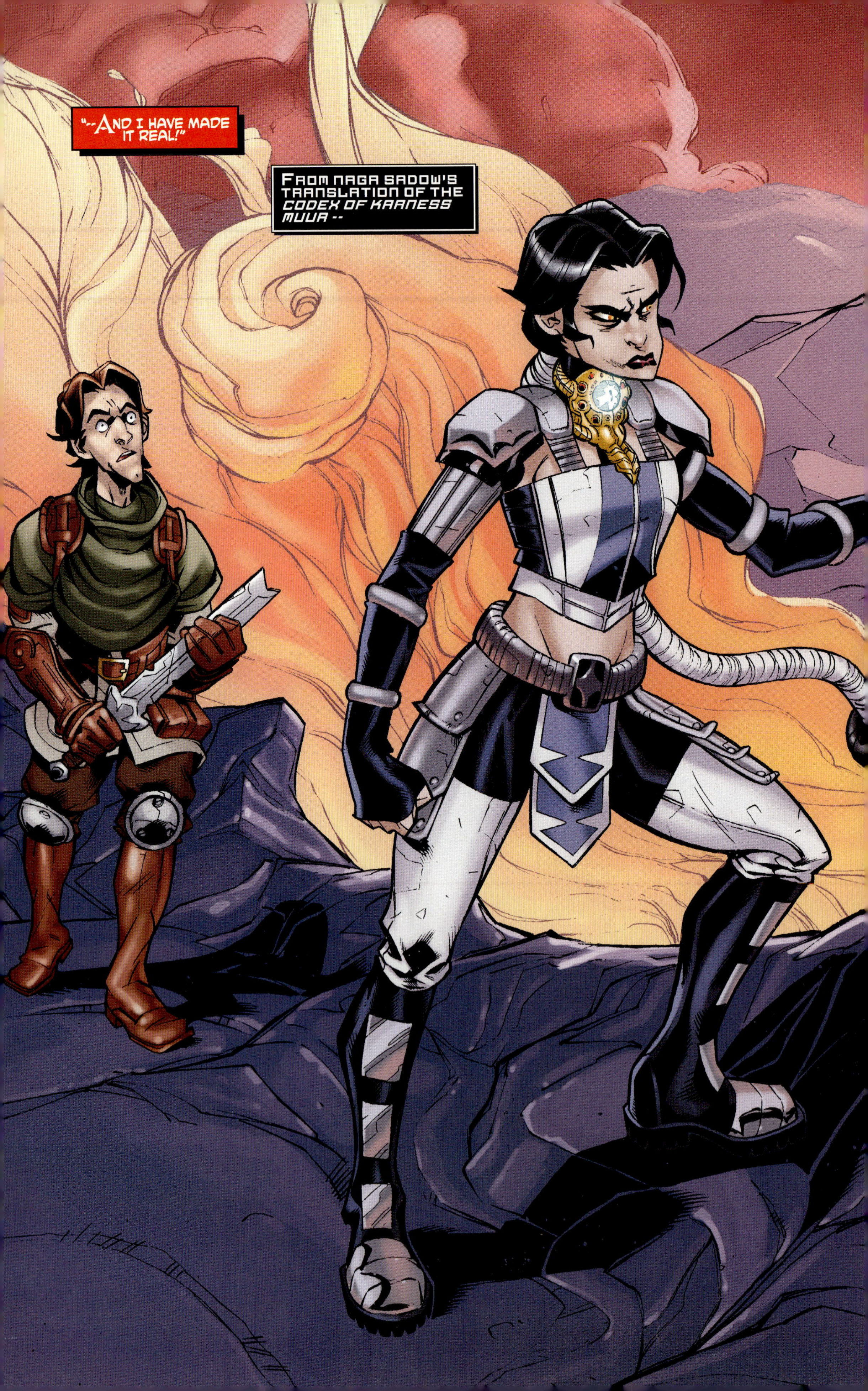
"--AND I HAVE MADE IT REAL!"
FROM NAGA SADOW'S TRANSLATION OF THE CODEX OF KAANESS MUUR --

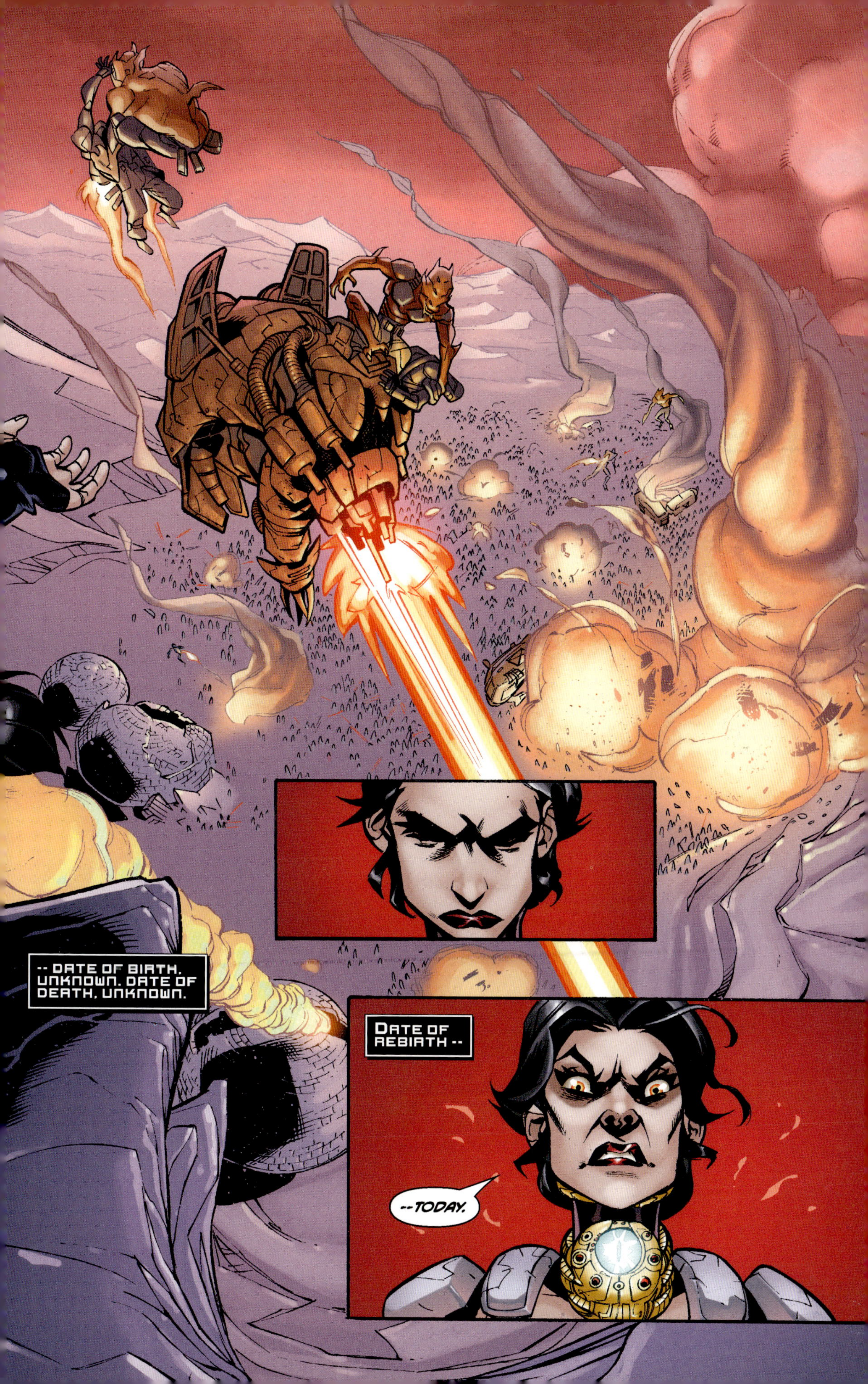
-- DATE OF BIRTH, UNKNOWN. DATE OF DEATH, UNKNOWN.
DATE OF REBIRTH --
--TODAY.

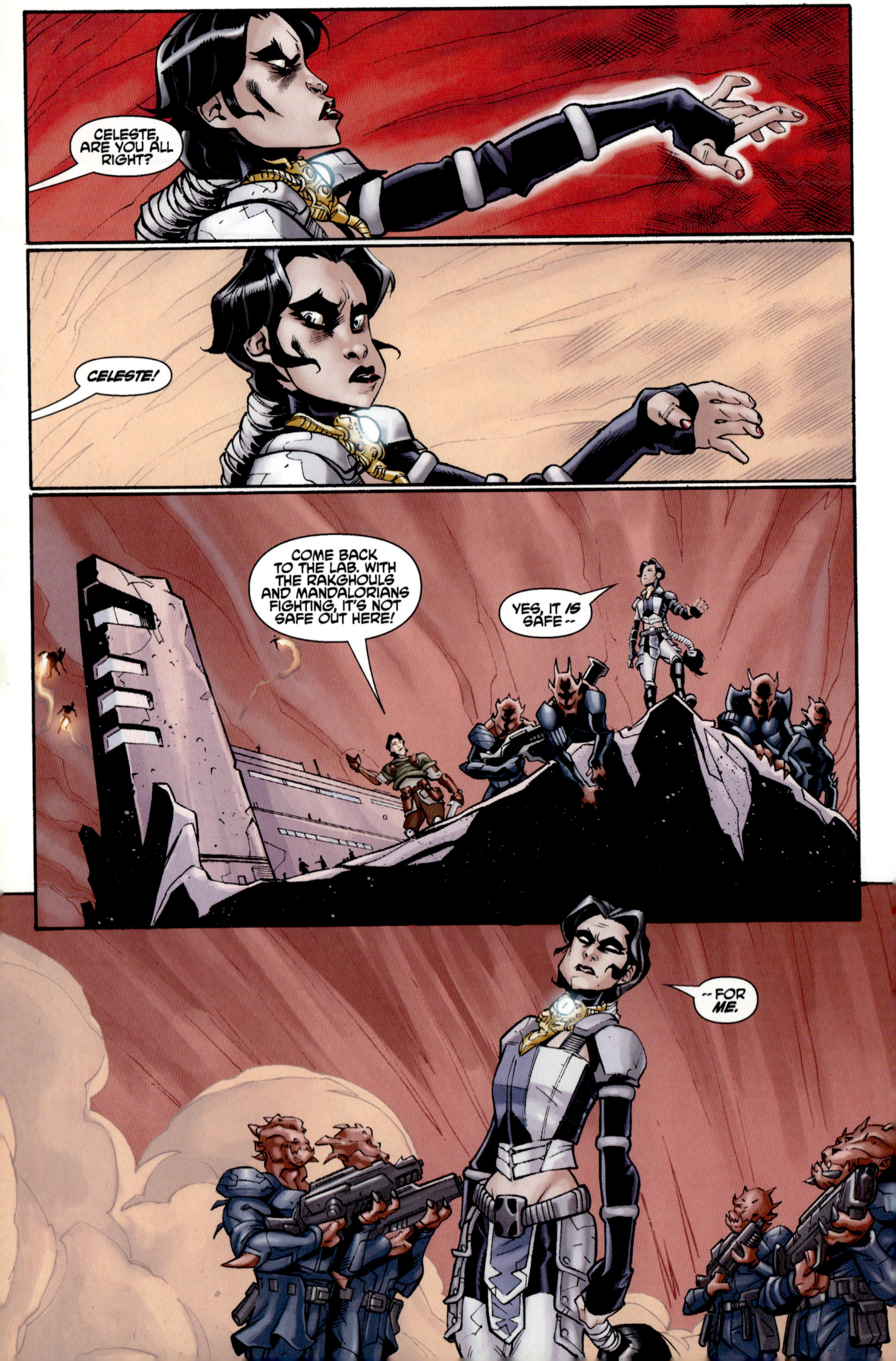
CELESTE, ARE YOU ALL RIGHT?
CELESTE!
COME BACK TO THE LAB. WITH THE RAKGHOULS AND MANDALORIANS FIGHTING, IT'S NOT SAFE OUT HERE!
YES, IT *IS* SAFE --
-- FOR *ME.*

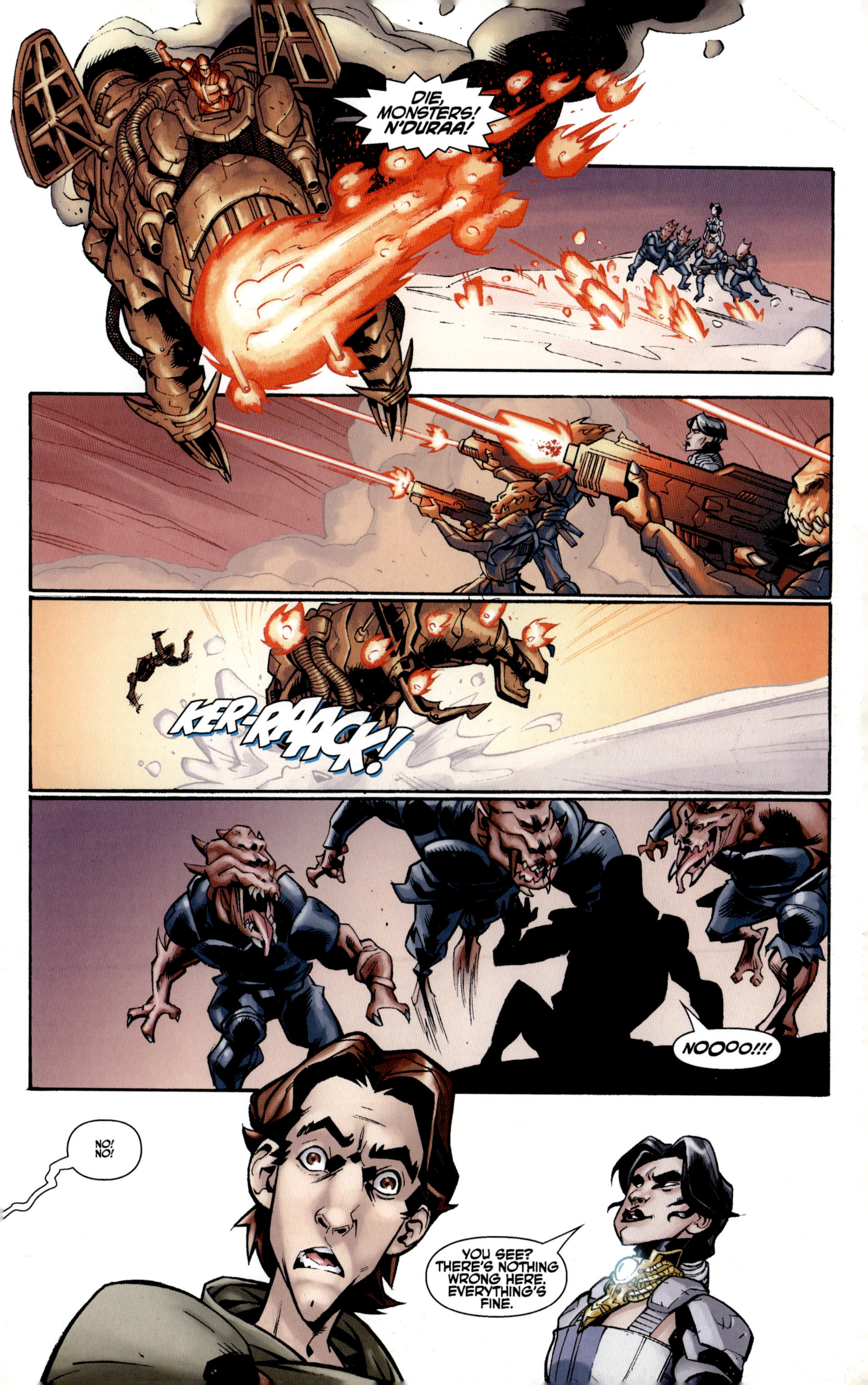
DIE, MONSTERS! N'DURAA!
KER-RAACK!
NOOOO!!!
NO! NO!
YOU SEE? THERE'S NOTHING WRONG HERE. EVERYTHING'S FINE.

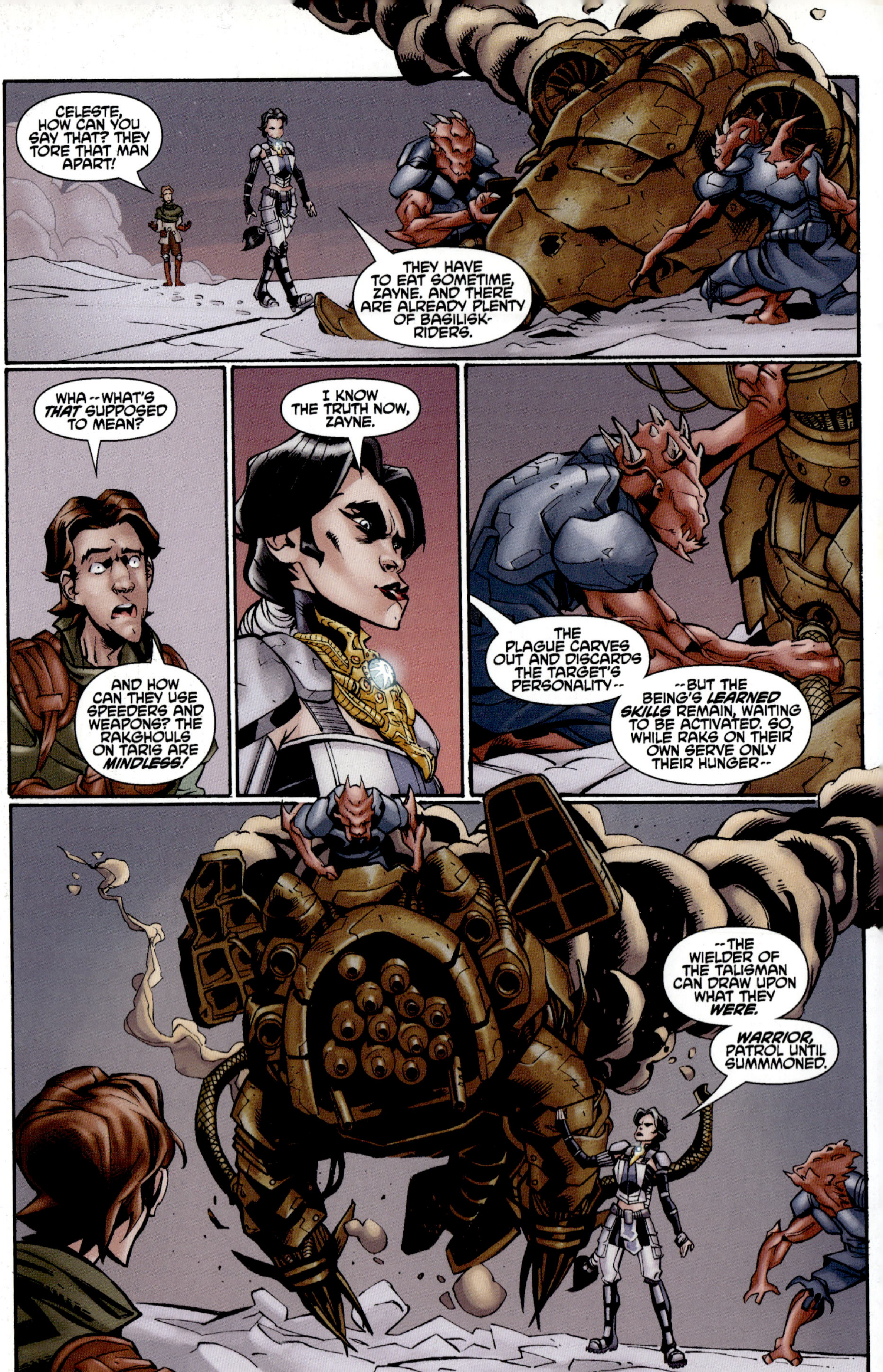

CELESTE, HOW CAN YOU SAY THAT? THEY TORE THAT MAN APART!
THEY HAVE TO EAT SOMETIME, ZAYNE. AND THERE ARE ALREADY PLENTY OF BASILISK-RIDERS.
WHA--WHAT'S THAT SUPPOSED TO MEAN?
AND HOW CAN THEY USE SPEEDERS AND WEAPONS? THE RAKGHOULS ON TARIS ARE MINDLESS!
I KNOW THE TRUTH NOW, ZAYNE.
THE PLAGUE CARVES OUT AND DISCARDS THE TARGET'S PERSONALITY--
--BUT THE BEING'S LEARNED SKILLS REMAIN, WAITING TO BE ACTIVATED. SO, WHILE RAKS ON THEIR OWN SERVE ONLY THEIR HUNGER--
--THE WIELDER OF THE TALISMAN CAN DRAW UPON WHAT THEY WERE.
WARRIOR, PATROL UNTIL SUMMMONED.

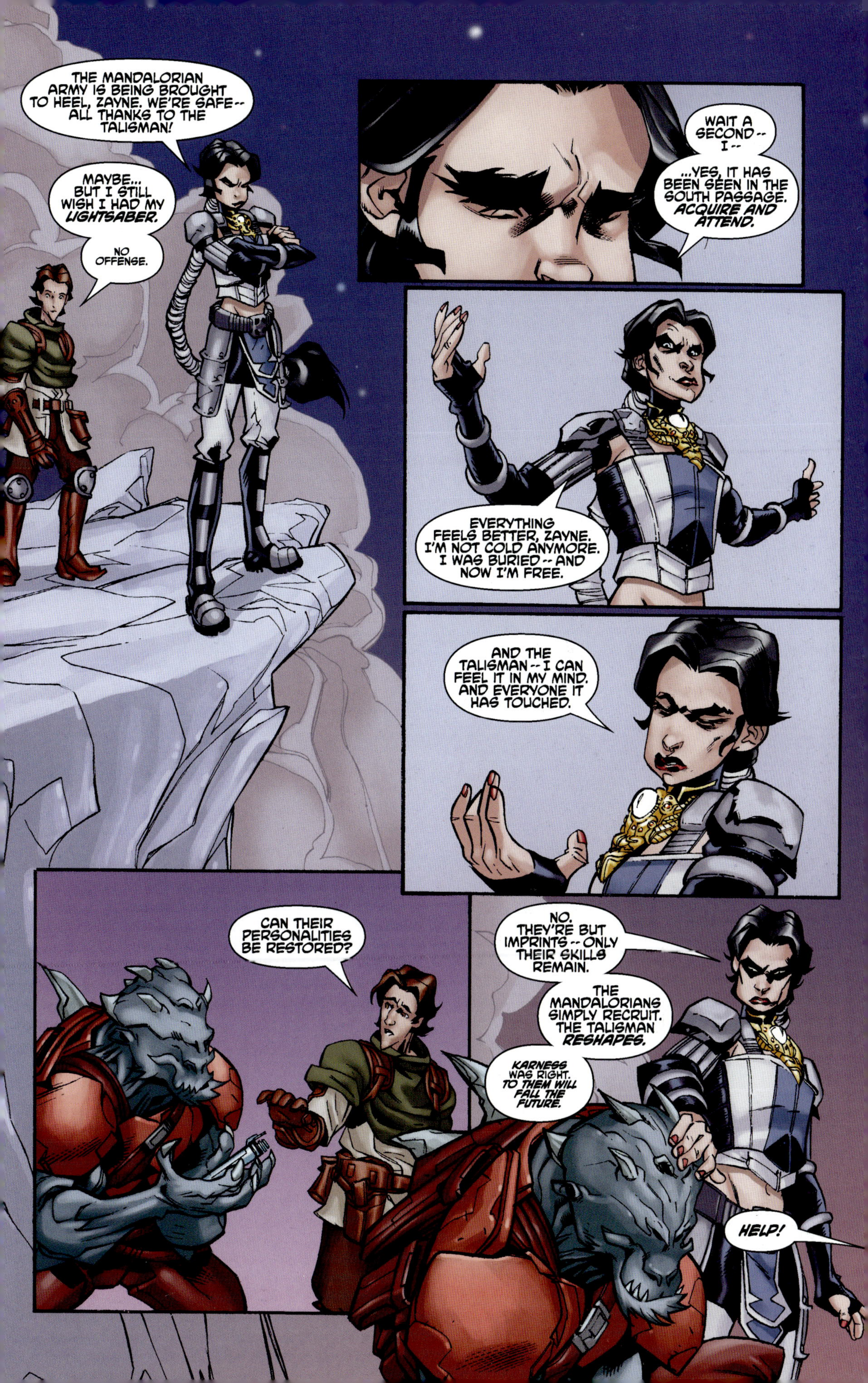
THE MANDALORIAN ARMY IS BEING BROUGHT TO HEEL, ZAYNE. WE'RE SAFE-- ALL THANKS TO THE TALISMAN!
MAYBE... BUT I STILL WISH I HAD MY LIGHTSABER.
NO OFFENSE.
WAIT A SECOND-- I--
...YES, IT HAS BEEN SEEN IN THE SOUTH PASSAGE. ACQUIRE AND ATTEND.
EVERYTHING FEELS BETTER, ZAYNE. I'M NOT COLD ANYMORE. I WAS BURIED--AND NOW I'M FREE.
AND THE TALISMAN--I CAN FEEL IT IN MY MIND. AND EVERYONE IT HAS TOUCHED.
CAN THEIR PERSONALITIES BE RESTORED?
NO. THEY'RE BUT IMPRINTS--ONLY THEIR SKILLS REMAIN.
THE MANDALORIANS SIMPLY RECRUIT. THE TALISMAN RESHAPES.
KARNESS WAS RIGHT. TO THEM WILL FALL THE FUTURE.
HELP!

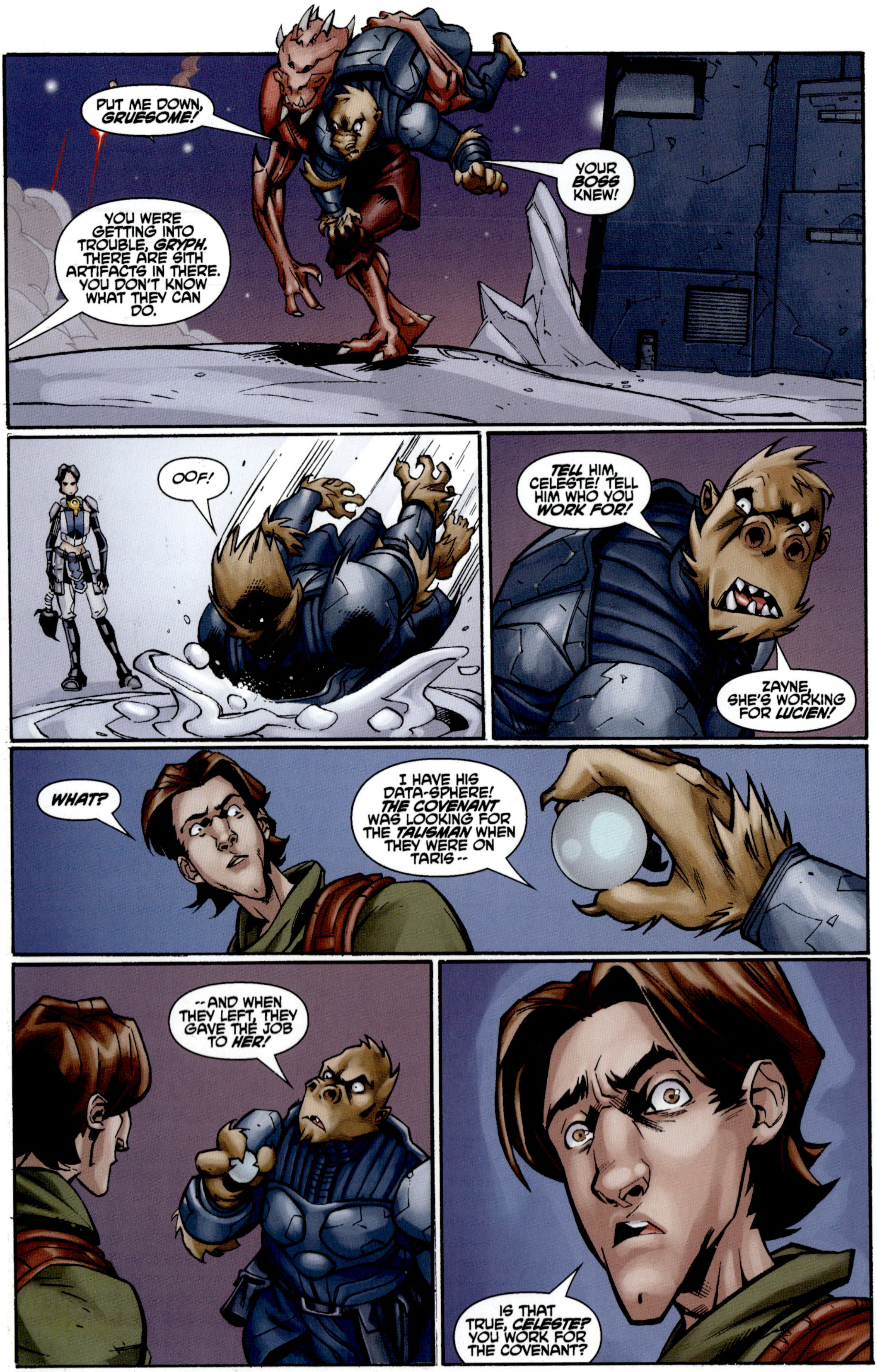
PUT ME DOWN, GRUESOME!
YOUR BOSS KNEW!
YOU WERE GETTING INTO TROUBLE, GRYPH. THERE ARE SITH ARTIFACTS IN THERE. YOU DON'T KNOW WHAT THEY CAN DO.
OOF!
TELL HIM, CELESTE! TELL HIM WHO YOU WORK FOR!
ZAYNE, SHE'S WORKING FOR LUCIEN!
WHAT?
I HAVE HIS DATA-SPHERE! THE COVENANT WAS LOOKING FOR THE TALISMAN WHEN THEY WERE ON TARIS --
--AND WHEN THEY LEFT, THEY GAVE THE JOB TO HER!
IS THAT TRUE, CELESTE? YOU WORK FOR THE COVENANT?

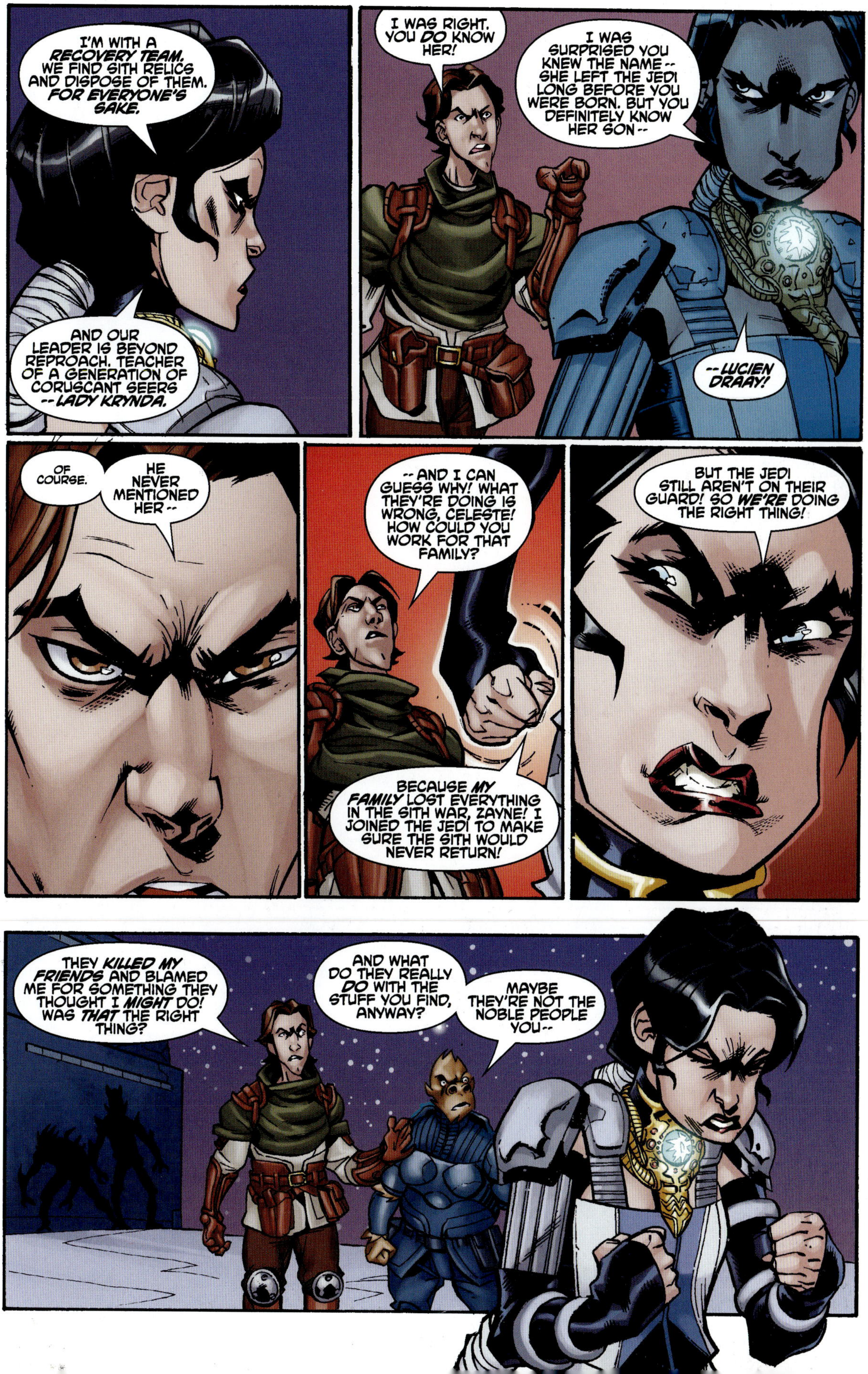
I'M WITH A RECOVERY TEAM. WE FIND SITH RELICS AND DISPOSE OF THEM. FOR EVERYONE'S SAKE.
AND OUR LEADER IS BEYOND REPROACH. TEACHER OF A GENERATION OF CORUSCANT SEERS --LADY KRYNDA.
I WAS RIGHT. YOU DO KNOW HER!
I WAS SURPRISED YOU KNEW THE NAME-- SHE LEFT THE JEDI LONG BEFORE YOU WERE BORN. BUT YOU DEFINITELY KNOW HER SON--
--LUCIEN DRAAY!
OF COURSE.
HE NEVER MENTIONED HER--
--AND I CAN GUESS WHY! WHAT THEY'RE DOING IS WRONG, CELESTE! HOW COULD YOU WORK FOR THAT FAMILY?
BECAUSE MY FAMILY LOST EVERYTHING IN THE SITH WAR, ZAYNE! I JOINED THE JEDI TO MAKE SURE THE SITH WOULD NEVER RETURN!
BUT THE JEDI STILL AREN'T ON THEIR GUARD! SO WE'RE DOING THE RIGHT THING!
THEY KILLED MY FRIENDS AND BLAMED ME FOR SOMETHING THEY THOUGHT I MIGHT DO! WAS THAT THE RIGHT THING?
AND WHAT DO THEY REALLY DO WITH THE STUFF YOU FIND, ANYWAY?
MAYBE THEY'RE NOT THE NOBLE PEOPLE YOU--

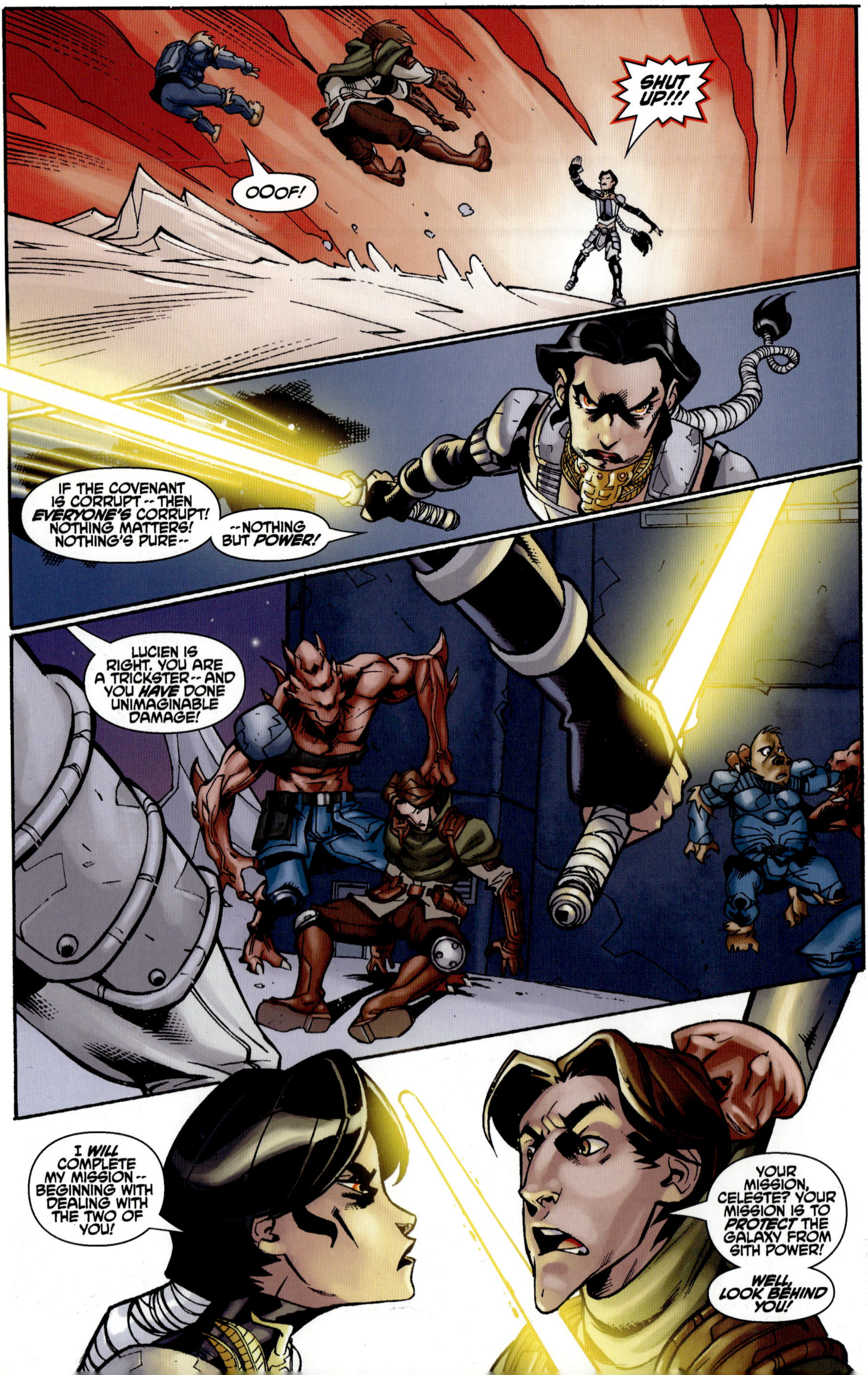

OOOF!
SHUT UP!!!
IF THE COVENANT IS CORRUPT -- THEN EVERYONE'S CORRUPT! NOTHING MATTERS! NOTHING'S PURE--
--NOTHING BUT POWER!
LUCIEN IS RIGHT. YOU ARE A TRICKSTER -- AND YOU HAVE DONE UNIMAGINABLE DAMAGE!
I WILL COMPLETE MY MISSION -- BEGINNING WITH DEALING WITH THE TWO OF YOU!
YOUR MISSION, CELESTE? YOUR MISSION IS TO PROTECT THE GALAXY FROM SITH POWER!
WELL, LOOK BEHIND YOU!

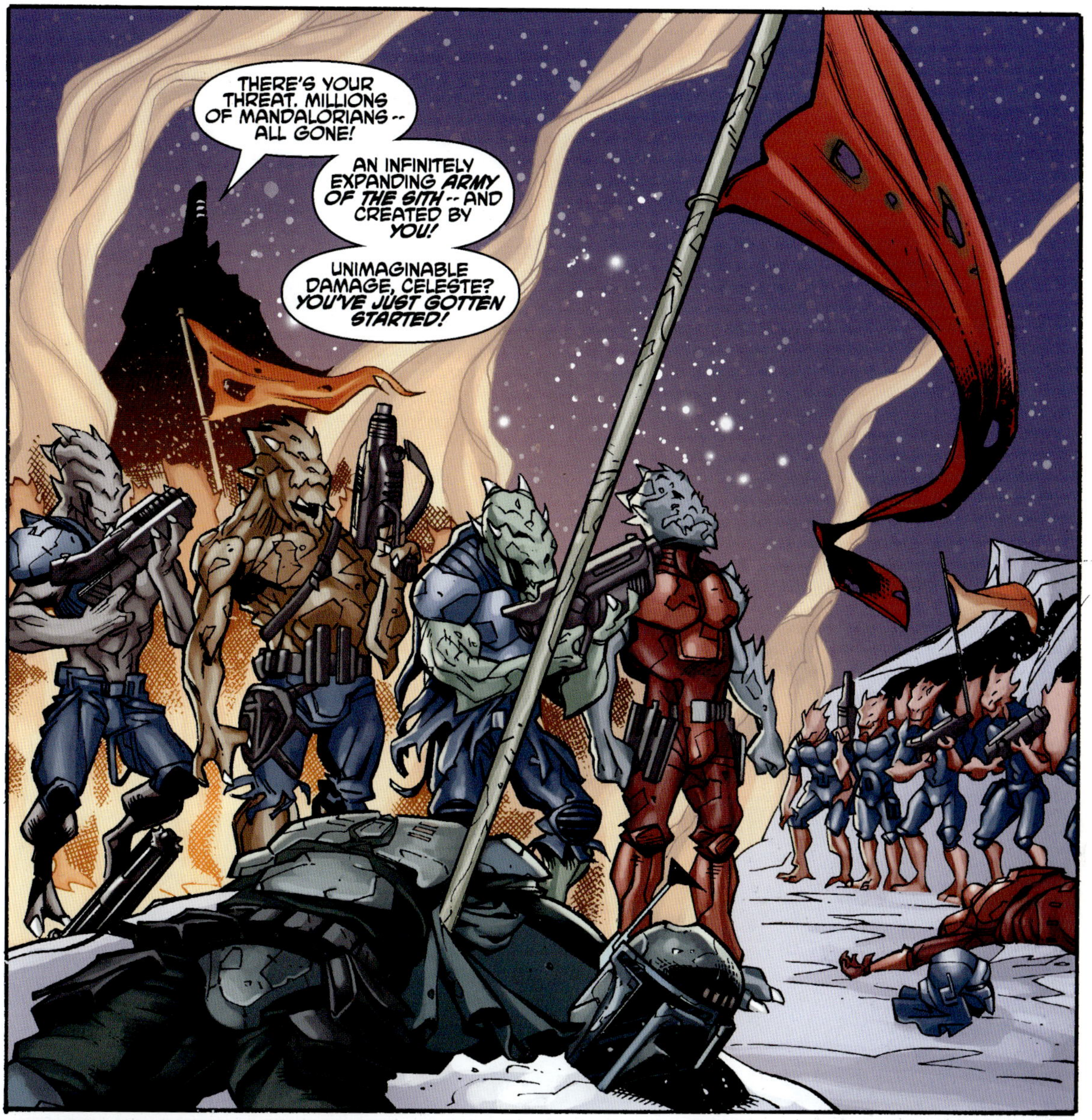
THERE'S YOUR THREAT. MILLIONS OF MANDALORIANS -- ALL GONE!
AN INFINITELY EXPANDING *ARMY OF THE SITH* -- AND CREATED BY *YOU!*
UNIMAGINABLE DAMAGE, CELESTE? *YOU'VE JUST GOTTEN STARTED!*

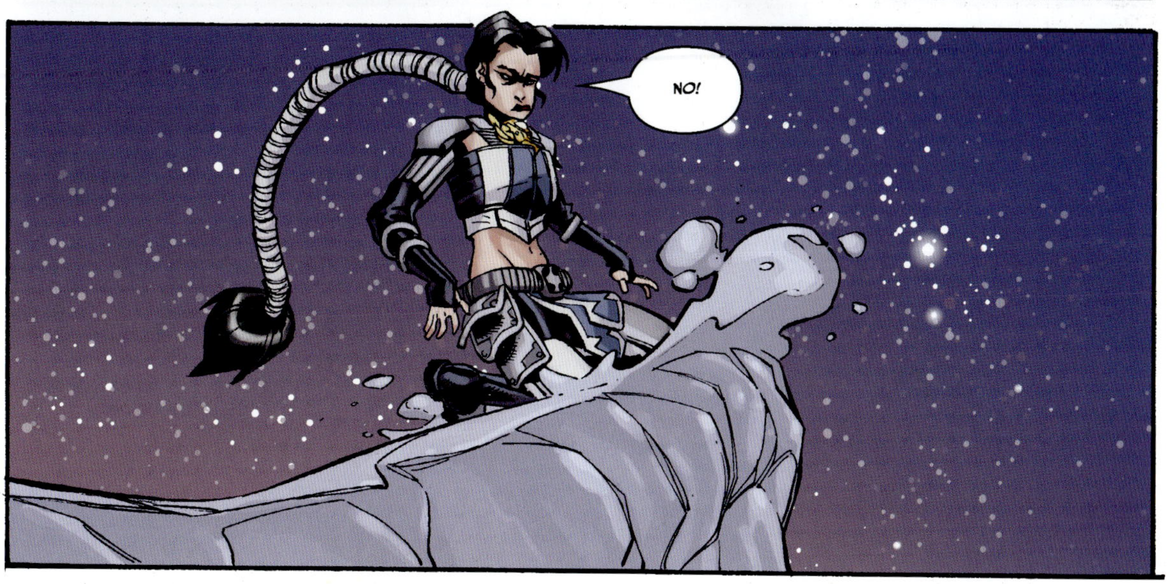
NO!

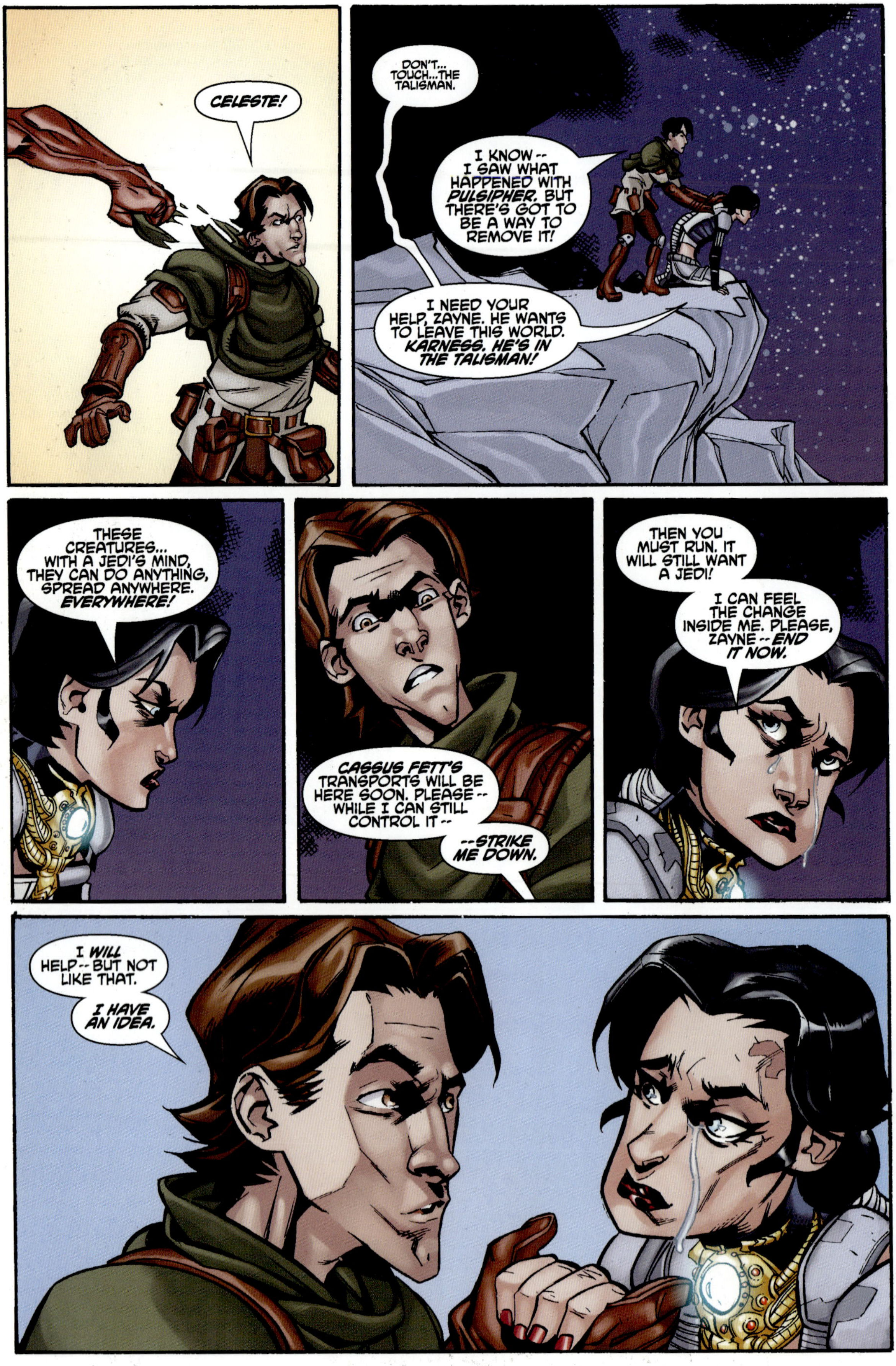
CELESTE!
DON'T... TOUCH...THE TALISMAN.
I KNOW -- I SAW WHAT HAPPENED WITH PULSIPHER. BUT THERE'S GOT TO BE A WAY TO REMOVE IT!
I NEED YOUR HELP, ZAYNE. HE WANTS TO LEAVE THIS WORLD. KARNESS. HE'S IN THE TALISMAN!
THESE CREATURES... WITH A JEDI'S MIND, THEY CAN DO ANYTHING, SPREAD ANYWHERE. EVERYWHERE!
CASSUS FETT'S TRANSPORTS WILL BE HERE SOON. PLEASE -- WHILE I CAN STILL CONTROL IT --
--STRIKE ME DOWN.
THEN YOU MUST RUN. IT WILL STILL WANT A JEDI!
I CAN FEEL THE CHANGE INSIDE ME. PLEASE, ZAYNE -- END IT NOW.
I WILL HELP -- BUT NOT LIKE THAT.
I HAVE AN IDEA.

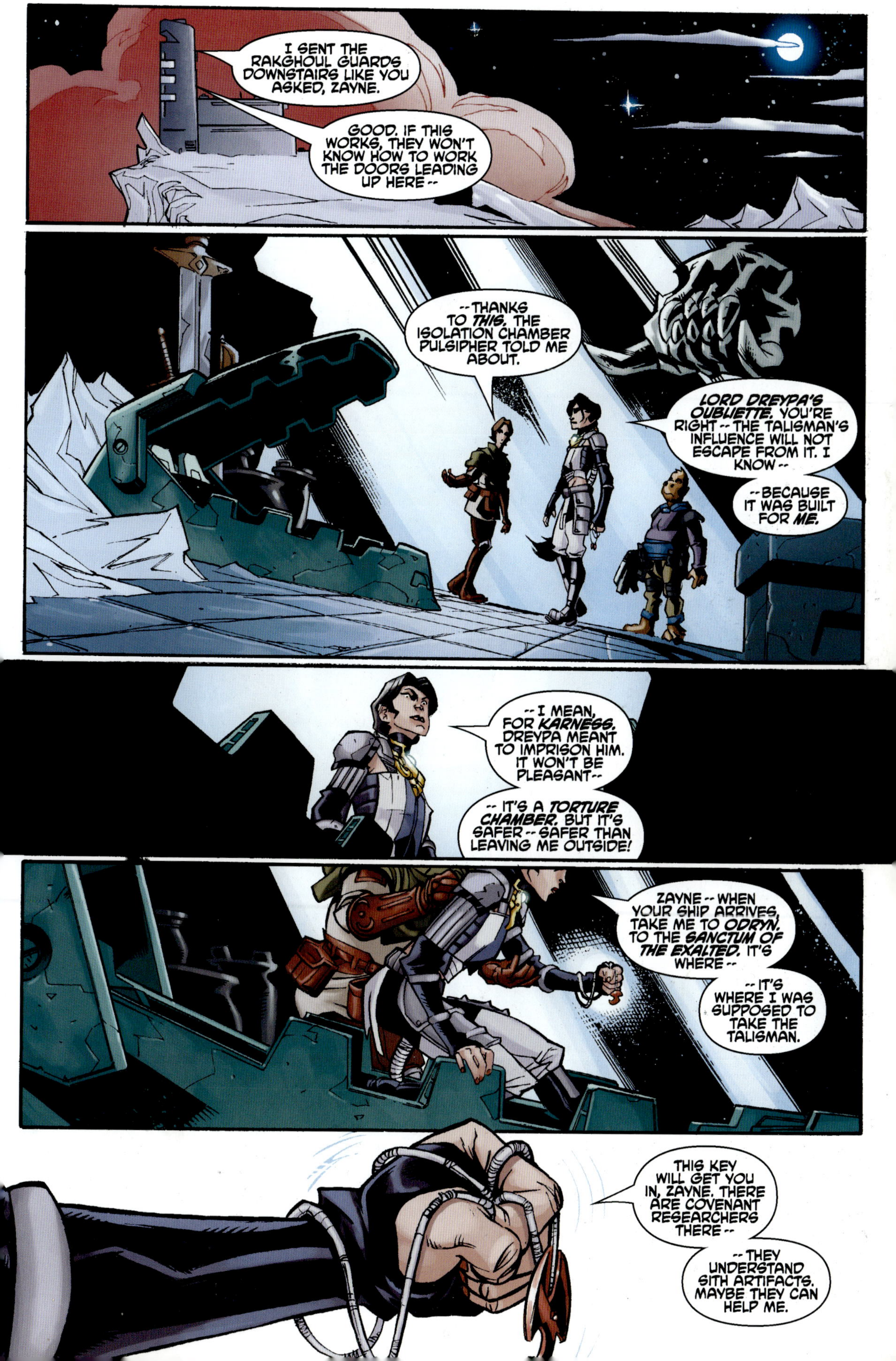
I SENT THE RAKGHOUL GUARDS DOWNSTAIRS LIKE YOU ASKED, ZAYNE.
GOOD. IF THIS WORKS, THEY WON'T KNOW HOW TO WORK THE DOORS LEADING UP HERE --
-- THANKS TO *THIS*. THE ISOLATION CHAMBER PULSIPHER TOLD ME ABOUT.
LORD DREYPA'S OUBLIETTE. YOU'RE RIGHT -- THE TALISMAN'S INFLUENCE WILL NOT ESCAPE FROM IT. I KNOW --
-- BECAUSE IT WAS BUILT FOR *ME.*
-- I MEAN, FOR *KARNESS.* DREYPA MEANT TO IMPRISON HIM. IT WON'T BE PLEASANT --
-- IT'S A *TORTURE CHAMBER.* BUT IT'S SAFER -- SAFER THAN LEAVING ME OUTSIDE!
ZAYNE -- WHEN YOUR SHIP ARRIVES, TAKE ME TO *ODRYN.* TO THE *SANCTUM OF THE EXALTED.* IT'S WHERE --
-- IT'S WHERE I WAS SUPPOSED TO TAKE THE TALISMAN.
THIS KEY WILL GET YOU IN, ZAYNE. THERE ARE COVENANT RESEARCHERS THERE --
-- THEY UNDERSTAND SITH ARTIFACTS. MAYBE THEY CAN HELP ME.

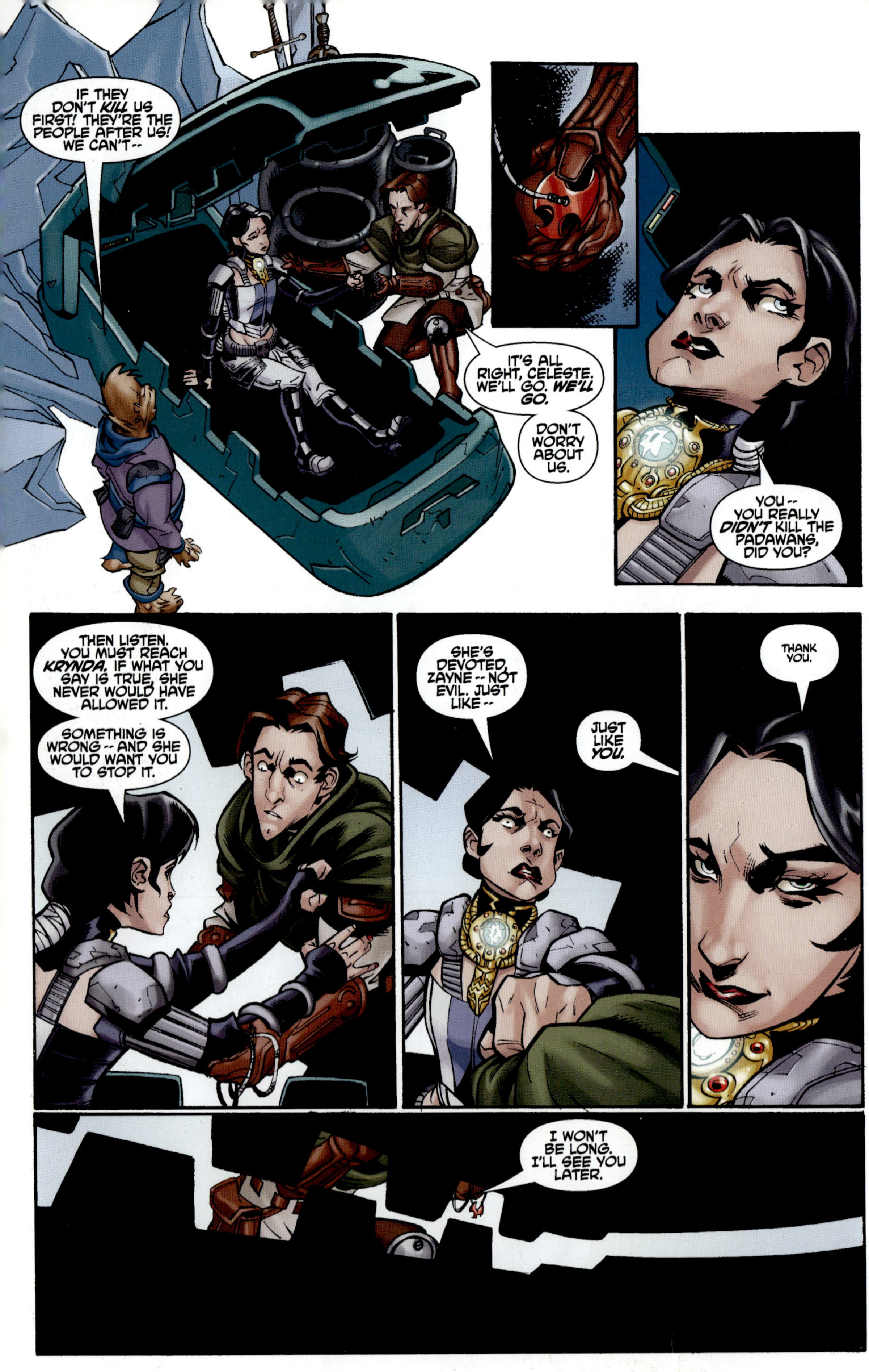
IF THEY DON'T KILL US FIRST! THEY'RE THE PEOPLE AFTER US! WE CAN'T--
IT'S ALL RIGHT, CELESTE. WE'LL GO. WE'LL GO.
DON'T WORRY ABOUT US.
YOU-- YOU REALLY DIDN'T KILL THE PADAWANS, DID YOU?
THEN LISTEN. YOU MUST REACH KRYNDA. IF WHAT YOU SAY IS TRUE, SHE NEVER WOULD HAVE ALLOWED IT.
SOMETHING IS WRONG-- AND SHE WOULD WANT YOU TO STOP IT.
SHE'S DEVOTED, ZAYNE-- NOT EVIL. JUST LIKE--
JUST LIKE YOU.
THANK YOU.
I WON'T BE LONG. I'LL SEE YOU LATER.

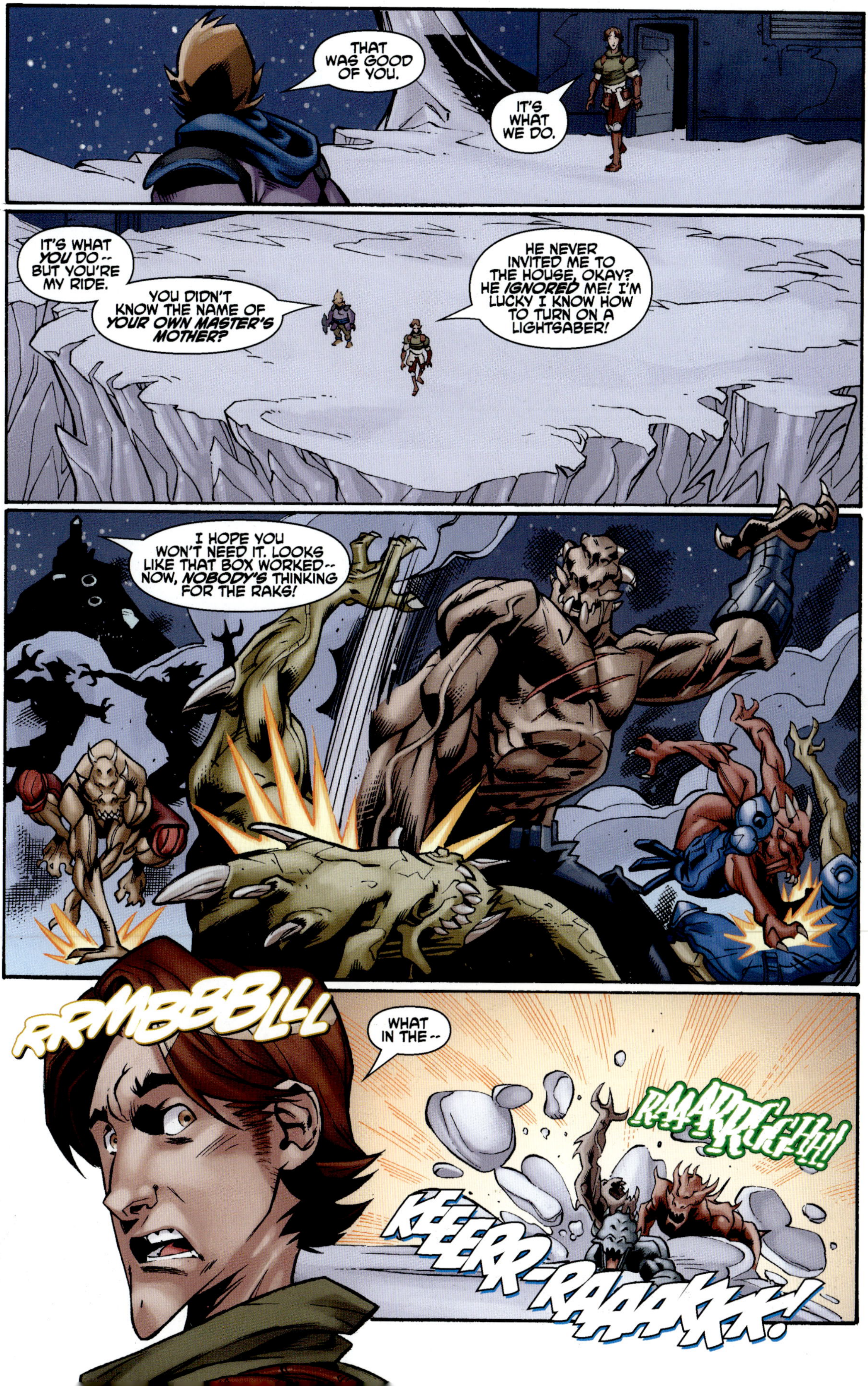
THAT WAS GOOD OF YOU.
IT'S WHAT WE DO.
IT'S WHAT *YOU* DO-- BUT YOU'RE MY RIDE.
YOU DIDN'T KNOW THE NAME OF *YOUR OWN MASTER'S MOTHER?*
HE NEVER INVITED ME TO THE HOUSE, OKAY? HE *IGNORED* ME! I'M LUCKY I KNOW HOW TO TURN ON A LIGHTSABER!
I HOPE YOU WON'T NEED IT. LOOKS LIKE THAT BOX WORKED-- NOW, *NOBODY'S* THINKING FOR THE RAKS!
RRMBBBLLL
WHAT IN THE--
RAAARRGHH!
KEEERR-RAAAKKK!

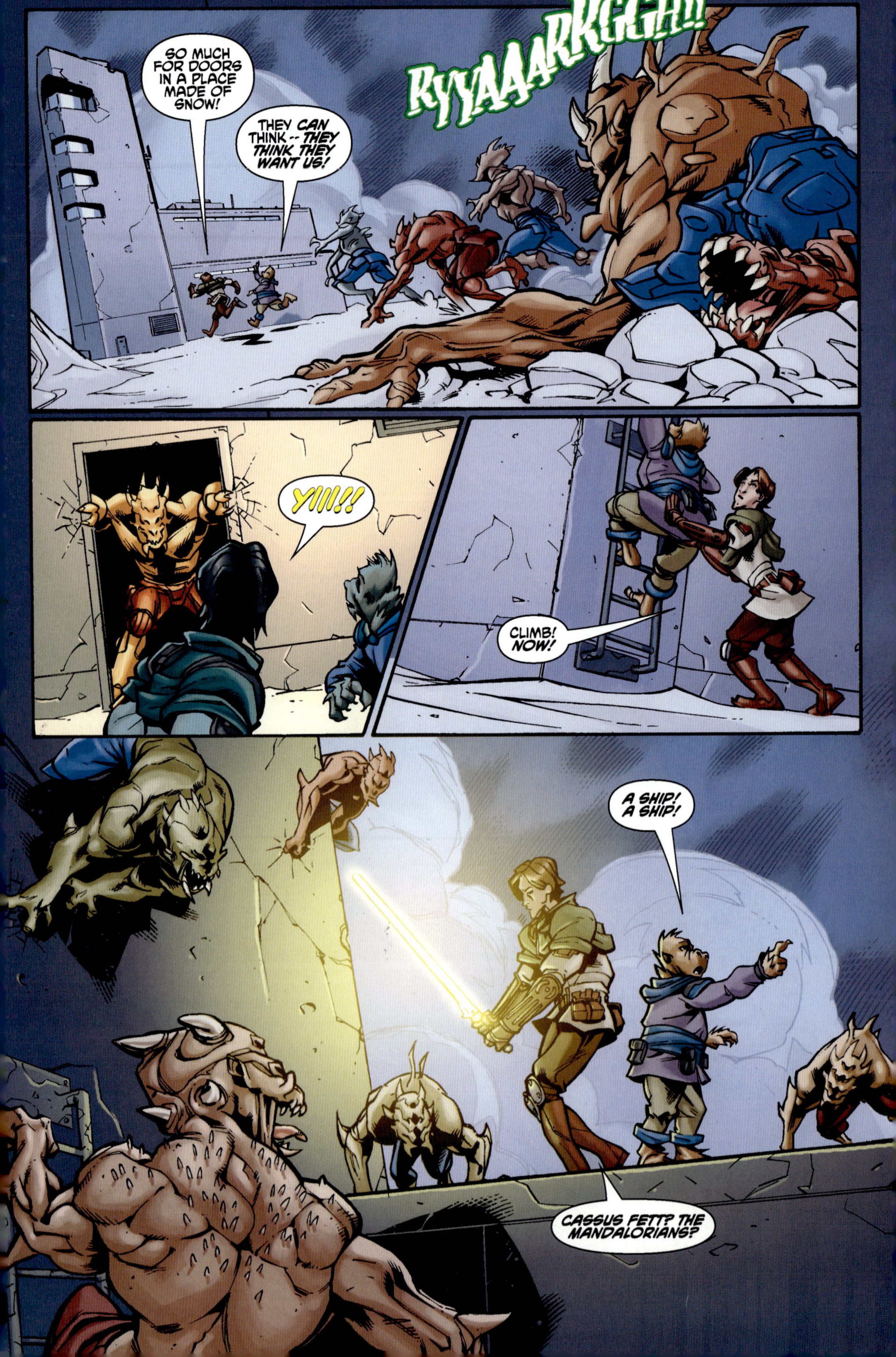
SO MUCH FOR DOORS IN A PLACE MADE OF SNOW!
THEY CAN THINK -- THEY THINK THEY WANT US!
RYYAAARRGGH!!
YIII!!
CLIMB! NOW!
A SHIP! A SHIP!
CASSUS FETT? THE MANDALORIANS?

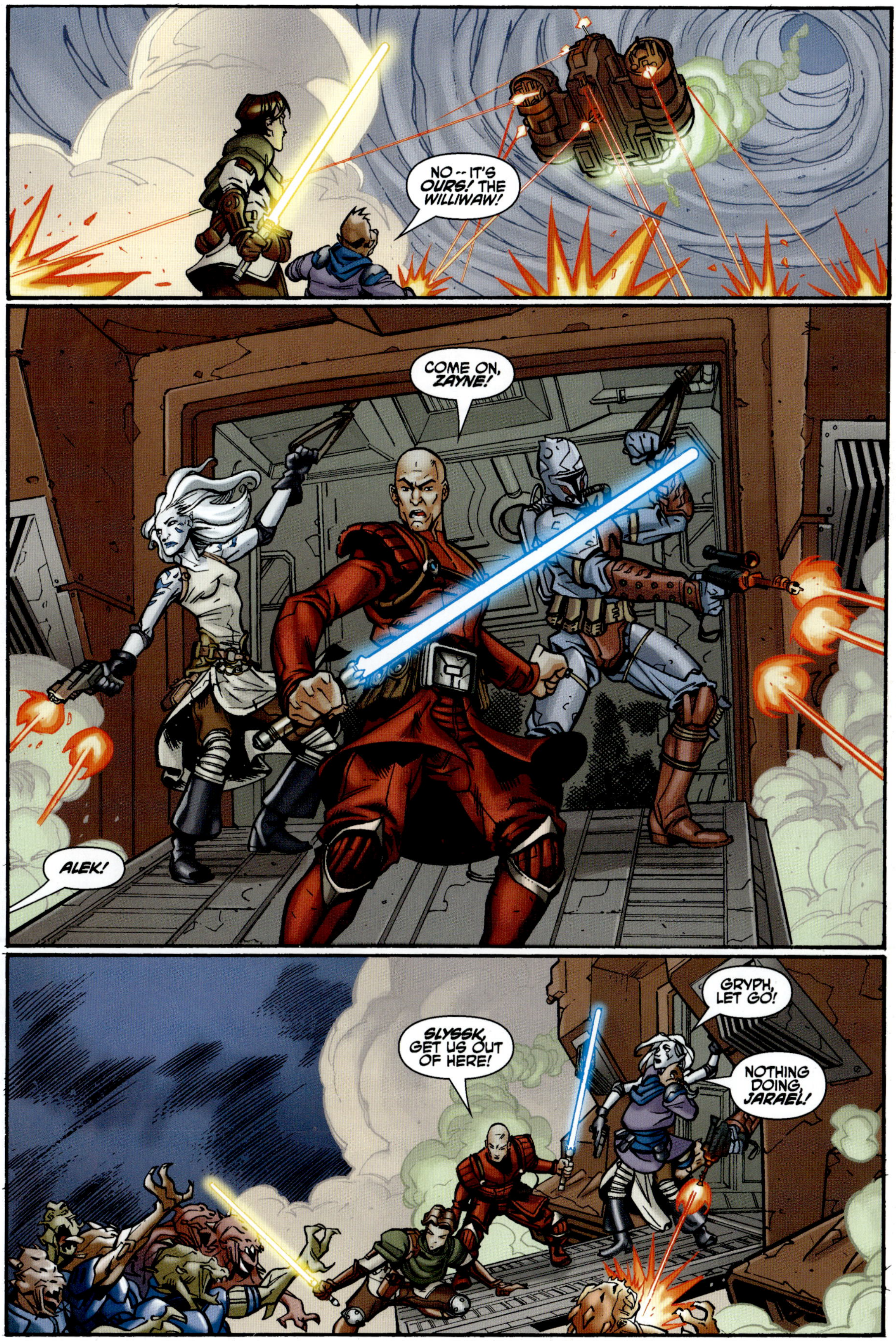

NO -- IT'S OURS! THE WILLIWAW!
COME ON, ZAYNE!
ALEK!
SLYSSK, GET US OUT OF HERE!
GRYPH, LET GO!
NOTHING DOING, JARAEL!

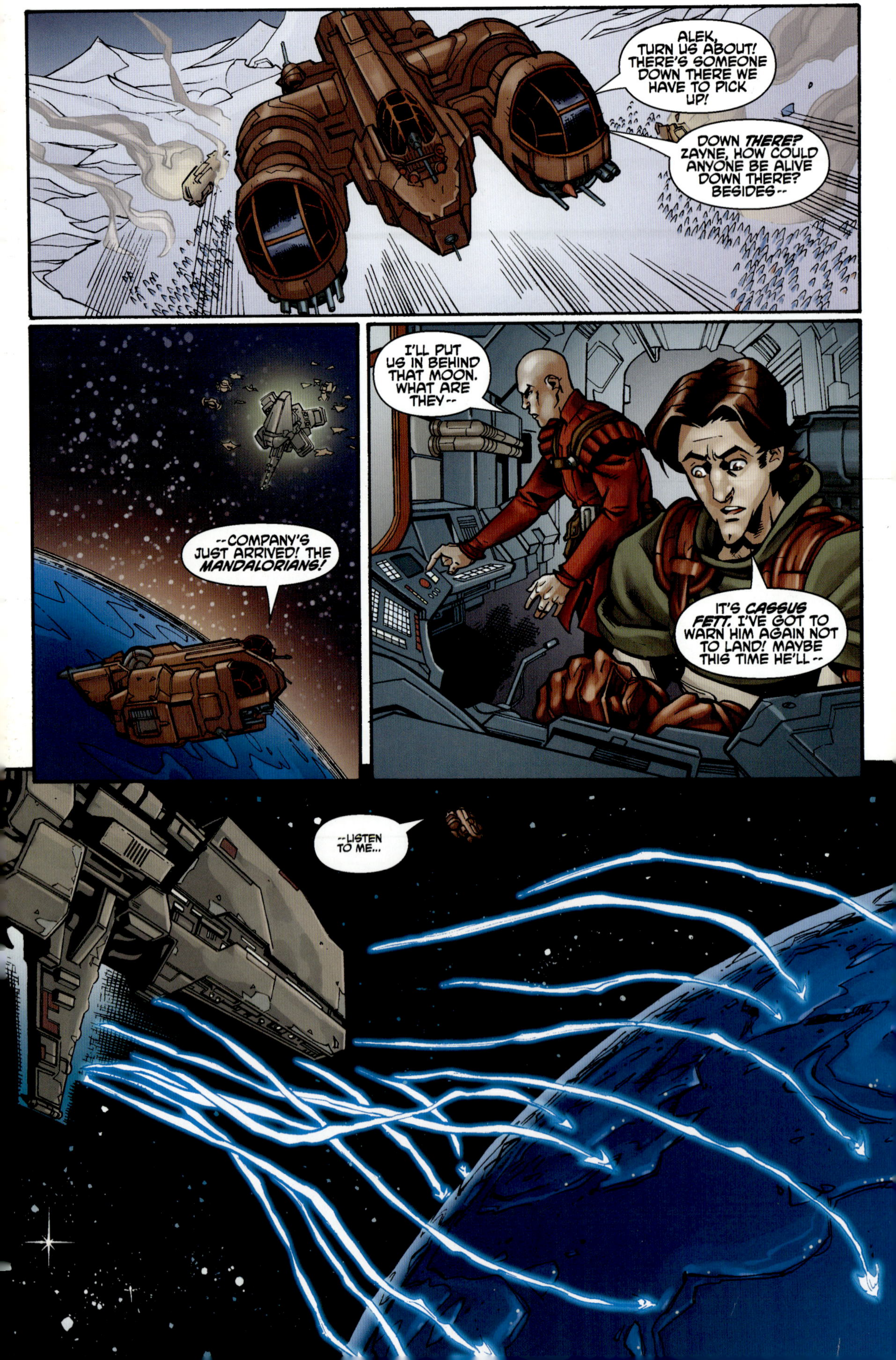
ALEK, TURN US ABOUT! THERE'S SOMEONE DOWN THERE WE HAVE TO PICK UP!
DOWN *THERE?* ZAYNE, HOW COULD ANYONE BE ALIVE DOWN THERE? BESIDES--
--COMPANY'S JUST ARRIVED! THE *MANDALORIANS!*
I'LL PUT US IN BEHIND THAT MOON. WHAT ARE THEY--
IT'S *CASSUS FETT.* I'VE GOT TO WARN HIM AGAIN NOT TO LAND! MAYBE THIS TIME HE'LL--
--LISTEN TO ME...

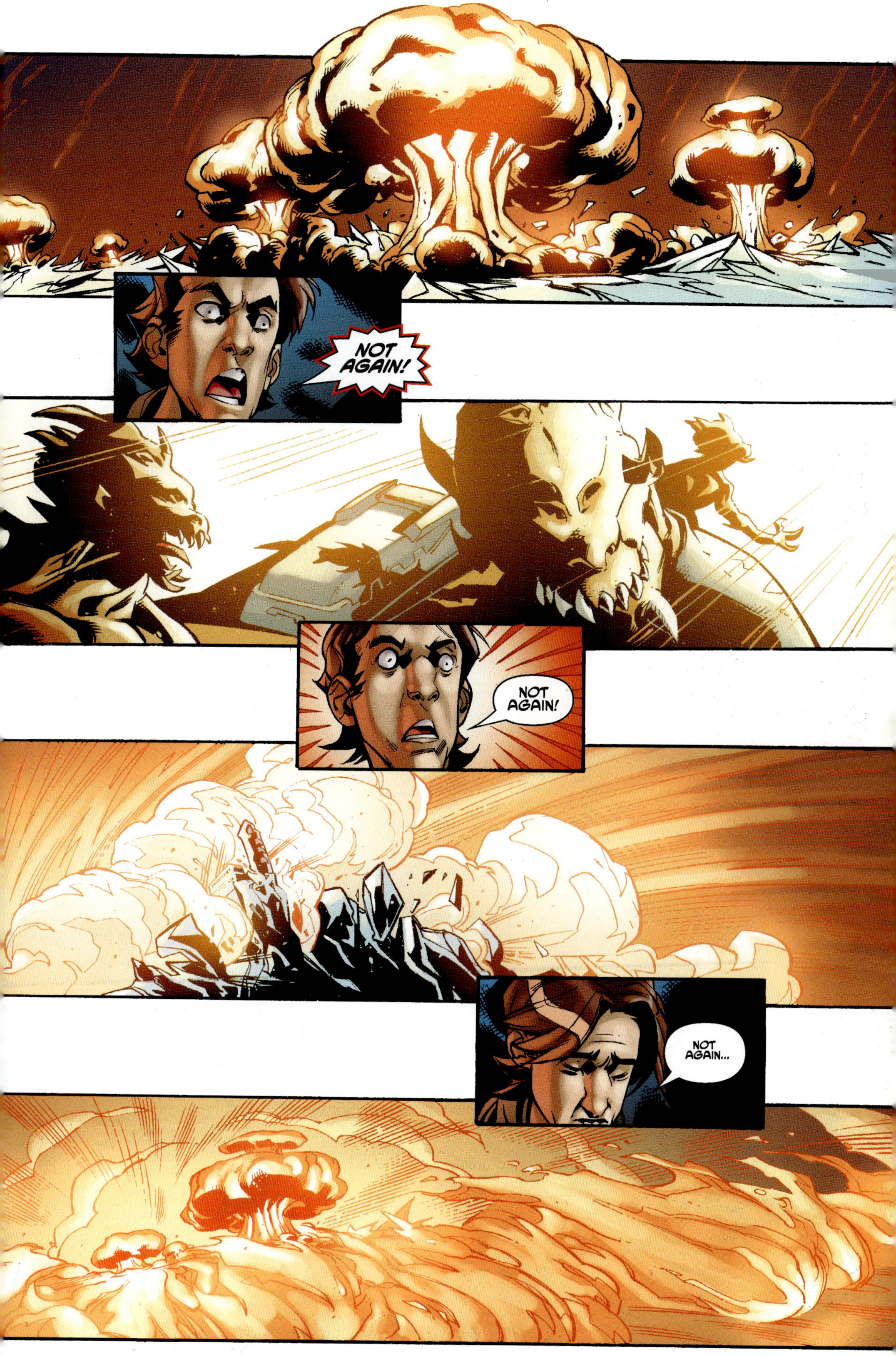
NOT AGAIN!
NOT AGAIN!
NOT AGAIN...

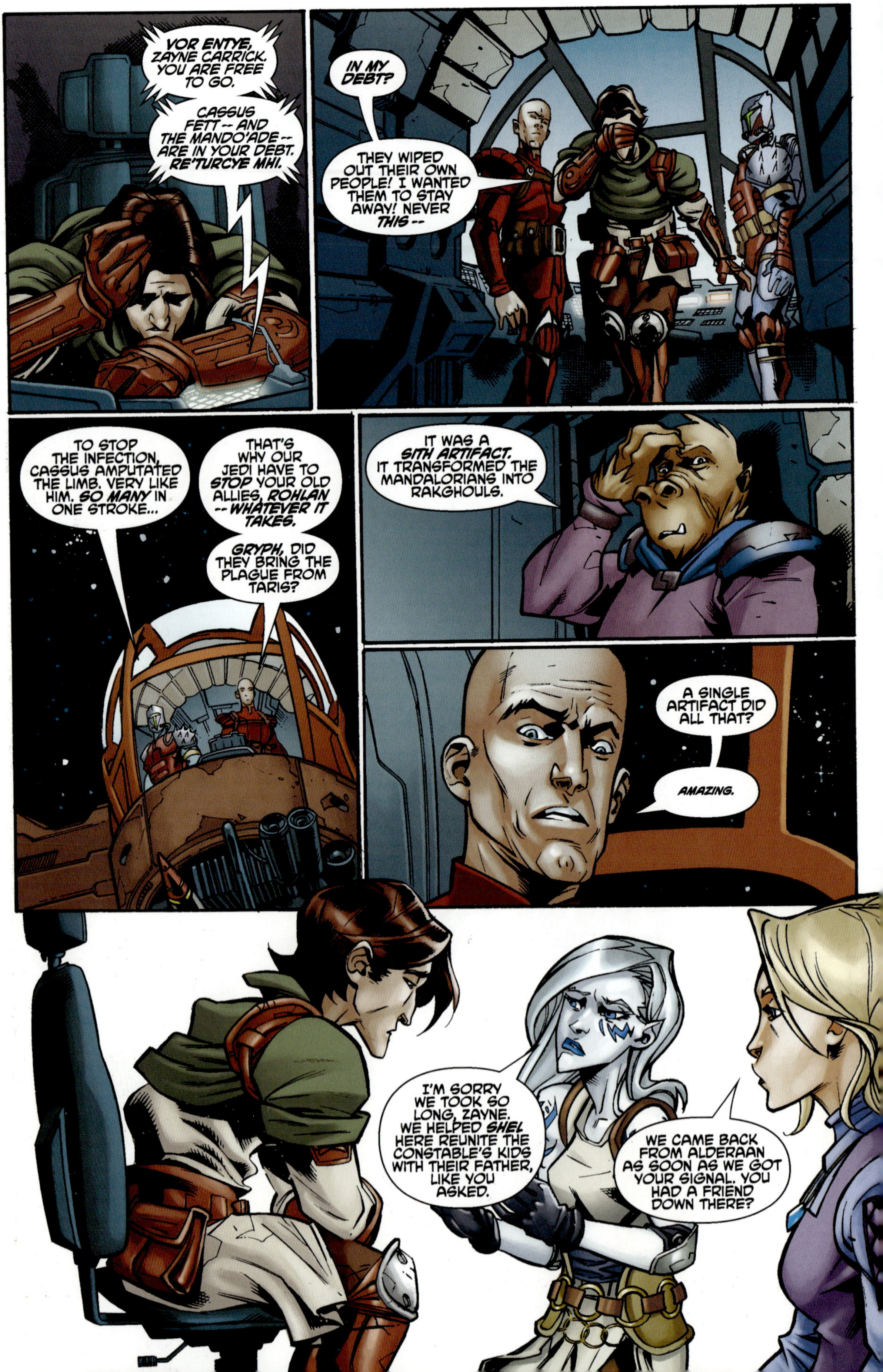
VOR ENTYE, ZAYNE CARRICK. YOU ARE FREE TO GO.
CASSUS FETT -- AND THE MANDO'ADE -- ARE IN YOUR DEBT. RE'TURCYE MHI.
IN MY DEBT?
THEY WIPED OUT THEIR OWN PEOPLE! I WANTED THEM TO STAY AWAY! NEVER THIS --
TO STOP THE INFECTION, CASSUS AMPUTATED THE LIMB. VERY LIKE HIM. SO MANY IN ONE STROKE...
THAT'S WHY OUR JEDI HAVE TO STOP YOUR OLD ALLIES, ROHLAN -- WHATEVER IT TAKES.
GRYPH, DID THEY BRING THE PLAGUE FROM TARIS?
IT WAS A SITH ARTIFACT. IT TRANSFORMED THE MANDALORIANS INTO RAKGHOULS.
A SINGLE ARTIFACT DID ALL THAT?
AMAZING.
I'M SORRY WE TOOK SO LONG, ZAYNE. WE HELPED SHEL HERE REUNITE THE CONSTABLE'S KIDS WITH THEIR FATHER, LIKE YOU ASKED.
WE CAME BACK FROM ALDERAAN AS SOON AS WE GOT YOUR SIGNAL. YOU HAD A FRIEND DOWN THERE?

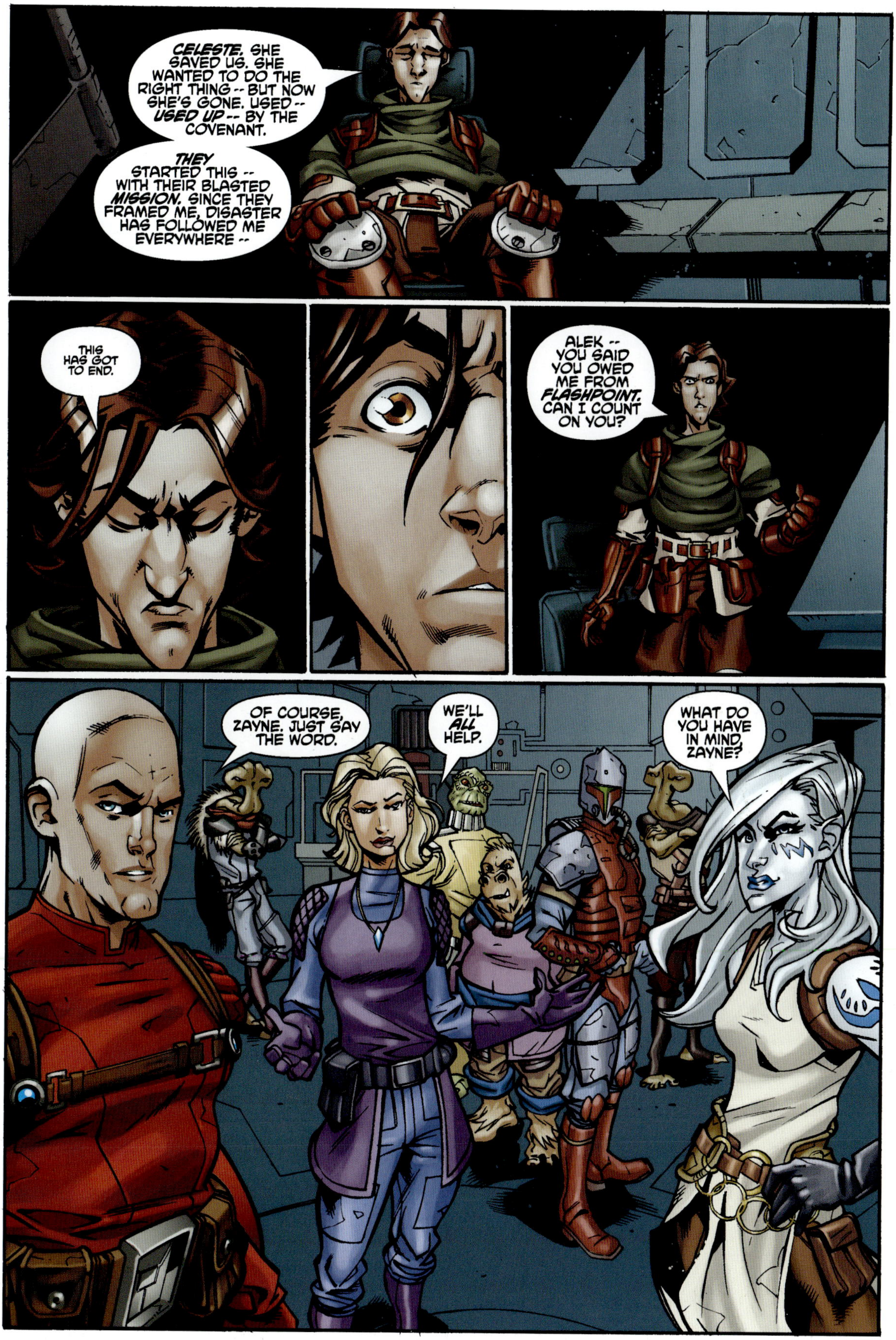
CELESTE. SHE SAVED US. SHE WANTED TO DO THE RIGHT THING -- BUT NOW SHE'S GONE. USED -- USED UP -- BY THE COVENANT.
THEY STARTED THIS -- WITH THEIR BLASTED MISSION. SINCE THEY FRAMED ME, DISASTER HAS FOLLOWED ME EVERYWHERE --
THIS HAS GOT TO END.
ALEK -- YOU SAID YOU OWED ME FROM FLASHPOINT. CAN I COUNT ON YOU?
OF COURSE, ZAYNE. JUST SAY THE WORD.
WE'LL ALL HELP.
WHAT DO YOU HAVE IN MIND, ZAYNE?

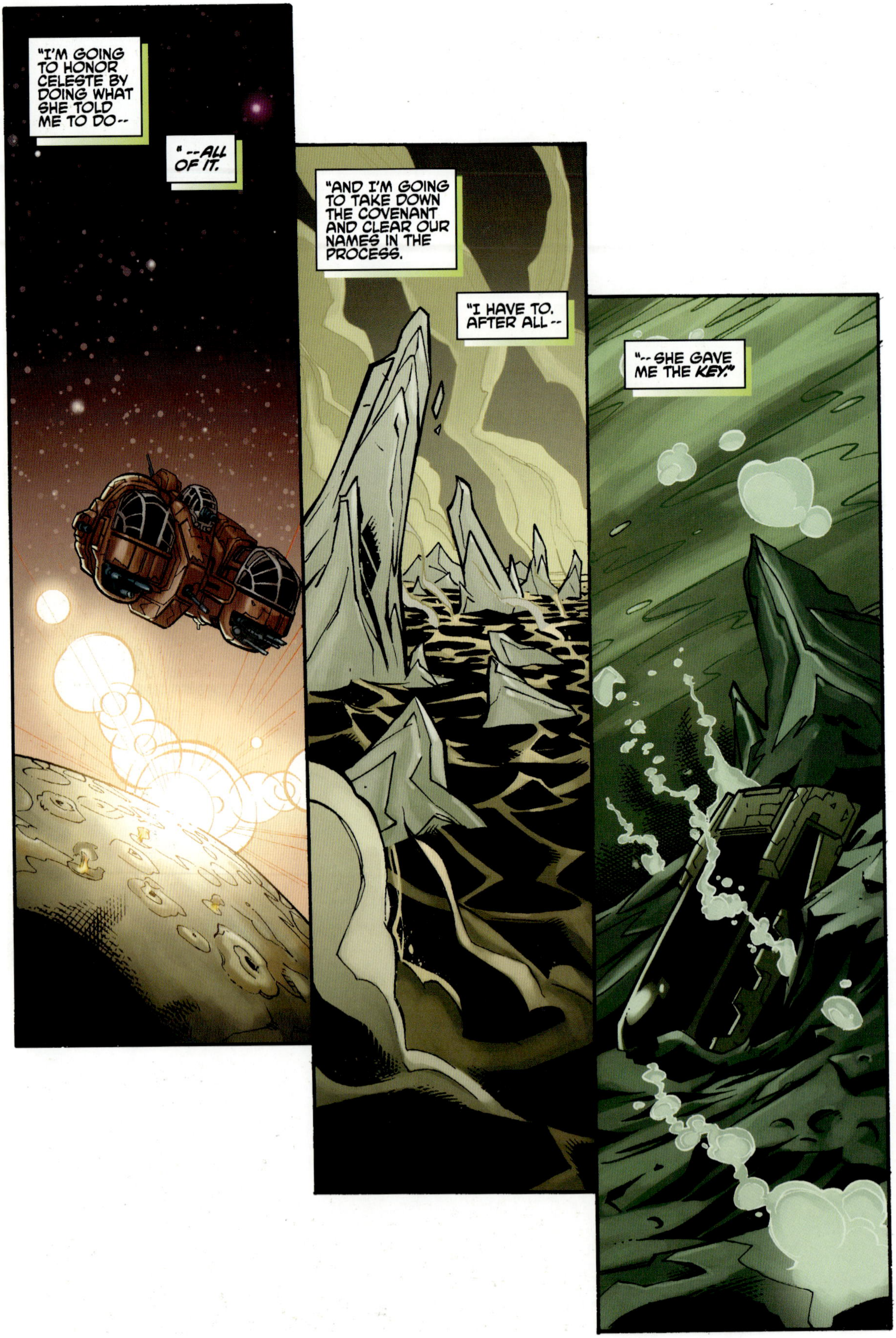
"I'M GOING TO HONOR CELESTE BY DOING WHAT SHE TOLD ME TO DO--
"--ALL OF IT.
"AND I'M GOING TO TAKE DOWN THE COVENANT AND CLEAR OUR NAMES IN THE PROCESS.
"I HAVE TO. AFTER ALL--
"--SHE GAVE ME THE KEY."

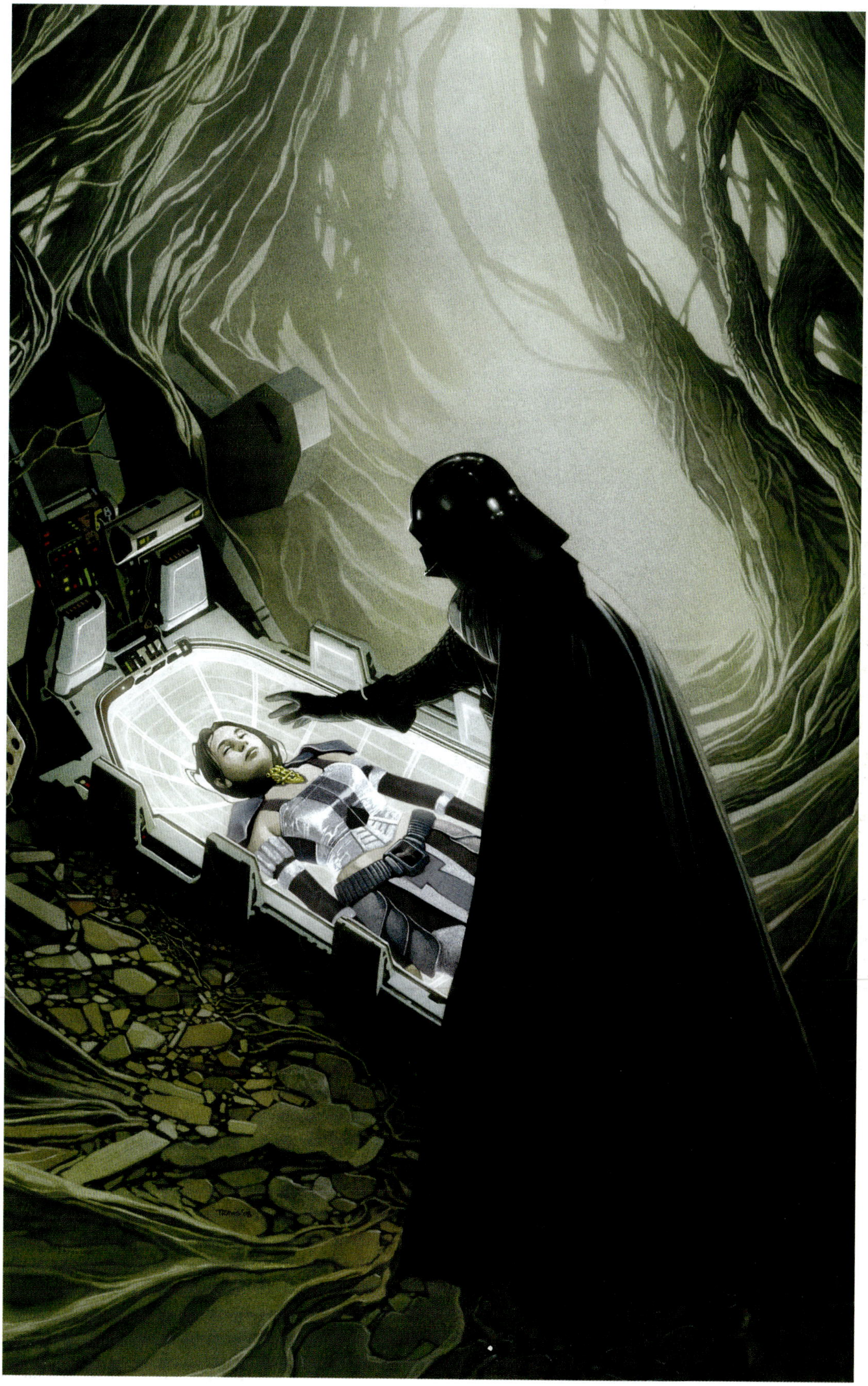

Illustration by **TRAVIS CHAREST**

DARK TIMES

VOLUME 3 The outlaw crew of the *Uhumele* has been through much in these recent dark times. In their efforts to sell the mysterious crate in their possession, one of the crew has been captured by the Empire, and another killed by the first buyer they approached. If not for the actions of Bomo Greenbark, the remainder of the company might have suffered a similar fate.

Now, Captain Heren has his hopes set on a new buyer for the ancient casket and its unknown contents . . .

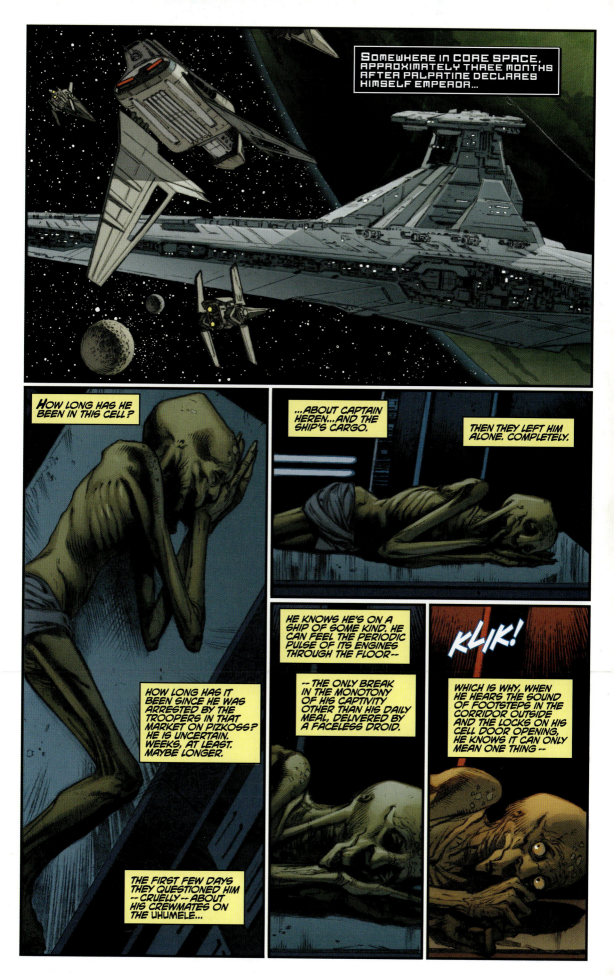

SOMEWHERE IN CORE SPACE, APPROXIMATELY THREE MONTHS AFTER PALPATINE DECLARES HIMSELF EMPEROR...

HOW LONG HAS HE BEEN IN THIS CELL?

...ABOUT CAPTAIN HEREN...AND THE SHIP'S CARGO.

THEN THEY LEFT HIM ALONE. COMPLETELY.

HOW LONG HAS IT BEEN SINCE HE WAS ARRESTED BY THE TROOPERS IN THAT MARKET ON PIZKOSS? HE IS UNCERTAIN. WEEKS, AT LEAST. MAYBE LONGER.

HE KNOWS HE'S ON A SHIP OF SOME KIND. HE CAN FEEL THE PERIODIC PULSE OF ITS ENGINES THROUGH THE FLOOR--

-- THE ONLY BREAK IN THE MONOTONY OF HIS CAPTIVITY OTHER THAN HIS DAILY MEAL, DELIVERED BY A FACELESS DROID.

KLIK!

WHICH IS WHY, WHEN HE HEARS THE SOUND OF FOOTSTEPS IN THE CORRIDOR OUTSIDE AND THE LOCKS ON HIS CELL DOOR OPENING, HE KNOWS IT CAN ONLY MEAN ONE THING --

THE FIRST FEW DAYS THEY QUESTIONED HIM -- CRUELLY -- ABOUT HIS CREWMATES ON THE UHUMELE...

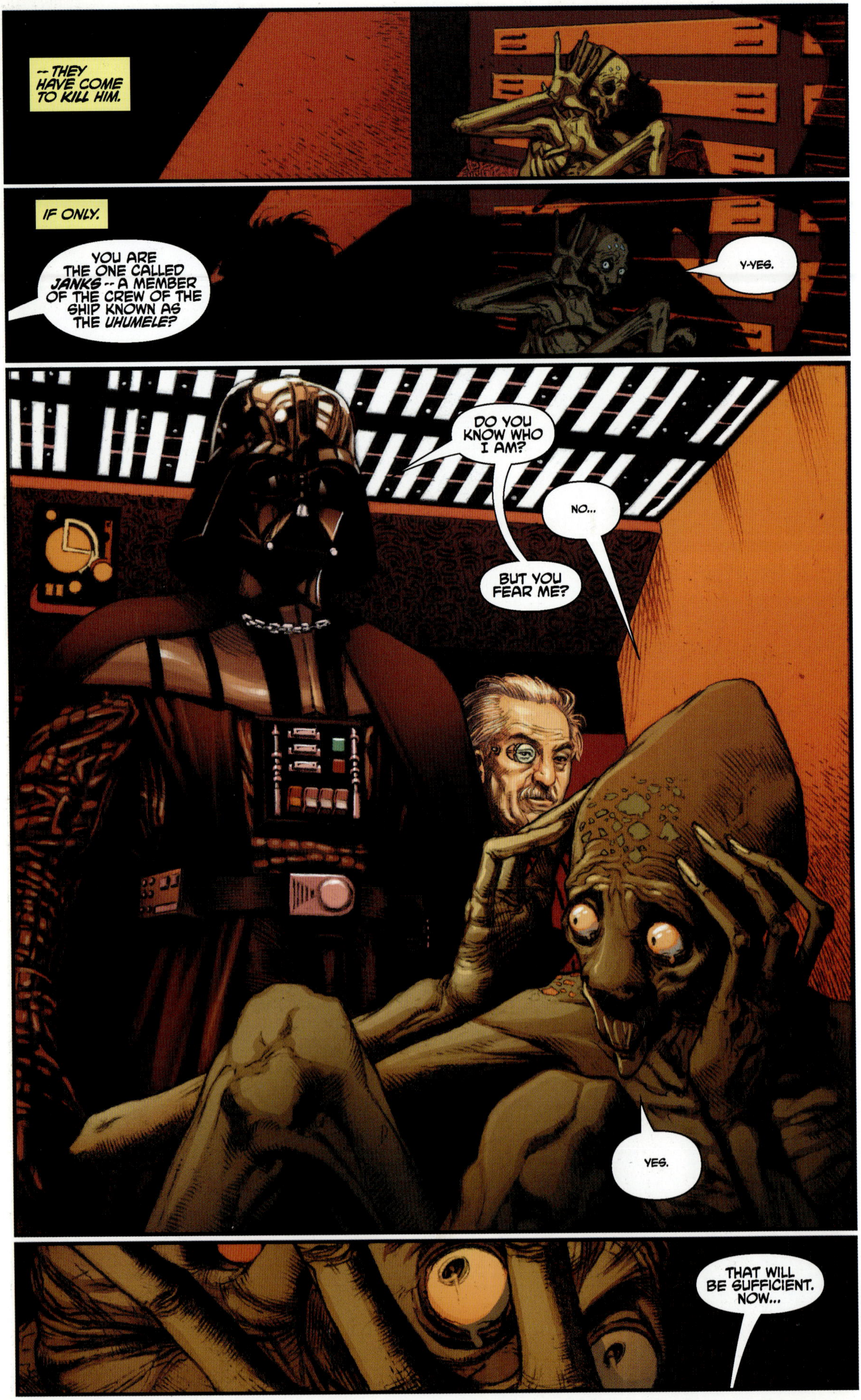

-- THEY HAVE COME TO KILL HIM.
IF ONLY.
YOU ARE THE ONE CALLED JANKS -- A MEMBER OF THE CREW OF THE SHIP KNOWN AS THE UHUMELE?
Y-YES.
DO YOU KNOW WHO I AM?
NO...
BUT YOU FEAR ME?
YES.
THAT WILL BE SUFFICIENT. NOW...

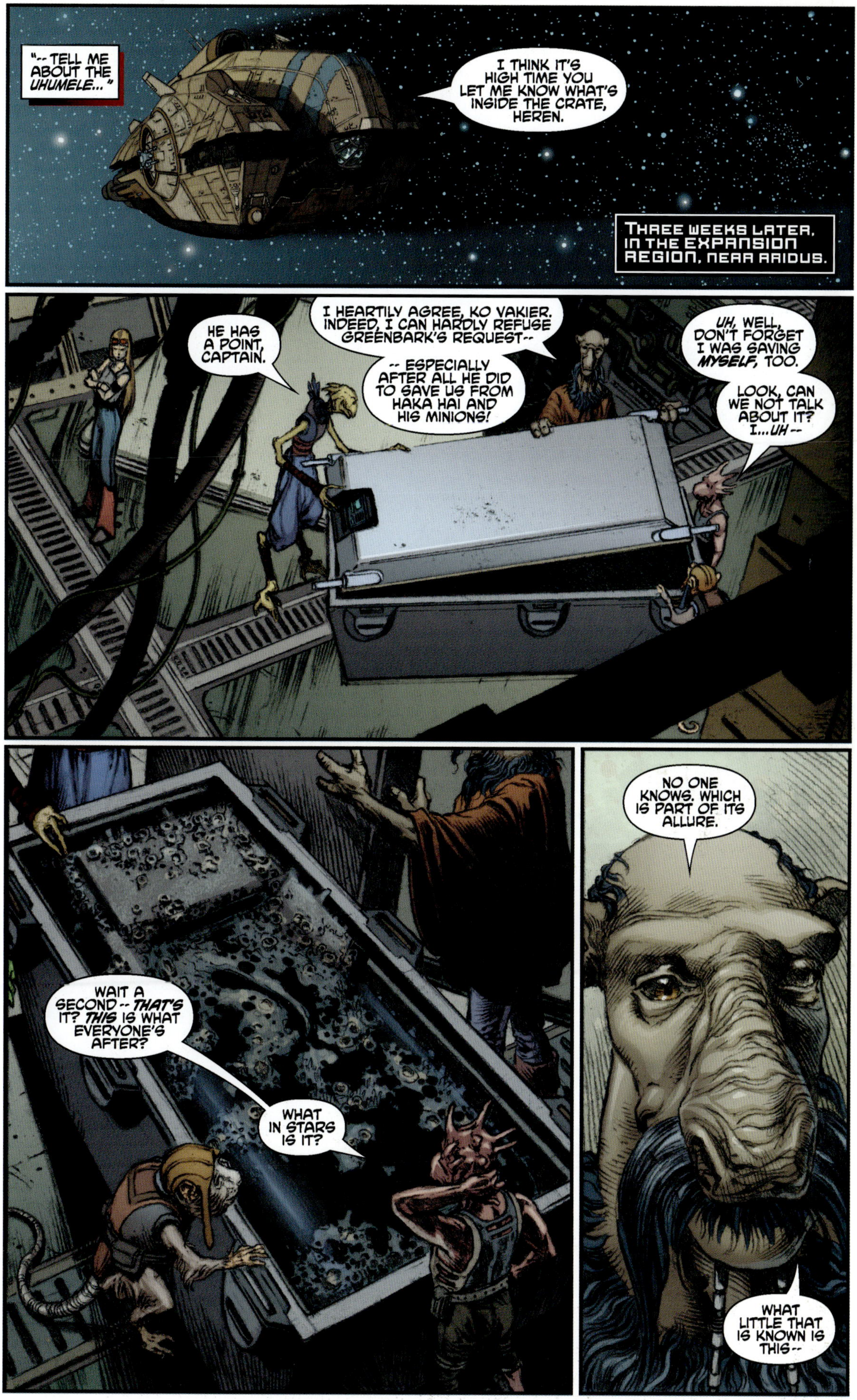
"-- TELL ME ABOUT THE *UHUMELE...*"
I THINK IT'S HIGH TIME YOU LET ME KNOW WHAT'S INSIDE THE CRATE, HEREN.
THREE WEEKS LATER, IN THE EXPANSION REGION, NEAR ARIDUS.
HE HAS A POINT, CAPTAIN.
I HEARTILY AGREE, KO VAKIER. INDEED, I CAN HARDLY REFUSE GREENBARK'S REQUEST--
-- ESPECIALLY AFTER ALL HE DID TO SAVE US FROM HAKA HAI AND HIS MINIONS!
UH, WELL, DON'T FORGET I WAS SAVING ***MYSELF,*** TOO.
LOOK, CAN WE NOT TALK ABOUT IT? I...*UH* --
WAIT A SECOND -- ***THAT'S*** IT? ***THIS*** IS WHAT EVERYONE'S AFTER?
WHAT IN STARS IS IT?
NO ONE KNOWS. WHICH IS PART OF ITS ALLURE.
WHAT LITTLE THAT IS KNOWN IS THIS --

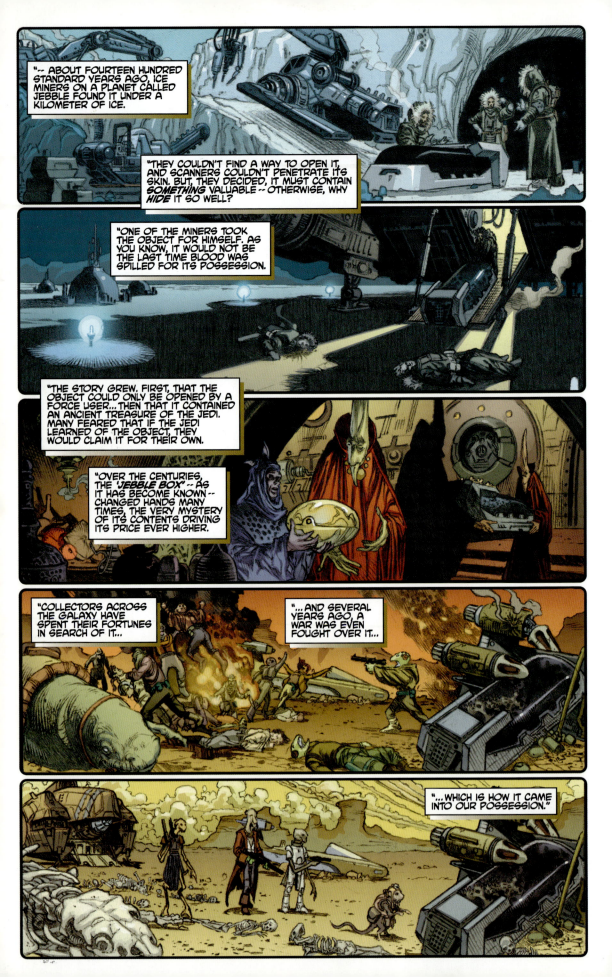

"-- ABOUT FOURTEEN HUNDRED STANDARD YEARS AGO, ICE MINERS ON A PLANET CALLED JEBBLE FOUND IT UNDER A KILOMETER OF ICE.

"THEY COULDN'T FIND A WAY TO OPEN IT, AND SCANNERS COULDN'T PENETRATE ITS SKIN. BUT, THEY DECIDED, IT MUST CONTAIN *SOMETHING* VALUABLE -- OTHERWISE, WHY *HIDE* IT SO WELL?

"ONE OF THE MINERS TOOK THE OBJECT FOR HIMSELF. AS YOU KNOW, IT WOULD NOT BE THE LAST TIME BLOOD WAS SPILLED FOR ITS POSSESSION.

"THE STORY GREW. FIRST, THAT THE OBJECT COULD ONLY BE OPENED BY A FORCE USER... THEN THAT IT CONTAINED AN ANCIENT TREASURE OF THE JEDI. MANY FEARED THAT IF THE JEDI LEARNED OF THE OBJECT, THEY WOULD CLAIM IT FOR THEIR OWN.

"OVER THE CENTURIES, THE *'JEBBLE BOX'* -- AS IT HAS BECOME KNOWN -- CHANGED HANDS MANY TIMES, THE VERY MYSTERY OF ITS CONTENTS DRIVING ITS PRICE EVER HIGHER.

"COLLECTORS ACROSS THE GALAXY HAVE SPENT THEIR FORTUNES IN SEARCH OF IT...

"...AND SEVERAL YEARS AGO, A WAR WAS EVEN FOUGHT OVER IT...

"...WHICH IS HOW IT CAME INTO OUR POSSESSION."

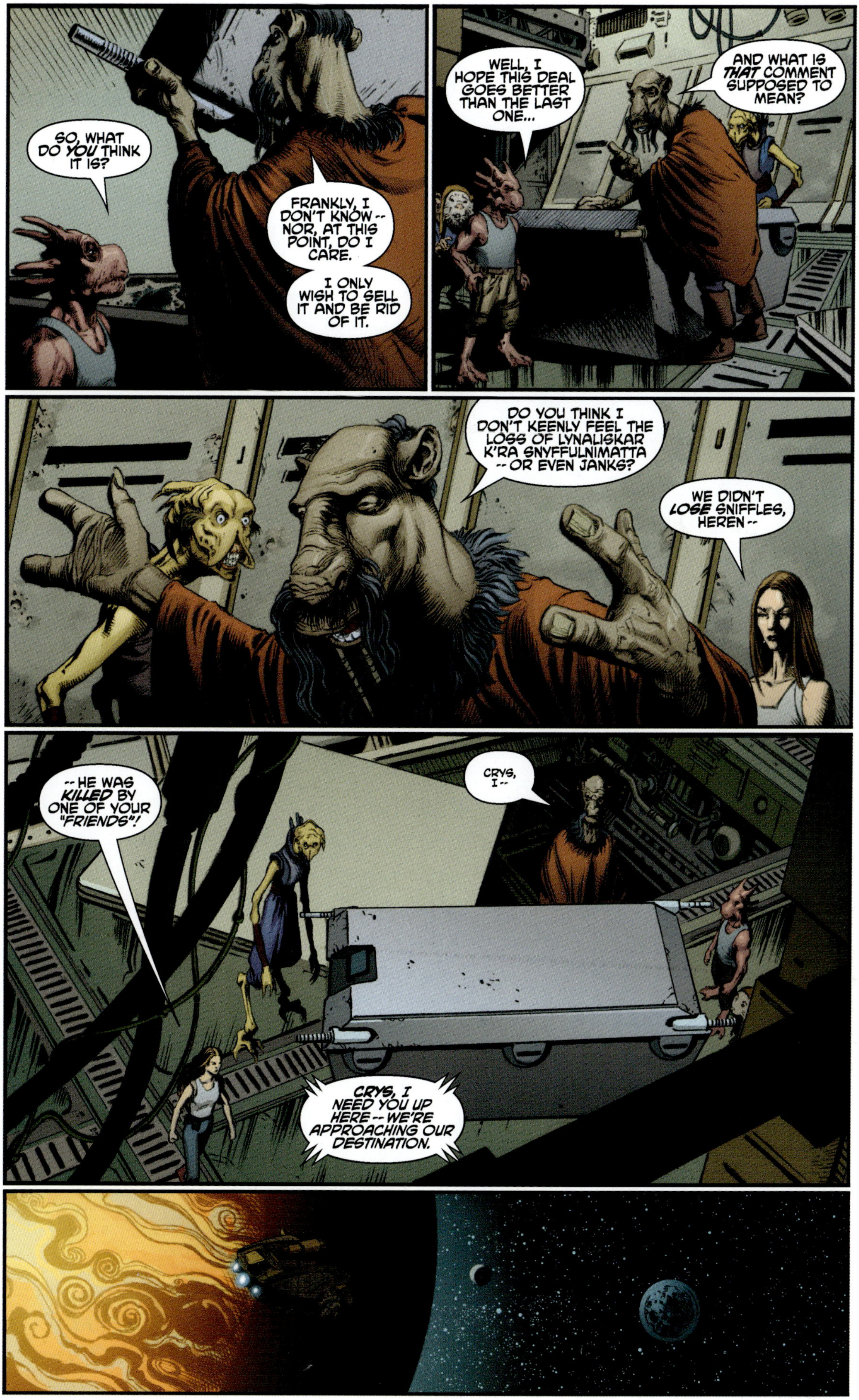
SO, WHAT DO YOU THINK IT IS?
FRANKLY, I DON'T KNOW -- NOR, AT THIS POINT, DO I CARE.
I ONLY WISH TO SELL IT AND BE RID OF IT.
WELL, I HOPE THIS DEAL GOES BETTER THAN THE LAST ONE...
AND WHAT IS THAT COMMENT SUPPOSED TO MEAN?
DO YOU THINK I DON'T KEENLY FEEL THE LOSS OF LYNALISKAR K'RA SNYFFULNIMATTA -- OR EVEN JANKS?
WE DIDN'T LOSE SNIFFLES, HEREN --
-- HE WAS KILLED BY ONE OF YOUR "FRIENDS"!
CRYS, I --
CRYS, I NEED YOU UP HERE -- WE'RE APPROACHING OUR DESTINATION.

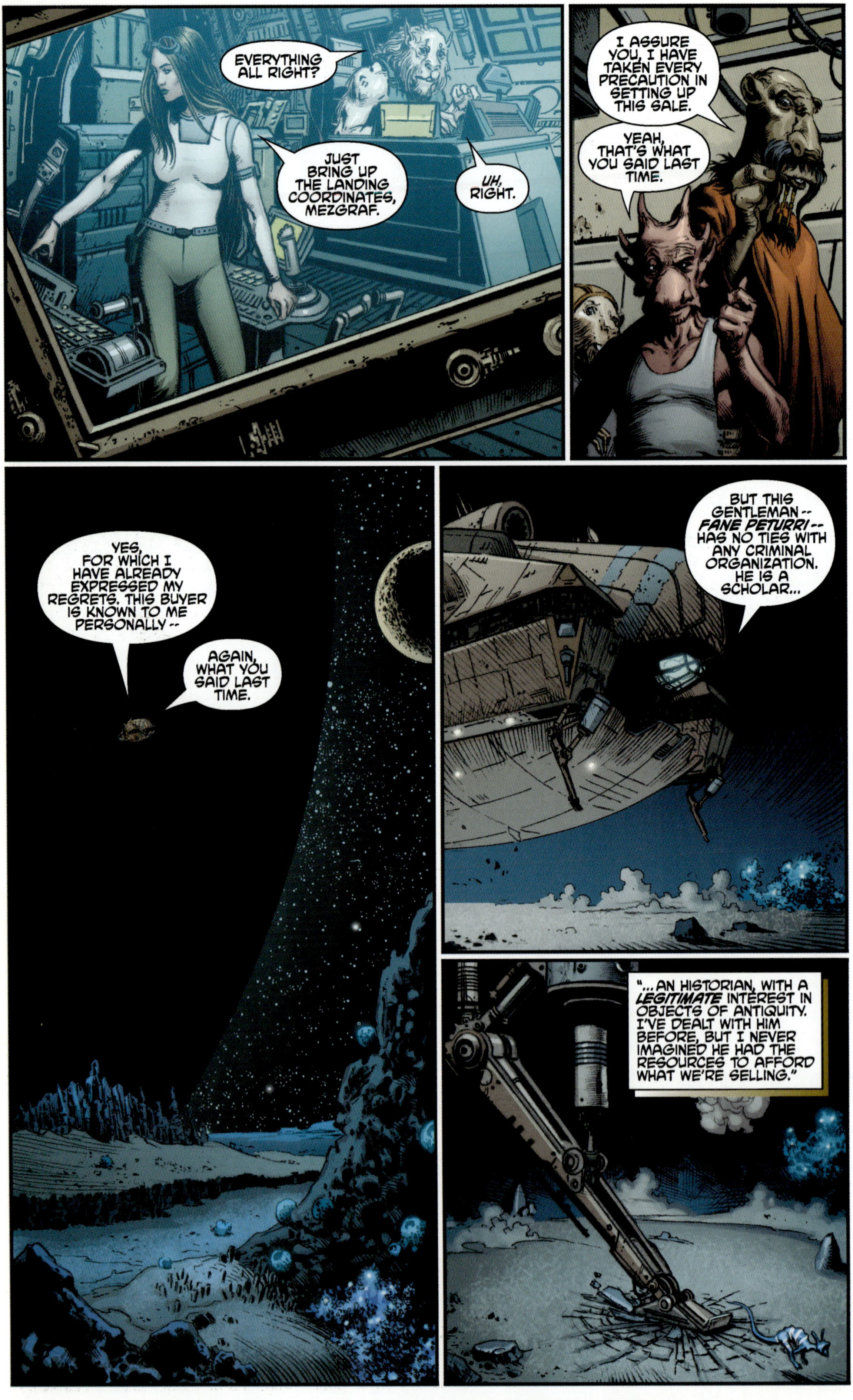
EVERYTHING ALL RIGHT?
JUST BRING UP THE LANDING COORDINATES, MEZGRAF.
UH, RIGHT.
I ASSURE YOU, I HAVE TAKEN EVERY PRECAUTION IN SETTING UP THIS SALE.
YEAH, THAT'S WHAT YOU SAID LAST TIME.
YES, FOR WHICH I HAVE ALREADY EXPRESSED MY REGRETS. THIS BUYER IS KNOWN TO ME PERSONALLY --
AGAIN, WHAT YOU SAID LAST TIME.
BUT THIS GENTLEMAN -- FANE PETURRI -- HAS NO TIES WITH ANY CRIMINAL ORGANIZATION. HE IS A SCHOLAR...
"...AN HISTORIAN, WITH A LEGITIMATE INTEREST IN OBJECTS OF ANTIQUITY. I'VE DEALT WITH HIM BEFORE, BUT I NEVER IMAGINED HE HAD THE RESOURCES TO AFFORD WHAT WE'RE SELLING."

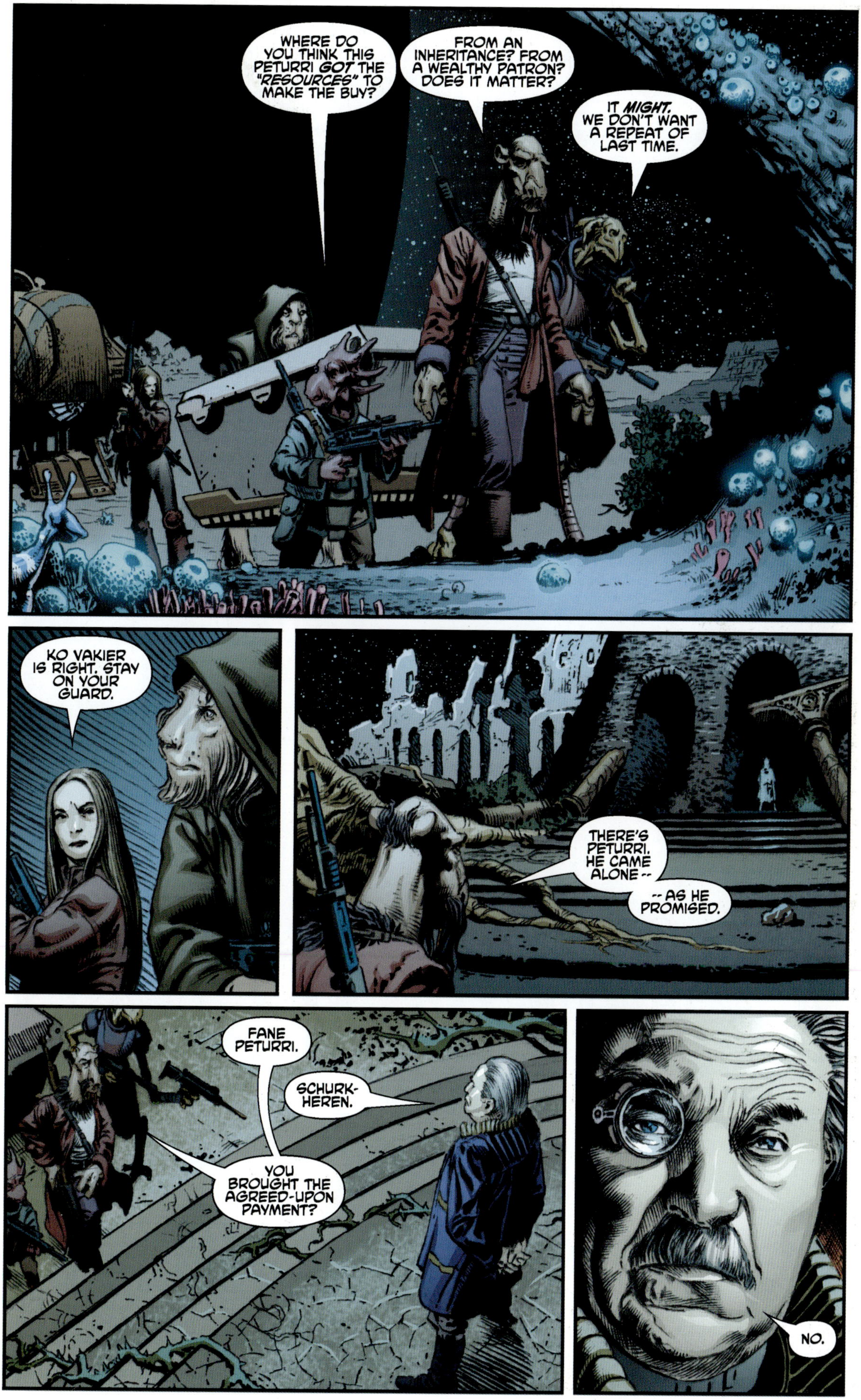
WHERE DO YOU THINK THIS PETURRI GOT THE "RESOURCES" TO MAKE THE BUY?
FROM AN INHERITANCE? FROM A WEALTHY PATRON? DOES IT MATTER?
IT MIGHT. WE DON'T WANT A REPEAT OF LAST TIME.
KO VAKIER IS RIGHT. STAY ON YOUR GUARD.
THERE'S PETURRI. HE CAME ALONE --
-- AS HE PROMISED.
FANE PETURRI.
SCHURK-HEREN.
YOU BROUGHT THE AGREED-UPON PAYMENT?
NO.

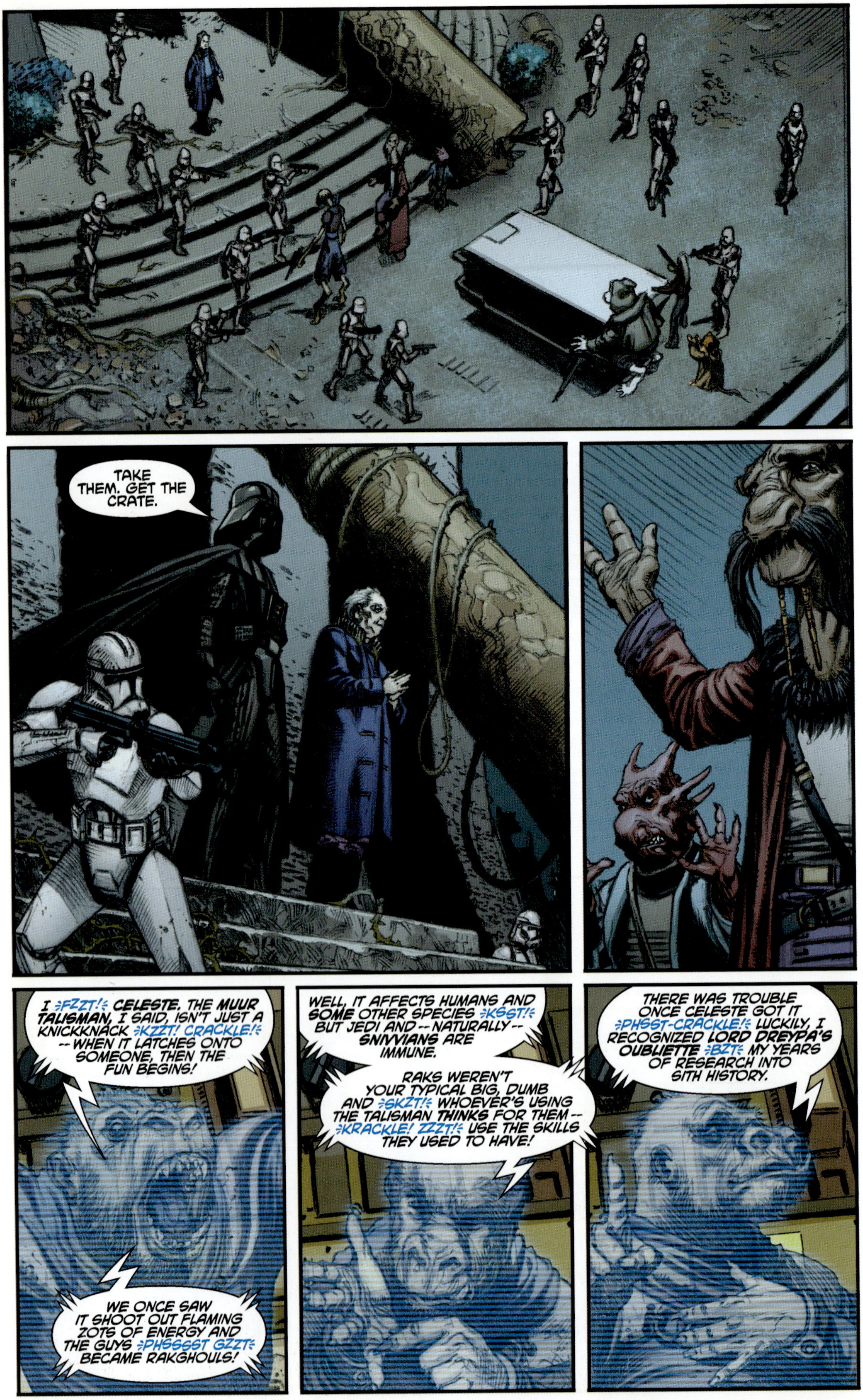
TAKE THEM. GET THE CRATE.
I FZZT! CELESTE. THE MUUR TALISMAN, I SAID, ISN'T JUST A KNICKKNACK KZZT! CRACKLE! -- WHEN IT LATCHES ONTO SOMEONE, THEN THE FUN BEGINS!
WE ONCE SAW IT SHOOT OUT FLAMING ZOTS OF ENERGY AND THE GUYS PHSSSST GZZT BECAME RAKGHOULS!
WELL, IT AFFECTS HUMANS AND SOME OTHER SPECIES KSST! BUT JEDI AND -- NATURALLY -- SNIVVIANS ARE IMMUNE.
RAKS WEREN'T YOUR TYPICAL BIG, DUMB AND SKZT! WHOEVER'S USING THE TALISMAN THINKS FOR THEM -- KRACKLE! ZZZT! USE THE SKILLS THEY USED TO HAVE!
THERE WAS TROUBLE ONCE CELESTE GOT IT PHSST-CRACKLE! LUCKILY, I RECOGNIZED LORD DREYPA'S OUBLIETTE BZT MY YEARS OF RESEARCH INTO SITH HISTORY.

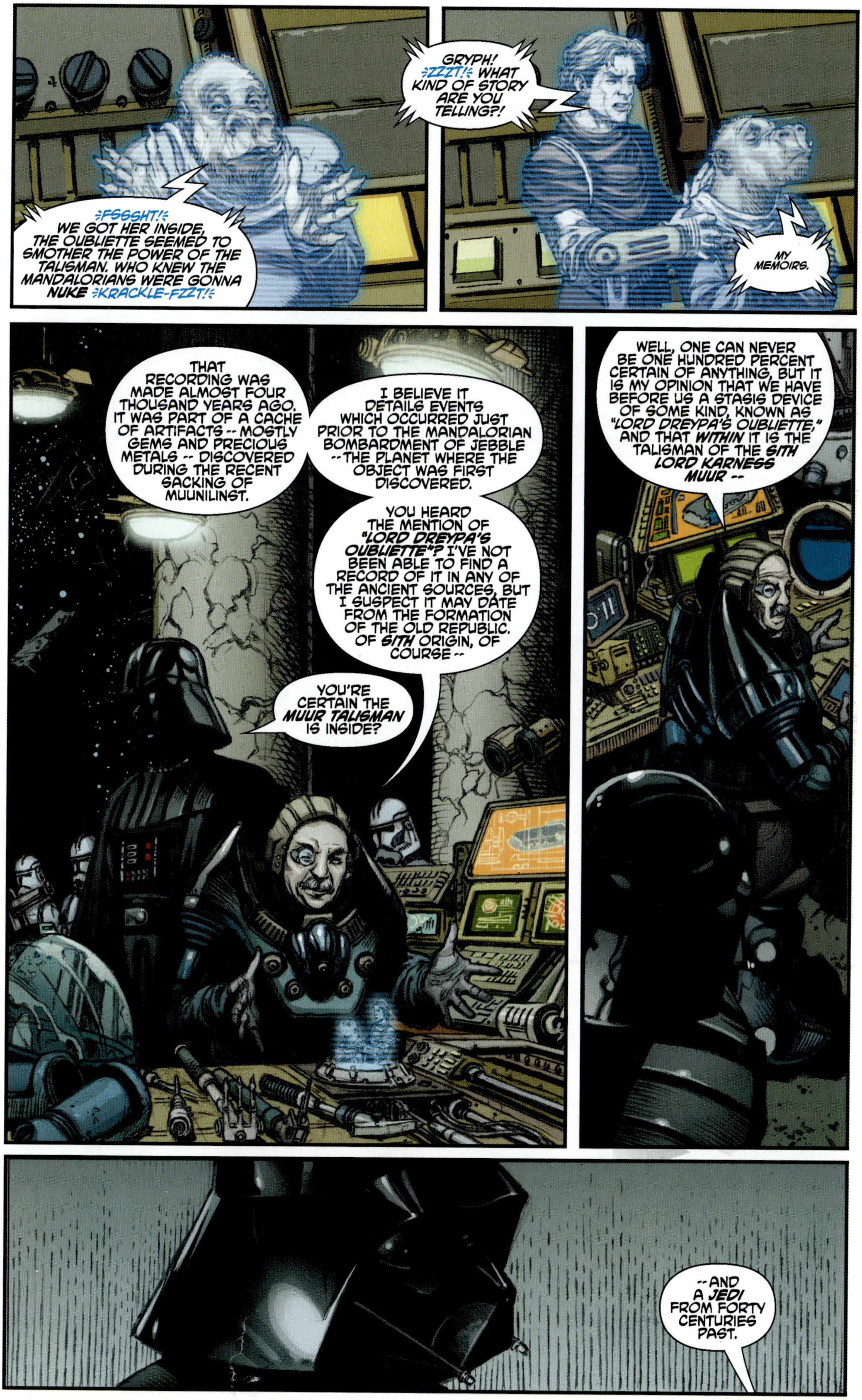

FSSSHT! WE GOT HER INSIDE. THE OUBLIETTE SEEMED TO SMOTHER THE POWER OF THE TALISMAN. WHO KNEW THE MANDALORIANS WERE GONNA NUKE KRACKLE-FZZT!
GRYPH! ZZZT! WHAT KIND OF STORY ARE YOU TELLING?!
MY MEMOIRS.
THAT RECORDING WAS MADE ALMOST FOUR THOUSAND YEARS AGO. IT WAS PART OF A CACHE OF ARTIFACTS -- MOSTLY GEMS AND PRECIOUS METALS -- DISCOVERED DURING THE RECENT SACKING OF MUUNILINST.
I BELIEVE IT DETAILS EVENTS WHICH OCCURRED JUST PRIOR TO THE MANDALORIAN BOMBARDMENT OF JEBBLE -- THE PLANET WHERE THE OBJECT WAS FIRST DISCOVERED.
YOU HEARD THE MENTION OF "LORD DREYPA'S OUBLIETTE"? I'VE NOT BEEN ABLE TO FIND A RECORD OF IT IN ANY OF THE ANCIENT SOURCES, BUT I SUSPECT IT MAY DATE FROM THE FORMATION OF THE OLD REPUBLIC. OF SITH ORIGIN, OF COURSE --
YOU'RE CERTAIN THE MUUR TALISMAN IS INSIDE?
WELL, ONE CAN NEVER BE ONE HUNDRED PERCENT CERTAIN OF ANYTHING, BUT IT IS MY OPINION THAT WE HAVE BEFORE US A STASIS DEVICE OF SOME KIND, KNOWN AS "LORD DREYPA'S OUBLIETTE," AND THAT WITHIN IT IS THE TALISMAN OF THE SITH LORD KARNESS MUUR --
--AND A JEDI FROM FORTY CENTURIES PAST.

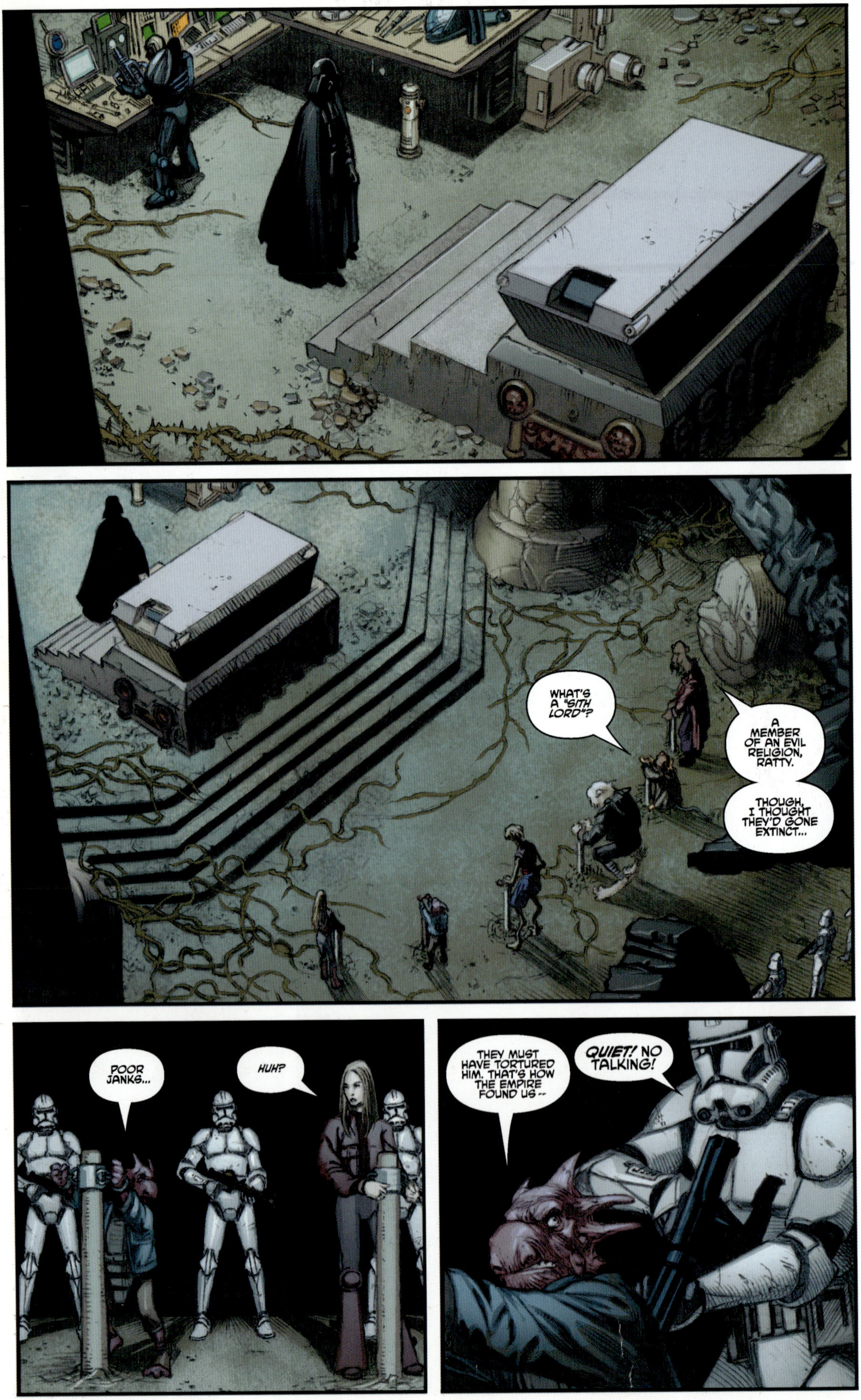
WHAT'S A "SITH LORD"?
A MEMBER OF AN EVIL RELIGION, RATTY.
THOUGH, I THOUGHT THEY'D GONE EXTINCT...
POOR JANKS...
HUH?
THEY MUST HAVE TORTURED HIM. THAT'S HOW THE EMPIRE FOUND US --
QUIET! NO TALKING!

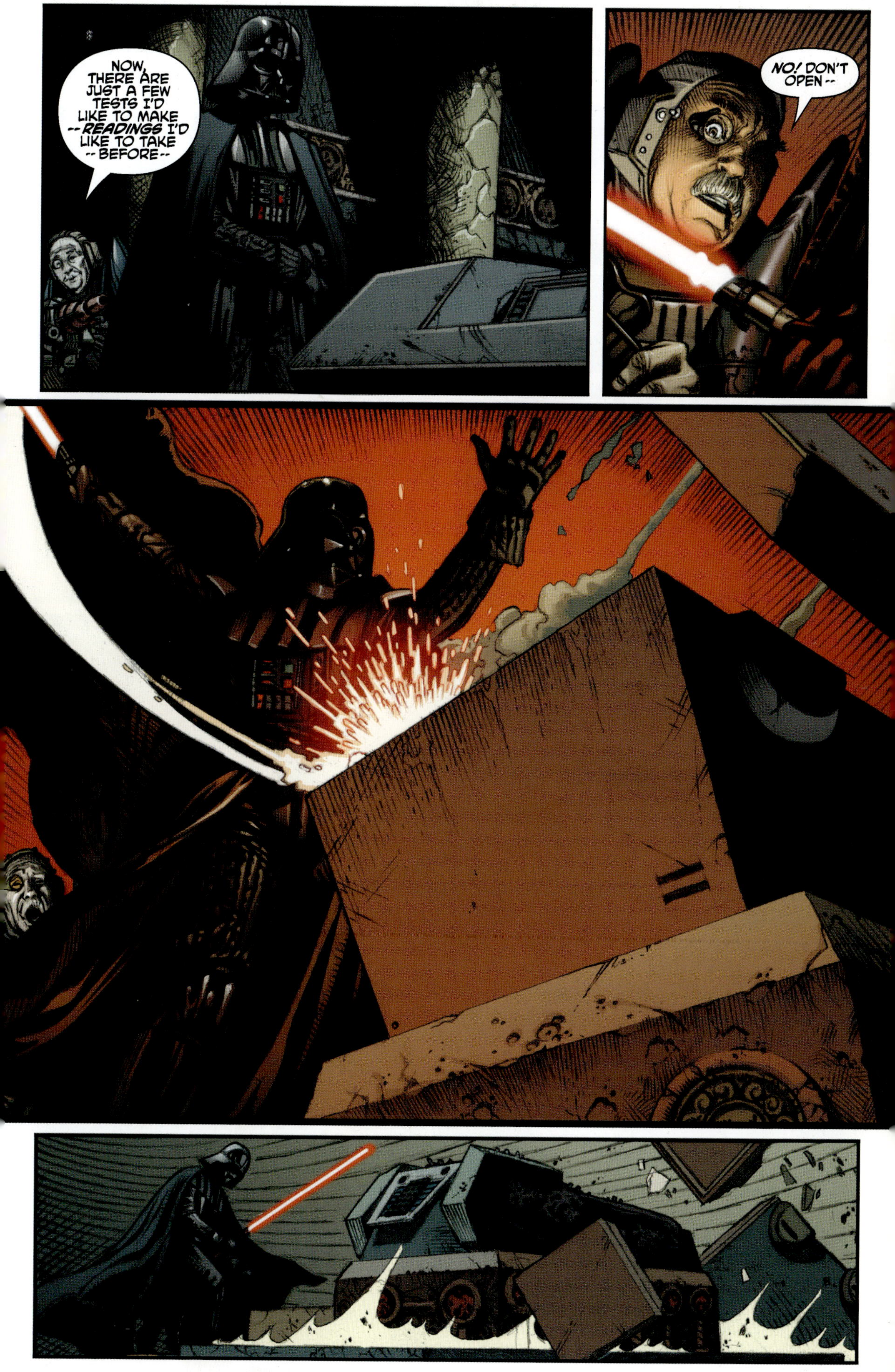
NOW, THERE ARE JUST A FEW TESTS I'D LIKE TO MAKE --READINGS I'D LIKE TO TAKE --BEFORE--
NO! DON'T OPEN--

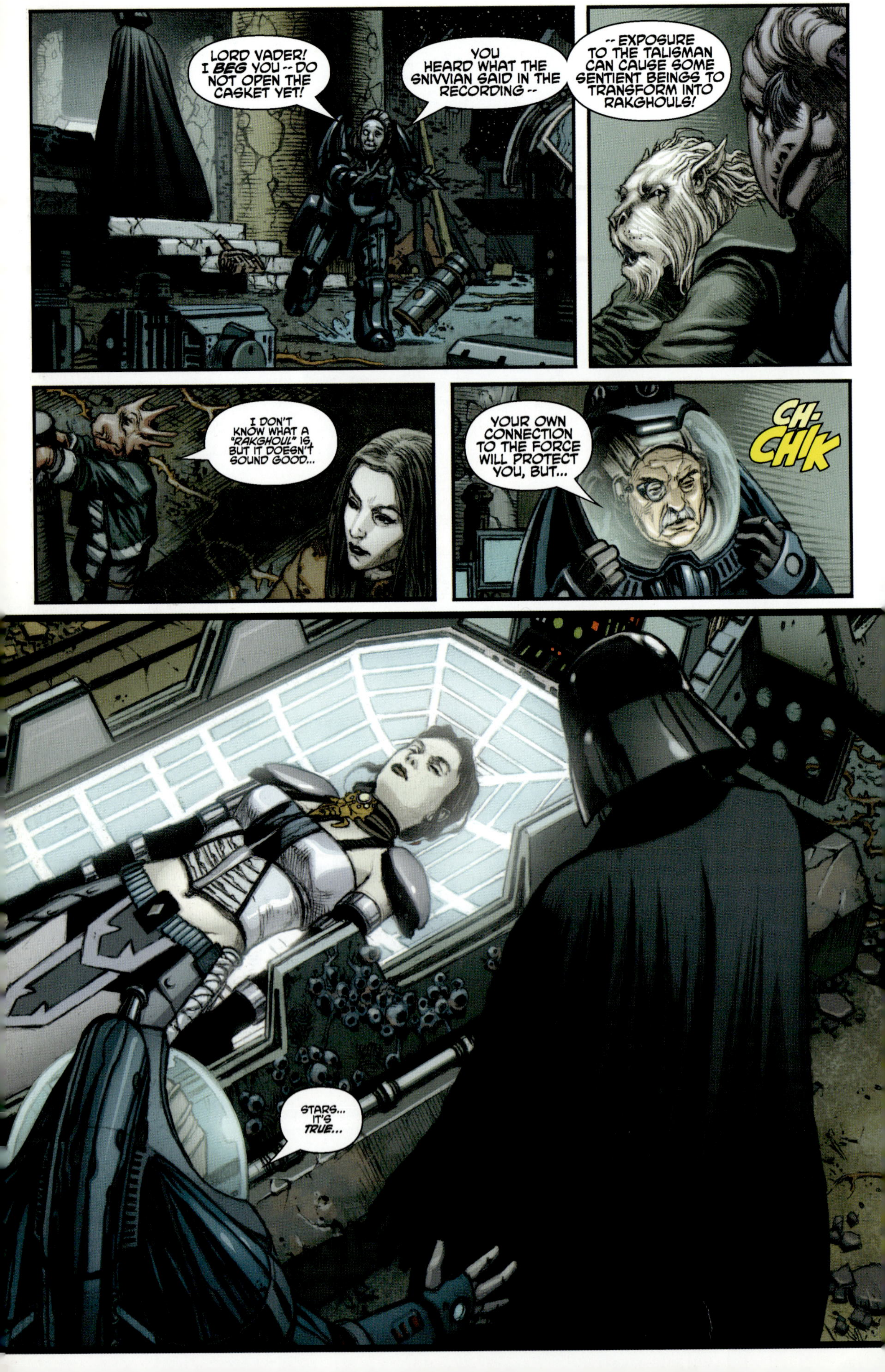
LORD VADER! I *BEG* YOU -- DO NOT OPEN THE CASKET YET!
YOU HEARD WHAT THE SNIVVIAN SAID IN THE RECORDING --
-- EXPOSURE TO THE TALISMAN CAN CAUSE SOME SENTIENT BEINGS TO TRANSFORM INTO RAKGHOULS!
I DON'T KNOW WHAT A *"RAKGHOUL"* IS, BUT IT DOESN'T SOUND GOOD...
YOUR OWN CONNECTION TO THE FORCE WILL PROTECT YOU, BUT...
CH-CHIK
STARS... IT'S *TRUE*...

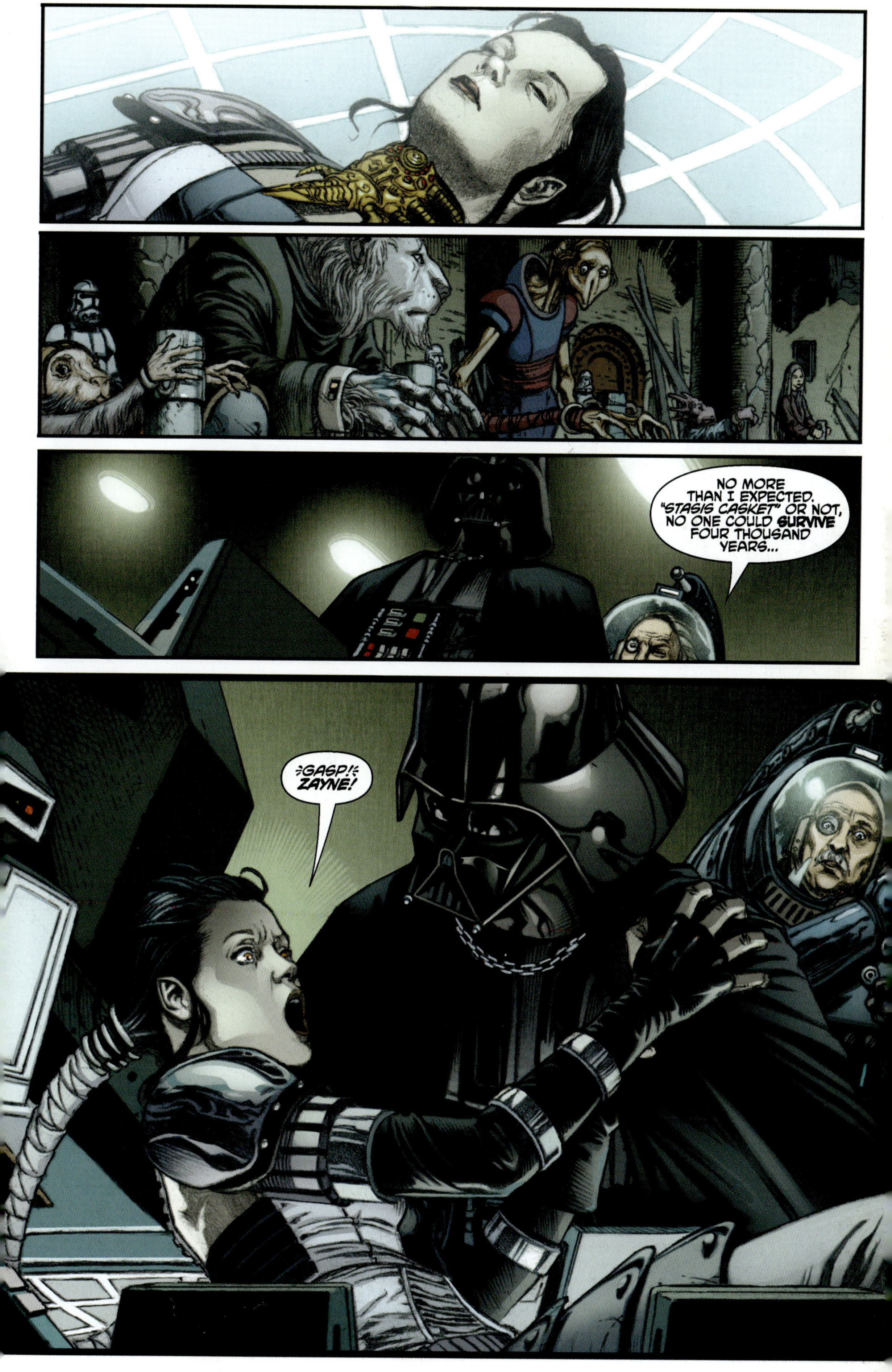
NO MORE THAN I EXPECTED. "STASIS CASKET" OR NOT, NO ONE COULD SURVIVE FOUR THOUSAND YEARS...
GASP! ZAYNE!

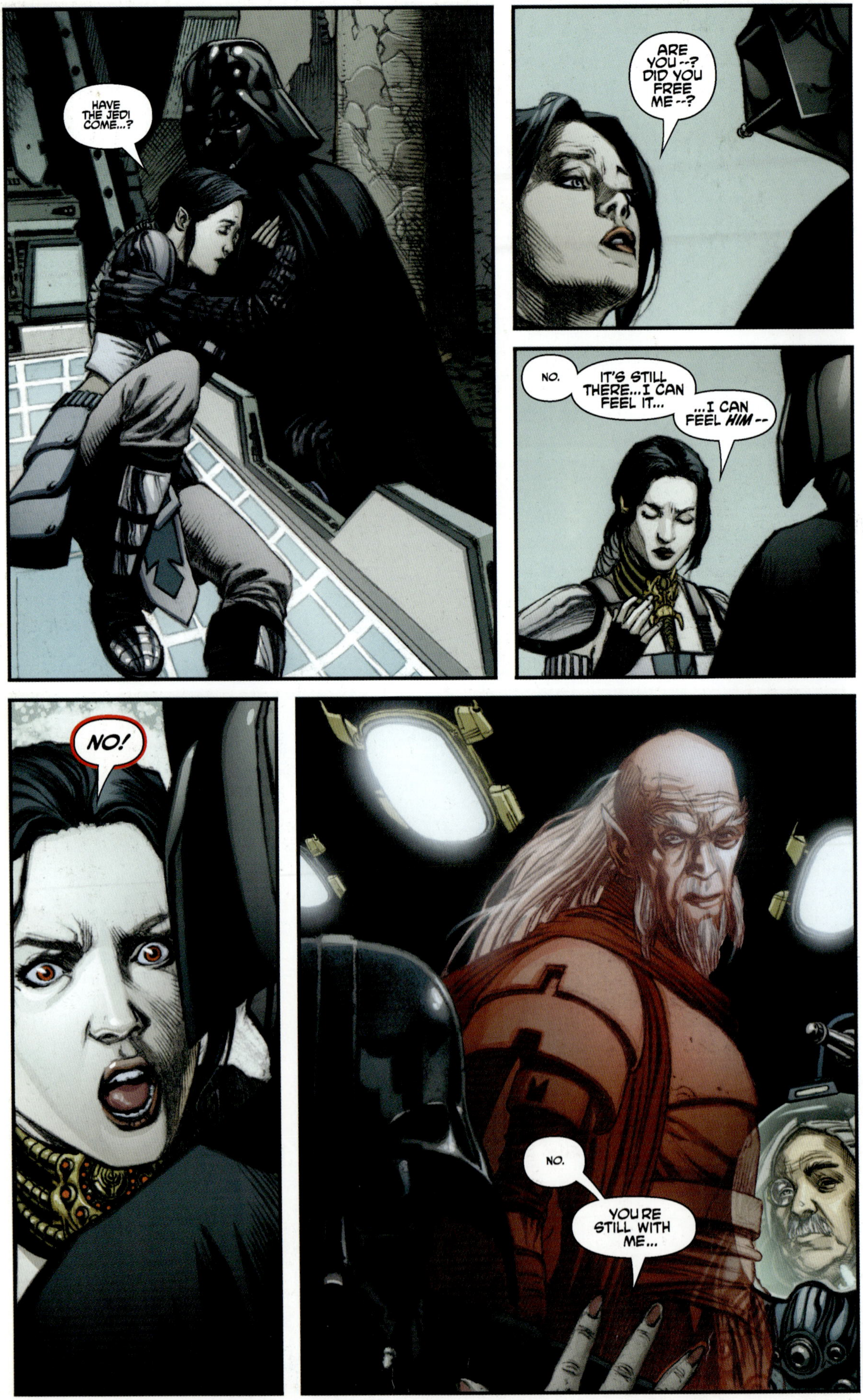
HAVE THE JEDI COME...?
ARE YOU--? DID YOU FREE ME--?
NO.
IT'S STILL THERE...I CAN FEEL IT...
...I CAN FEEL HIM--
NO!
NO.
YOU'RE STILL WITH ME...

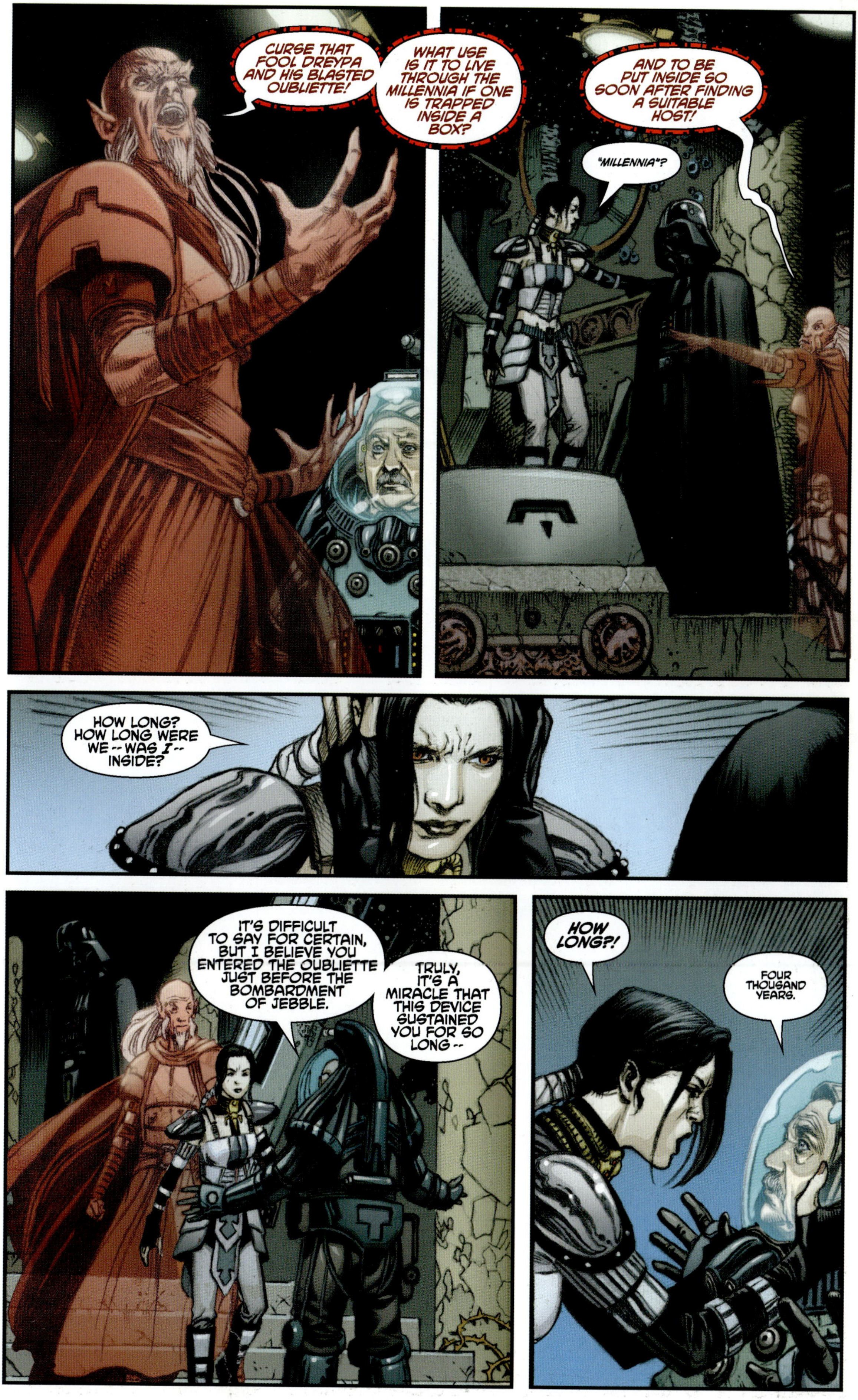

CURSE THAT FOOL DREYPA AND HIS BLASTED OUBLIETTE!
WHAT USE IS IT TO LIVE THROUGH THE MILLENNIA IF ONE IS TRAPPED INSIDE A BOX?
AND TO BE PUT INSIDE SO SOON AFTER FINDING A SUITABLE HOST!
"MILLENNIA"?
HOW LONG? HOW LONG WERE WE -- WAS I -- INSIDE?
IT'S DIFFICULT TO SAY FOR CERTAIN, BUT I BELIEVE YOU ENTERED THE OUBLIETTE JUST BEFORE THE BOMBARDMENT OF JEBBLE.
TRULY, IT'S A MIRACLE THAT THIS DEVICE SUSTAINED YOU FOR SO LONG --
HOW LONG?!
FOUR THOUSAND YEARS.

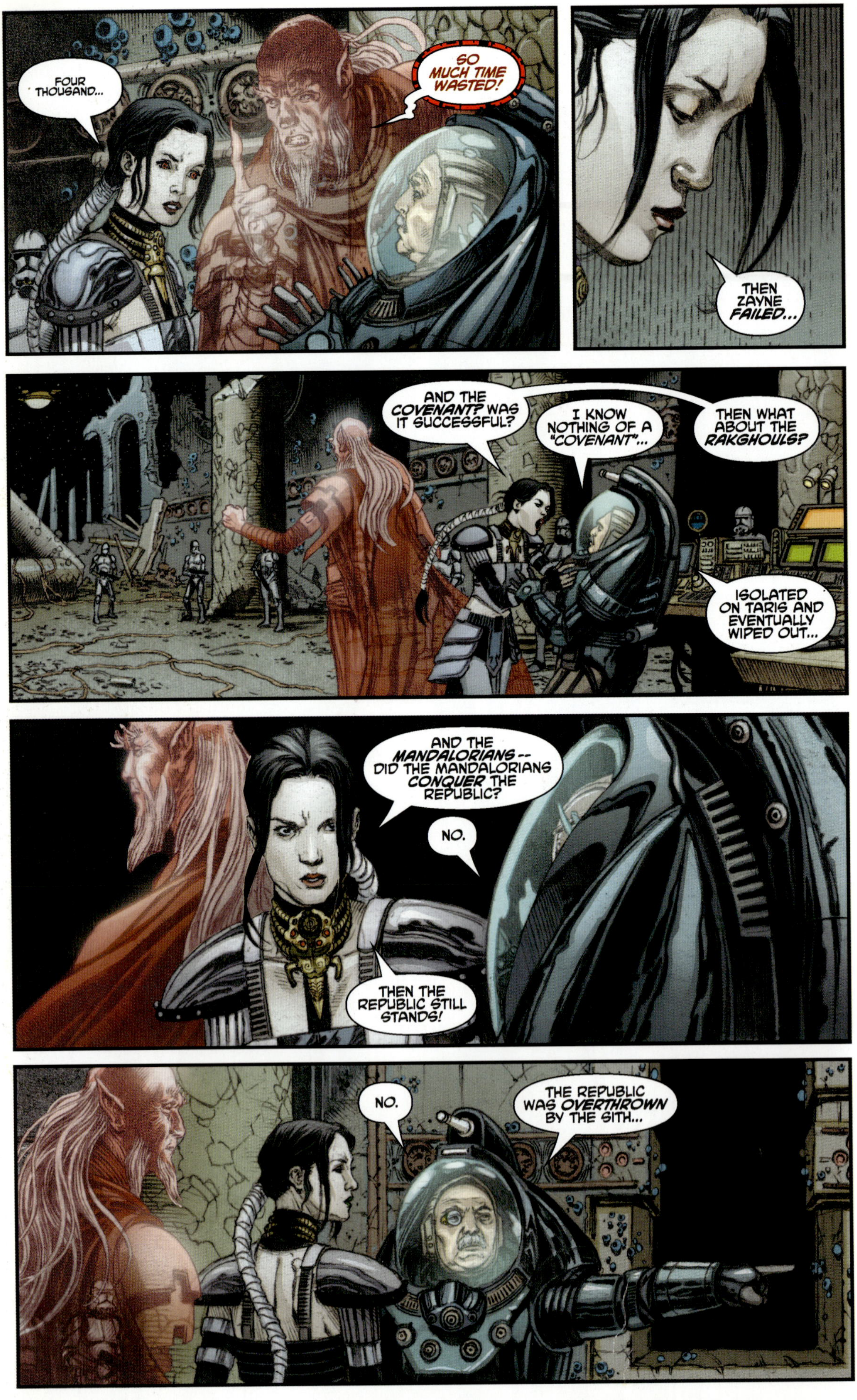

FOUR THOUSAND...
SO MUCH TIME WASTED!
THEN ZAYNE FAILED...
AND THE COVENANT? WAS IT SUCCESSFUL?
I KNOW NOTHING OF A "COVENANT"...
THEN WHAT ABOUT THE RAKGHOULS?
ISOLATED ON TARIS AND EVENTUALLY WIPED OUT...
AND THE MANDALORIANS -- DID THE MANDALORIANS CONQUER THE REPUBLIC?
NO.
THEN THE REPUBLIC STILL STANDS!
NO.
THE REPUBLIC WAS OVERTHROWN BY THE SITH...

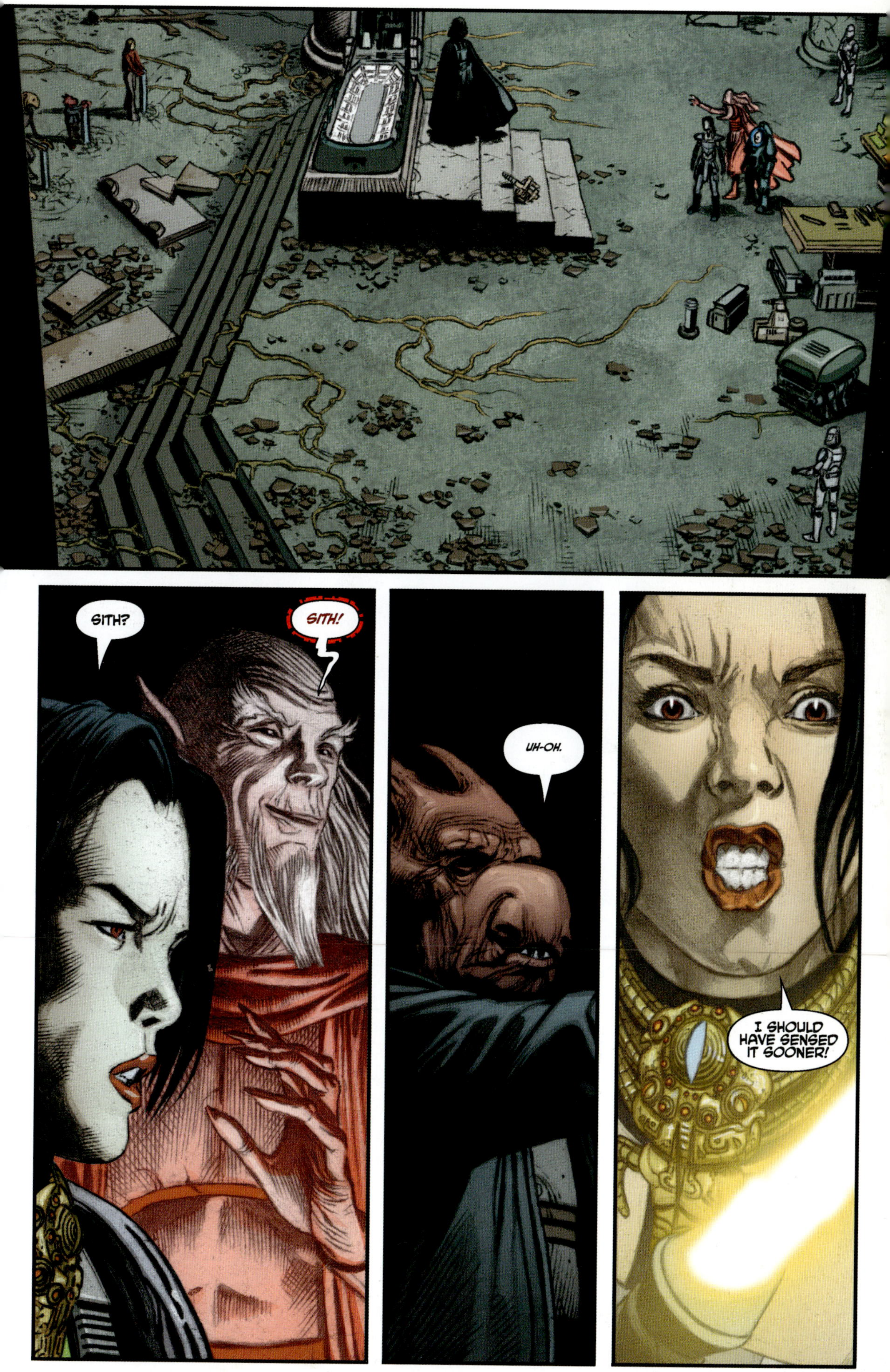
SITH?
SITH!
UH-OH.
I SHOULD HAVE SENSED IT SOONER!

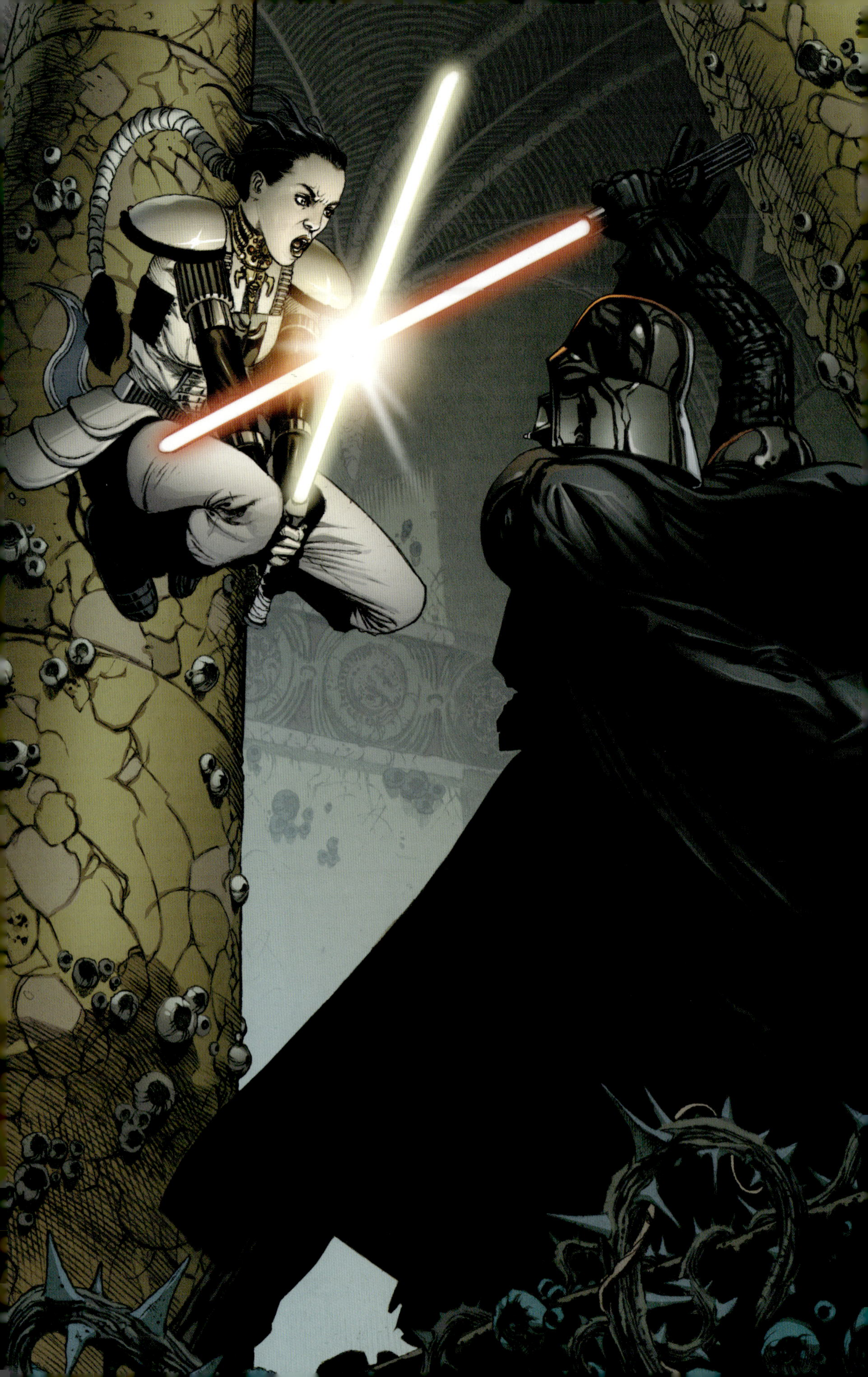

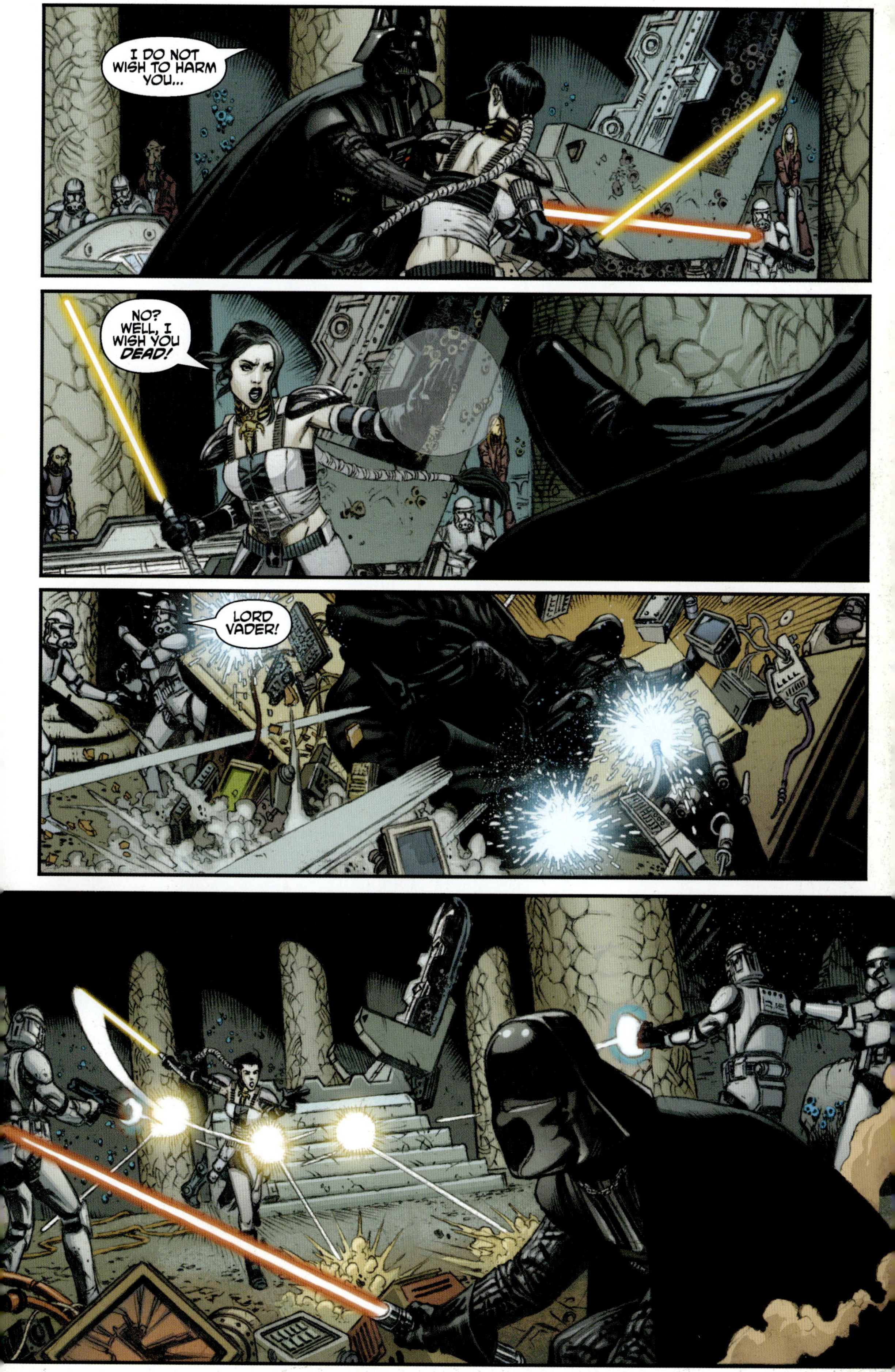
I DO NOT WISH TO HARM YOU...
NO? WELL, I WISH YOU *DEAD!*
LORD VADER!

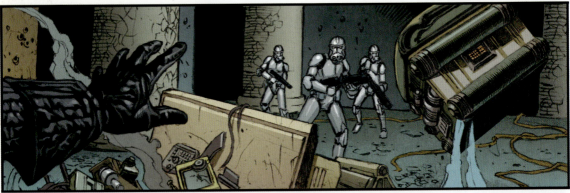

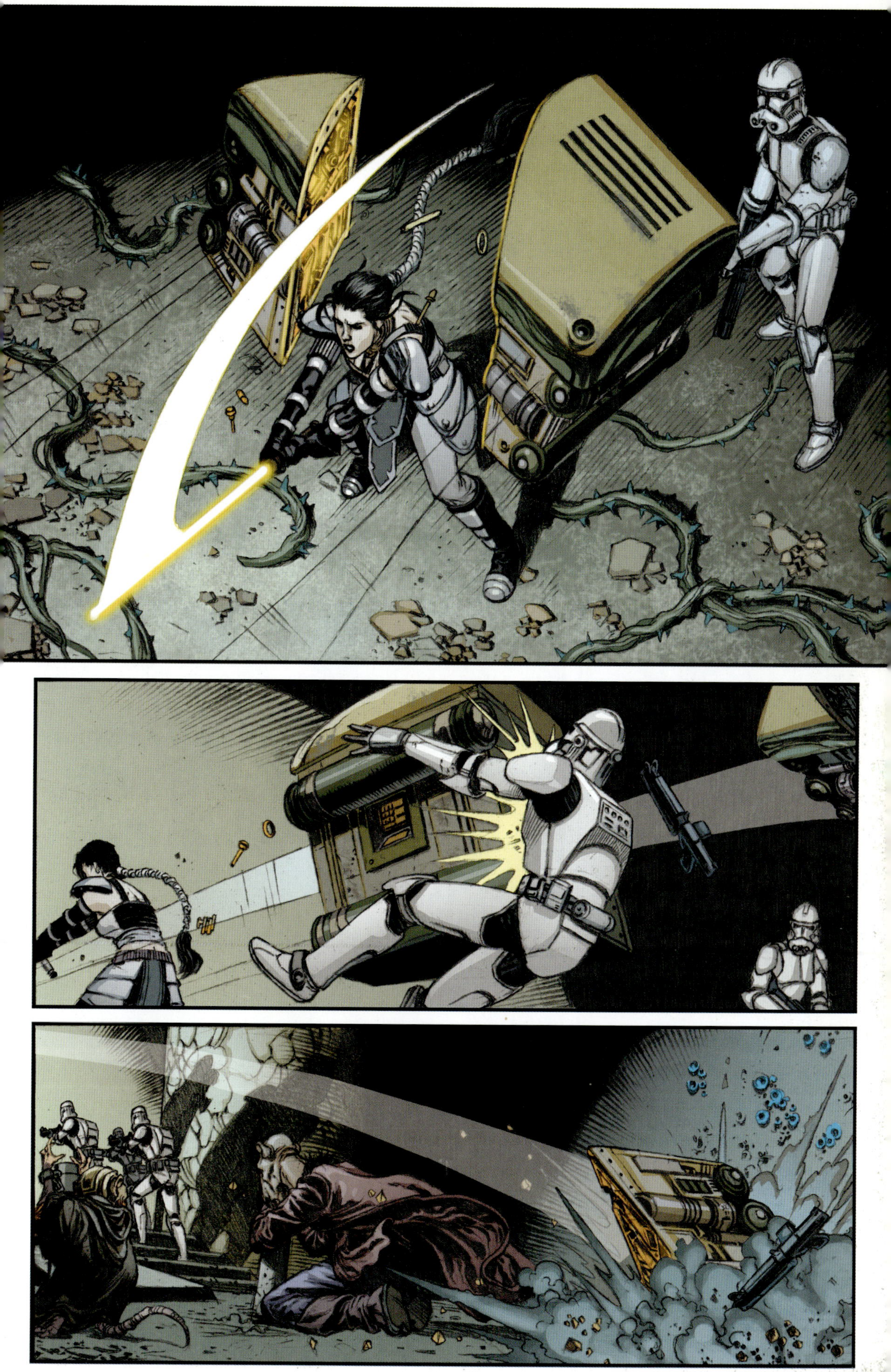

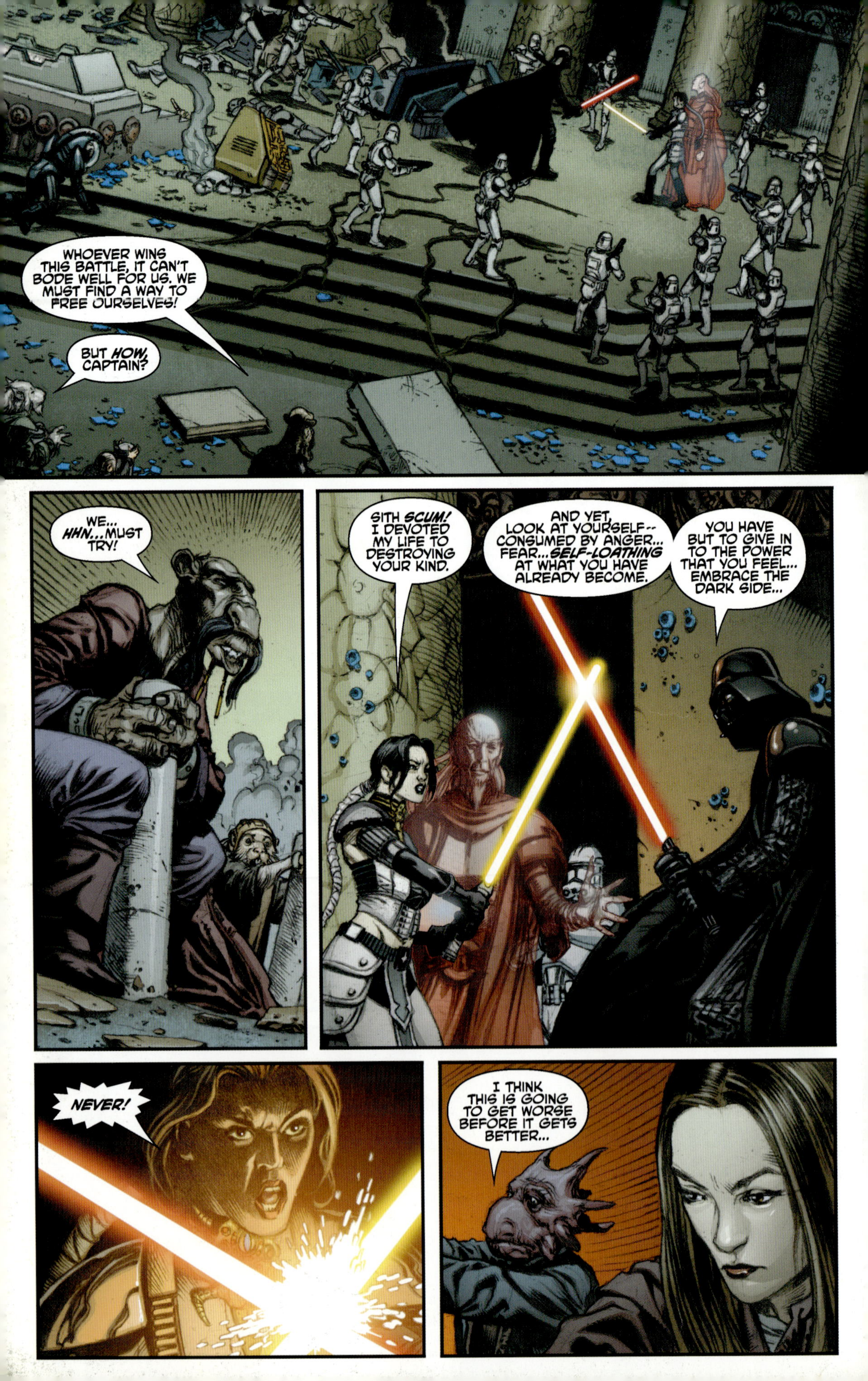
WHOEVER WINS THIS BATTLE, IT CAN'T BODE WELL FOR US. WE MUST FIND A WAY TO FREE OURSELVES!
BUT *HOW*, CAPTAIN?
WE... *HHN*... MUST TRY!
SITH *SCUM!* I DEVOTED MY LIFE TO DESTROYING YOUR KIND.
AND YET, LOOK AT YOURSELF-- CONSUMED BY ANGER... FEAR... *SELF-LOATHING* AT WHAT YOU HAVE ALREADY BECOME.
YOU HAVE BUT TO GIVE IN TO THE POWER THAT YOU FEEL... EMBRACE THE DARK SIDE...
NEVER!
I THINK THIS IS GOING TO GET WORSE BEFORE IT GETS BETTER...

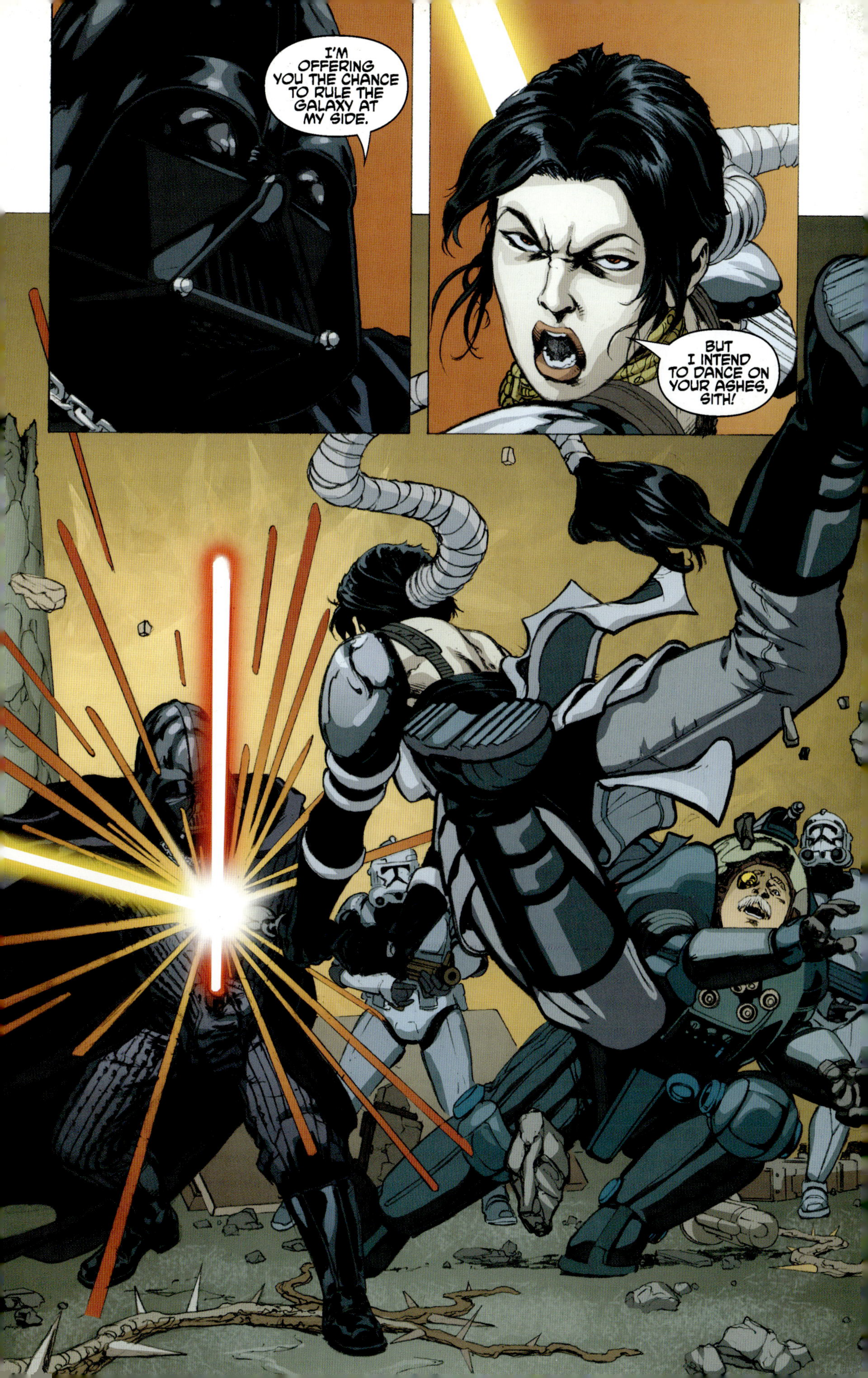
I'M OFFERING YOU THE CHANCE TO RULE THE GALAXY AT MY SIDE.
BUT I INTEND TO DANCE ON YOUR ASHES, SITH!

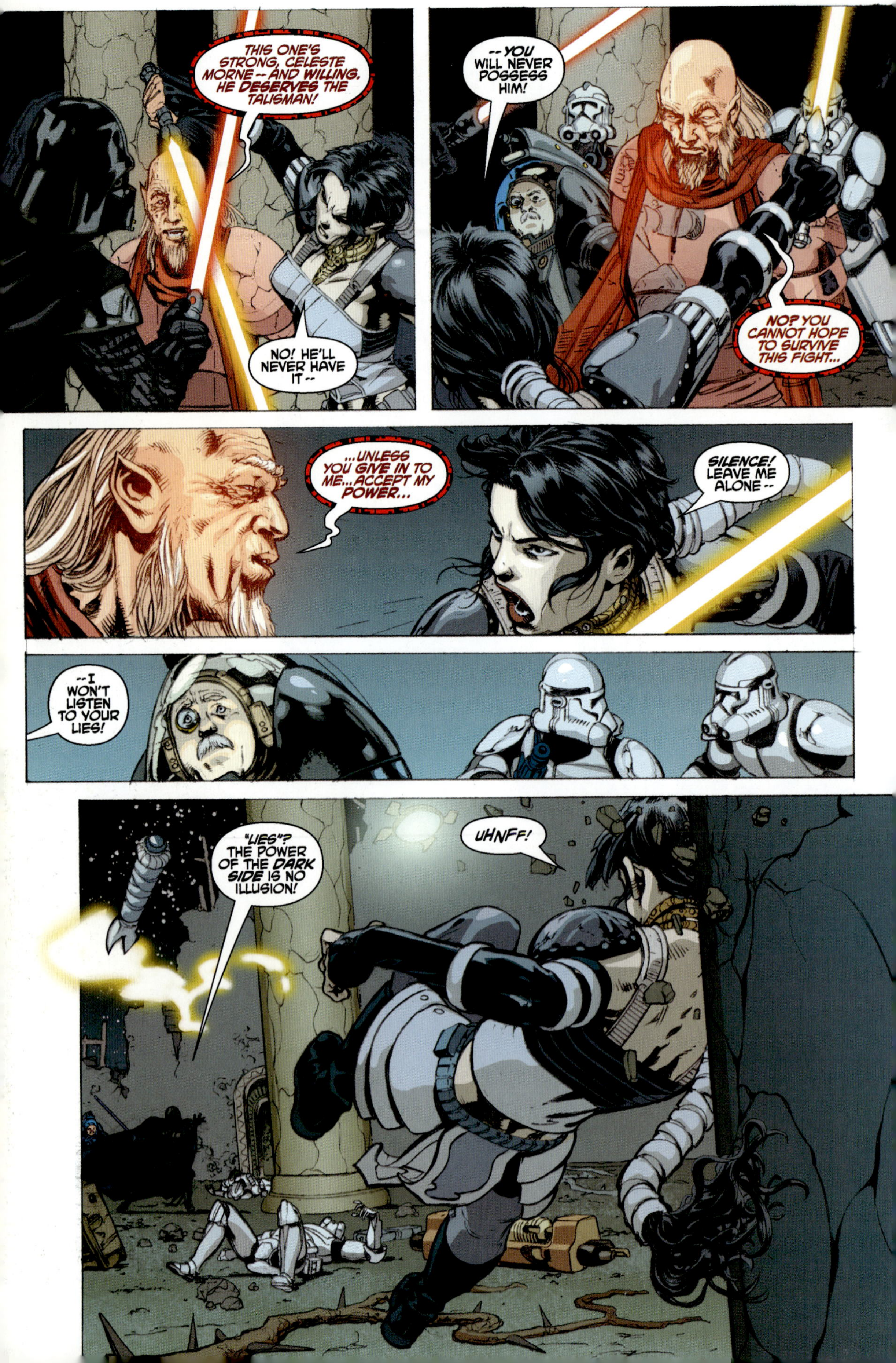
THIS ONE'S STRONG, CELESTE MORNE -- AND WILLING. HE DESERVES THE TALISMAN!
NO! HE'LL NEVER HAVE IT --
-- YOU WILL NEVER POSSESS HIM!
NO? YOU CANNOT HOPE TO SURVIVE THIS FIGHT...
...UNLESS YOU GIVE IN TO ME...ACCEPT MY POWER...
SILENCE! LEAVE ME ALONE --
-- I WON'T LISTEN TO YOUR LIES!
"LIES"? THE POWER OF THE DARK SIDE IS NO ILLUSION!
UHNFF!

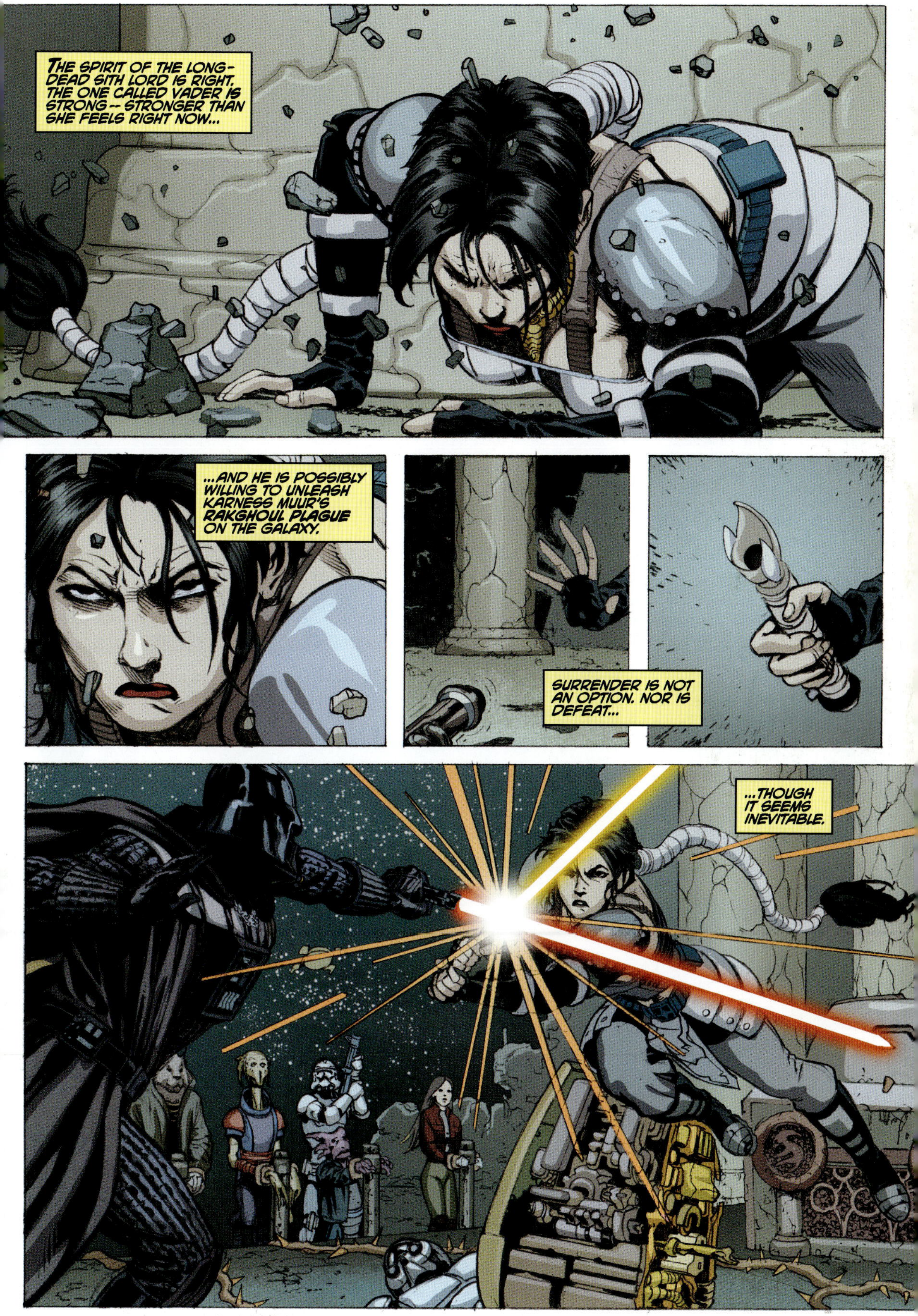
THE SPIRIT OF THE LONG-DEAD SITH LORD IS RIGHT. THE ONE CALLED VADER IS STRONG -- STRONGER THAN SHE FEELS RIGHT NOW...
...AND HE IS POSSIBLY WILLING TO UNLEASH KARNESS MUUR'S RAKGHOUL PLAGUE ON THE GALAXY.
SURRENDER IS NOT AN OPTION. NOR IS DEFEAT...
...THOUGH IT SEEMS INEVITABLE.

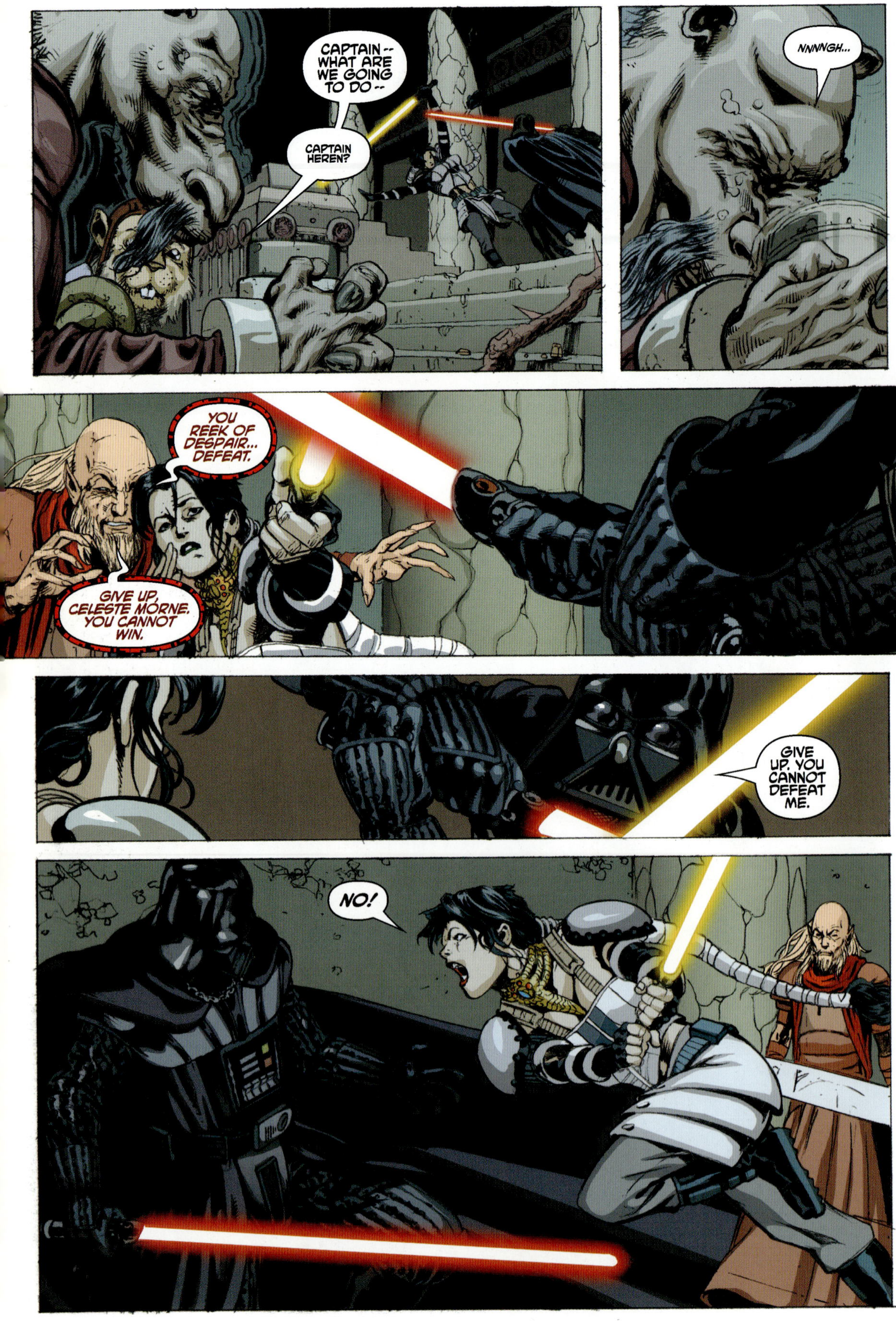
CAPTAIN -- WHAT ARE WE GOING TO DO --
CAPTAIN HEREN?
NNNNGH...
YOU REEK OF DESPAIR... DEFEAT.
GIVE UP, CELESTE MORNE. YOU CANNOT WIN.
GIVE UP. YOU CANNOT DEFEAT ME.
NO!

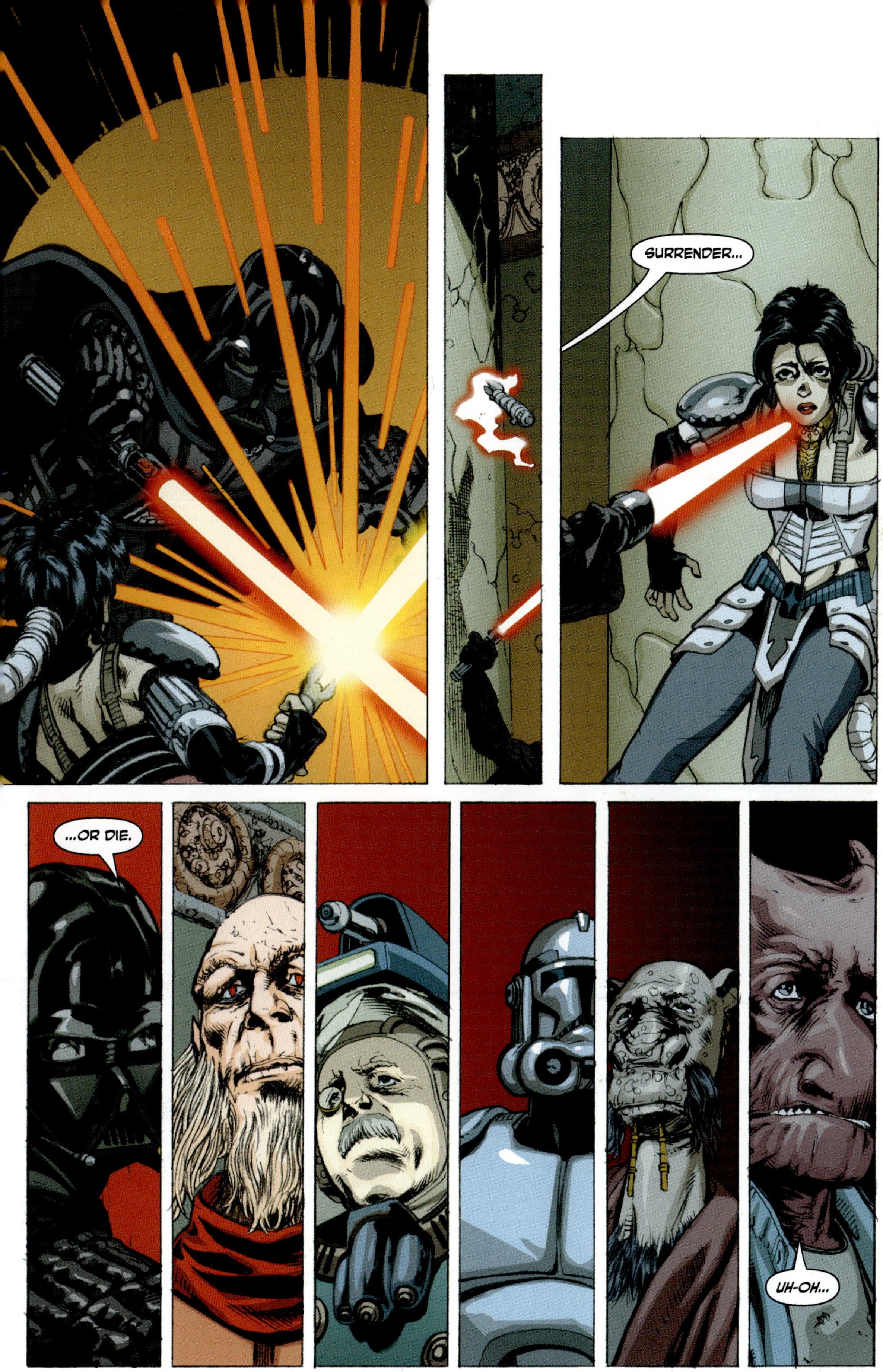
SURRENDER...
...OR DIE.
UH-OH...

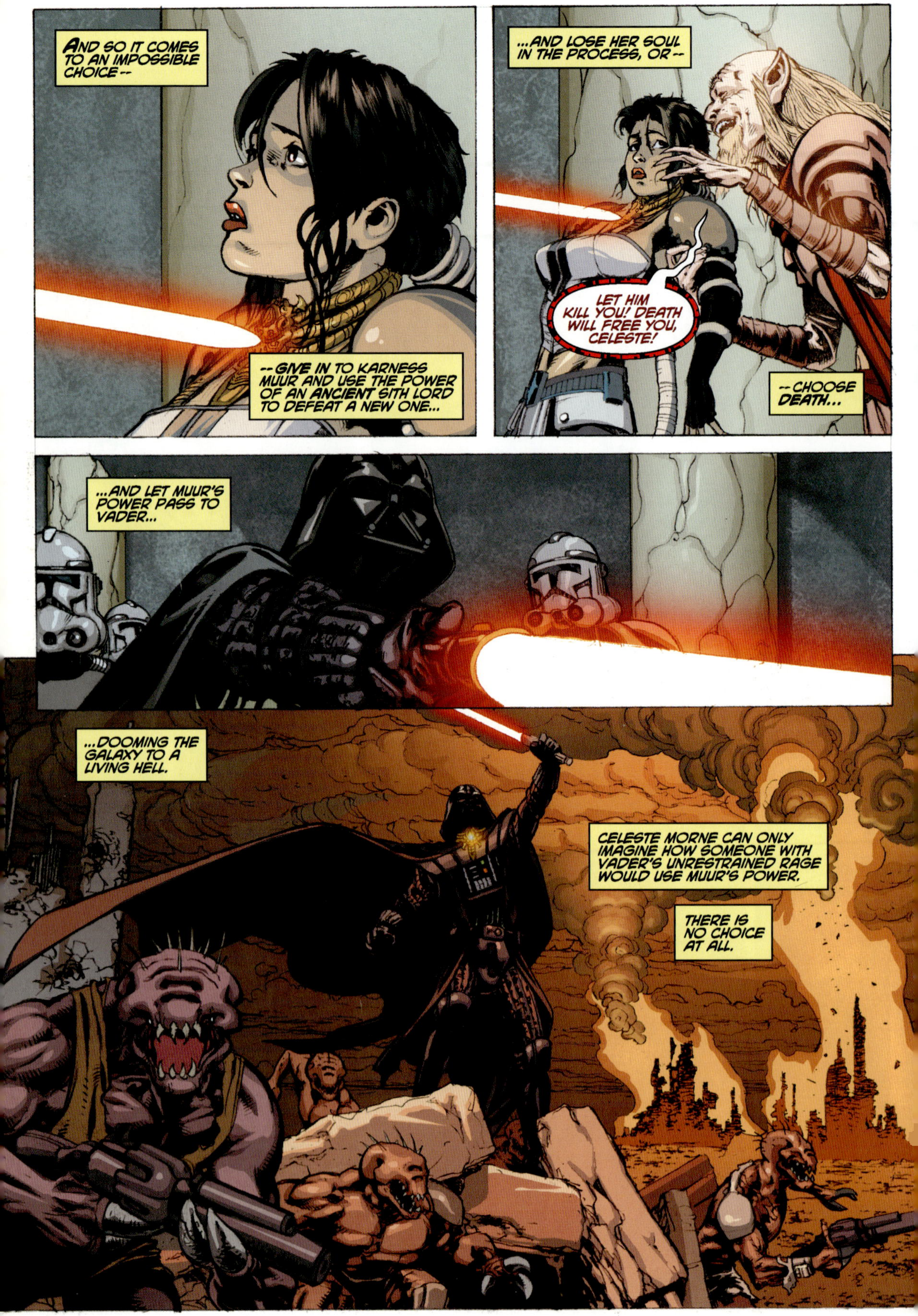
AND SO IT COMES TO AN IMPOSSIBLE CHOICE--
--GIVE IN TO KARNESS MUUR AND USE THE POWER OF AN ANCIENT SITH LORD TO DEFEAT A NEW ONE...
...AND LOSE HER SOUL IN THE PROCESS, OR--
LET HIM KILL YOU! DEATH WILL FREE YOU, CELESTE!
--CHOOSE DEATH...
...AND LET MUUR'S POWER PASS TO VADER...
...DOOMING THE GALAXY TO A LIVING HELL.
CELESTE MORNE CAN ONLY IMAGINE HOW SOMEONE WITH VADER'S UNRESTRAINED RAGE WOULD USE MUUR'S POWER.
THERE IS NO CHOICE AT ALL.

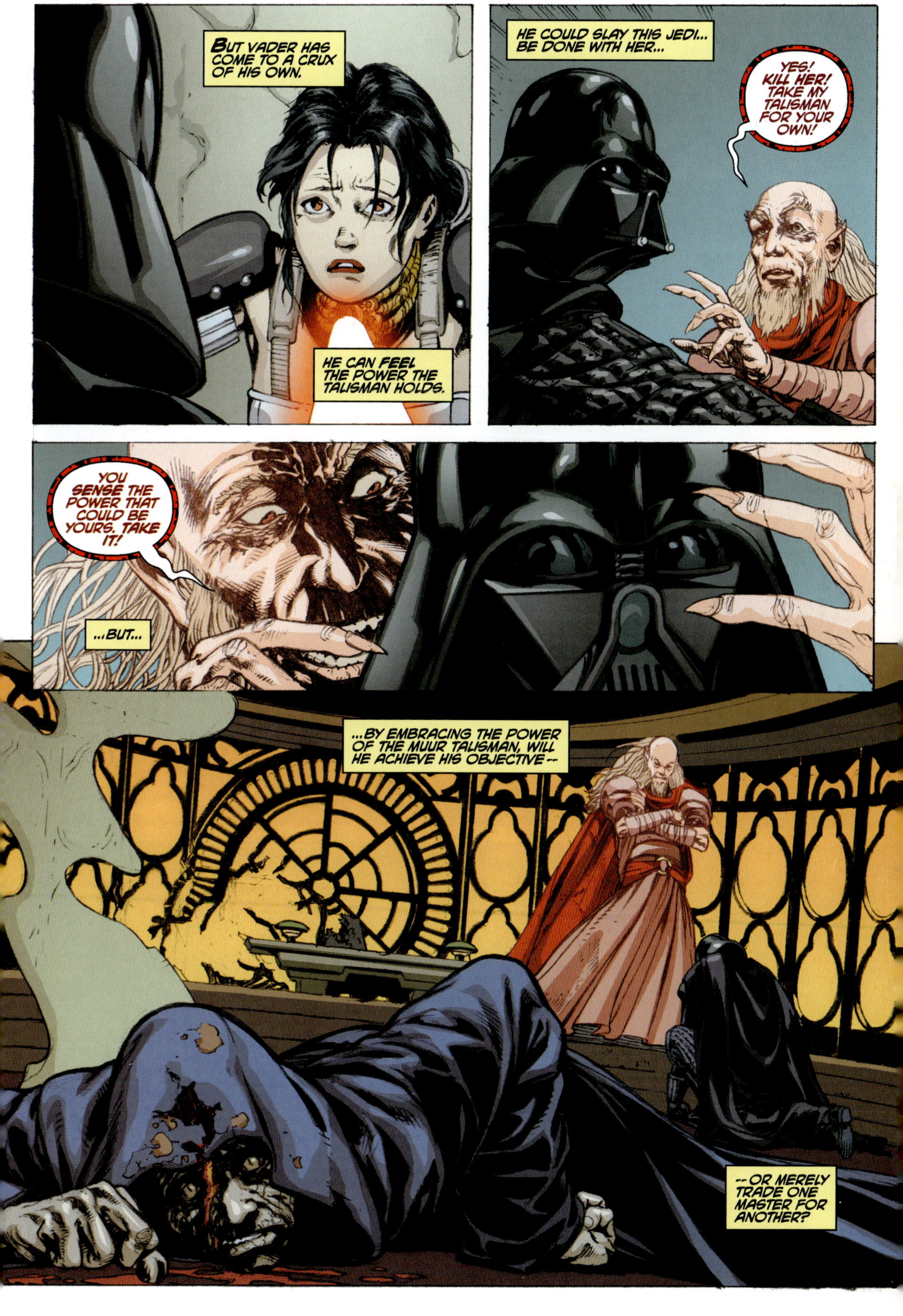
BUT VADER HAS COME TO A CRUX OF HIS OWN.
HE CAN FEEL THE POWER THE TALISMAN HOLDS.
HE COULD SLAY THIS JEDI... BE DONE WITH HER...
YES! KILL HER! TAKE MY TALISMAN FOR YOUR OWN!
YOU SENSE THE POWER THAT COULD BE YOURS. TAKE IT!
...BUT...
...BY EMBRACING THE POWER OF THE MUUR TALISMAN, WILL HE ACHIEVE HIS OBJECTIVE--
--OR MERELY TRADE ONE MASTER FOR ANOTHER?

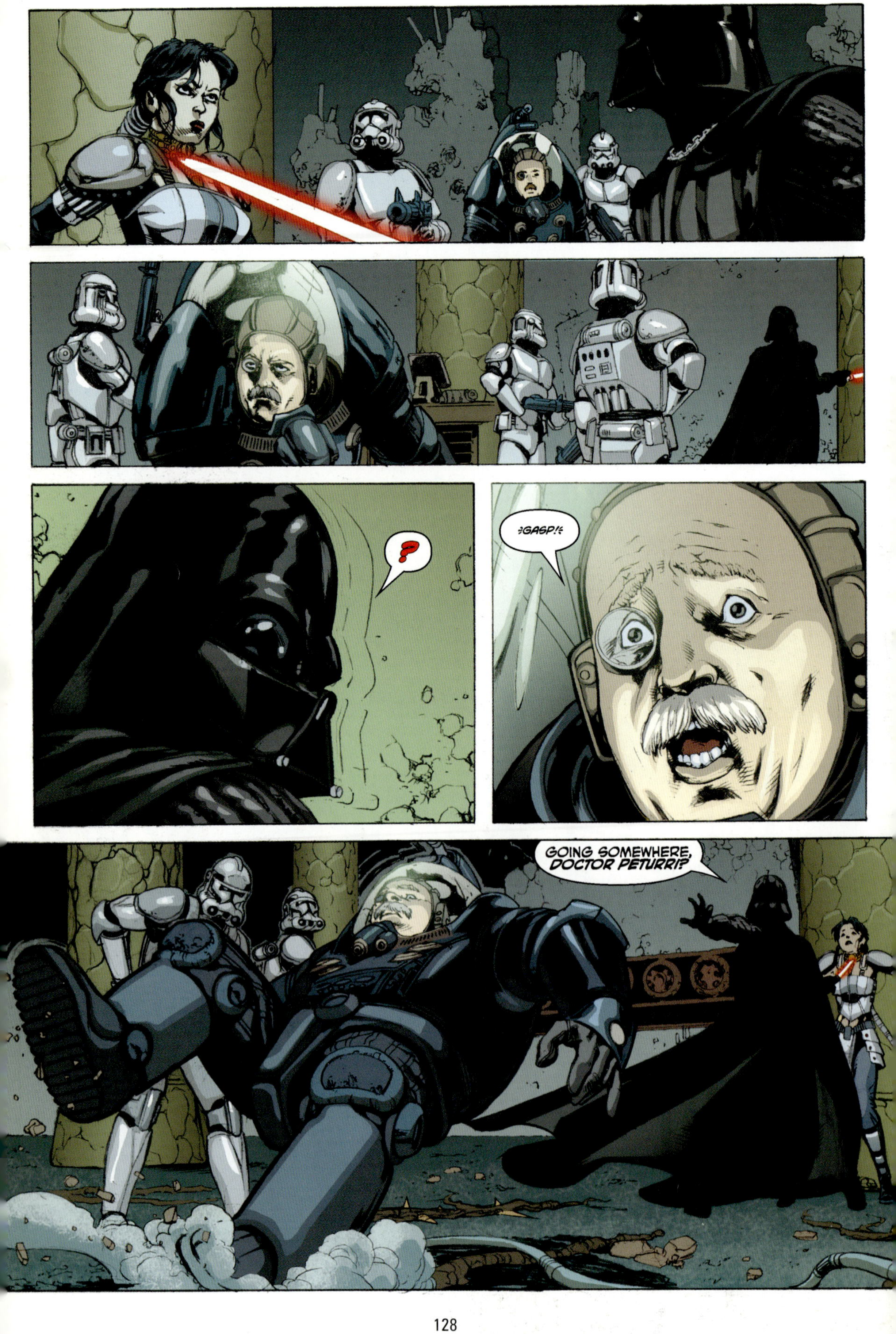
?
GASP!
GOING SOMEWHERE, DOCTOR PETURRI?

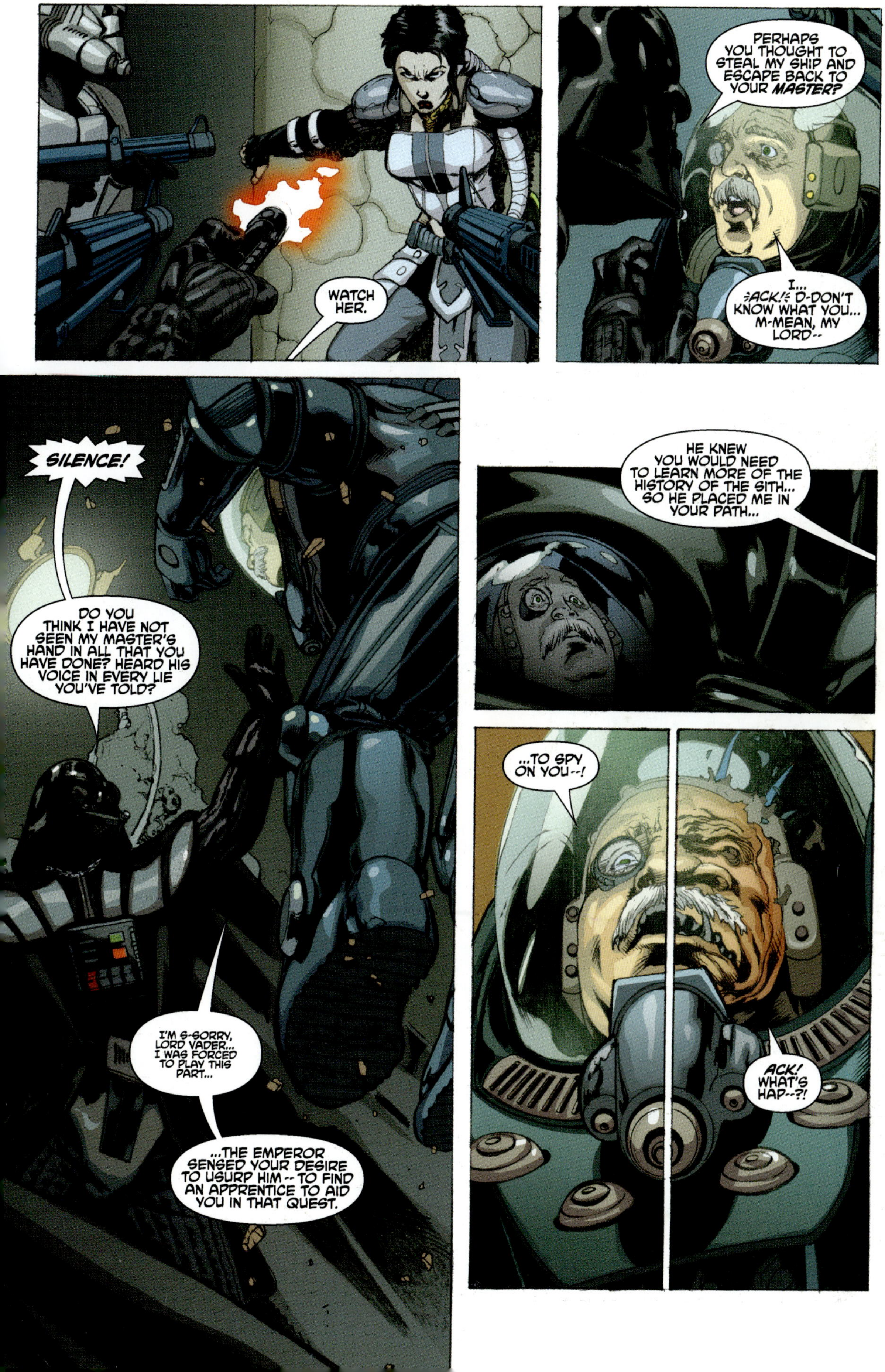
WATCH HER.
PERHAPS YOU THOUGHT TO STEAL MY SHIP AND ESCAPE BACK TO YOUR MASTER?
I... ACK! D-DON'T KNOW WHAT YOU... M-MEAN, MY LORD--
SILENCE!
DO YOU THINK I HAVE NOT SEEN MY MASTER'S HAND IN ALL THAT YOU HAVE DONE? HEARD HIS VOICE IN EVERY LIE YOU'VE TOLD?
I'M S-SORRY, LORD VADER... I WAS FORCED TO PLAY THIS PART...
...THE EMPEROR SENSED YOUR DESIRE TO USURP HIM -- TO FIND AN APPRENTICE TO AID YOU IN THAT QUEST.
HE KNEW YOU WOULD NEED TO LEARN MORE OF THE HISTORY OF THE SITH... SO HE PLACED ME IN YOUR PATH...
...TO SPY ON YOU--!
ACK! WHAT'S HAP--?!

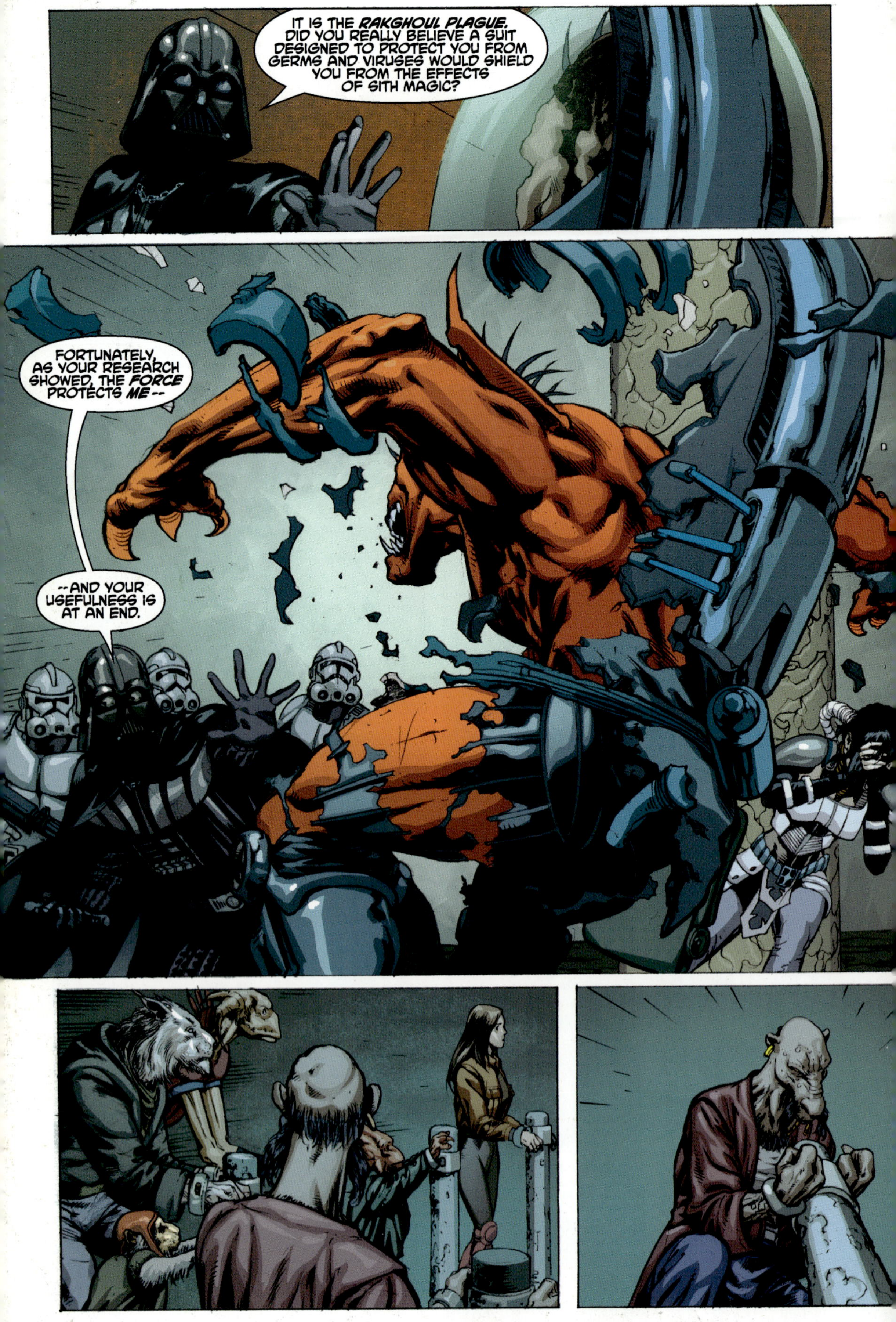
IT IS THE *RAKGHOUL PLAGUE.* DID YOU REALLY BELIEVE A SUIT DESIGNED TO PROTECT YOU FROM GERMS AND VIRUSES WOULD SHIELD YOU FROM THE EFFECTS OF SITH MAGIC?
FORTUNATELY, AS YOUR RESEARCH SHOWED, THE *FORCE* PROTECTS *ME*--
--AND YOUR USEFULNESS IS AT AN END.

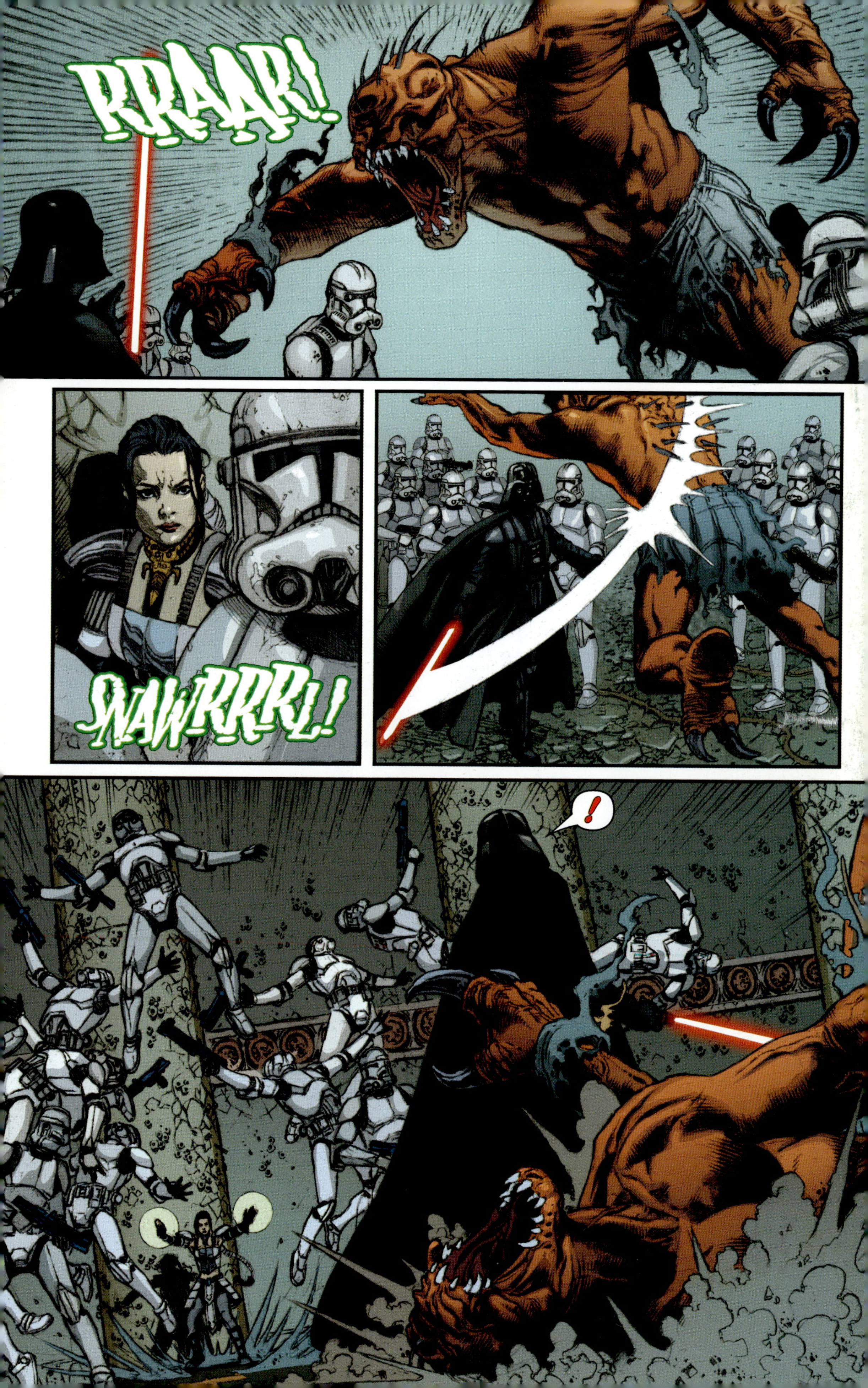
RRAAR!
SNAWRRRL!
!

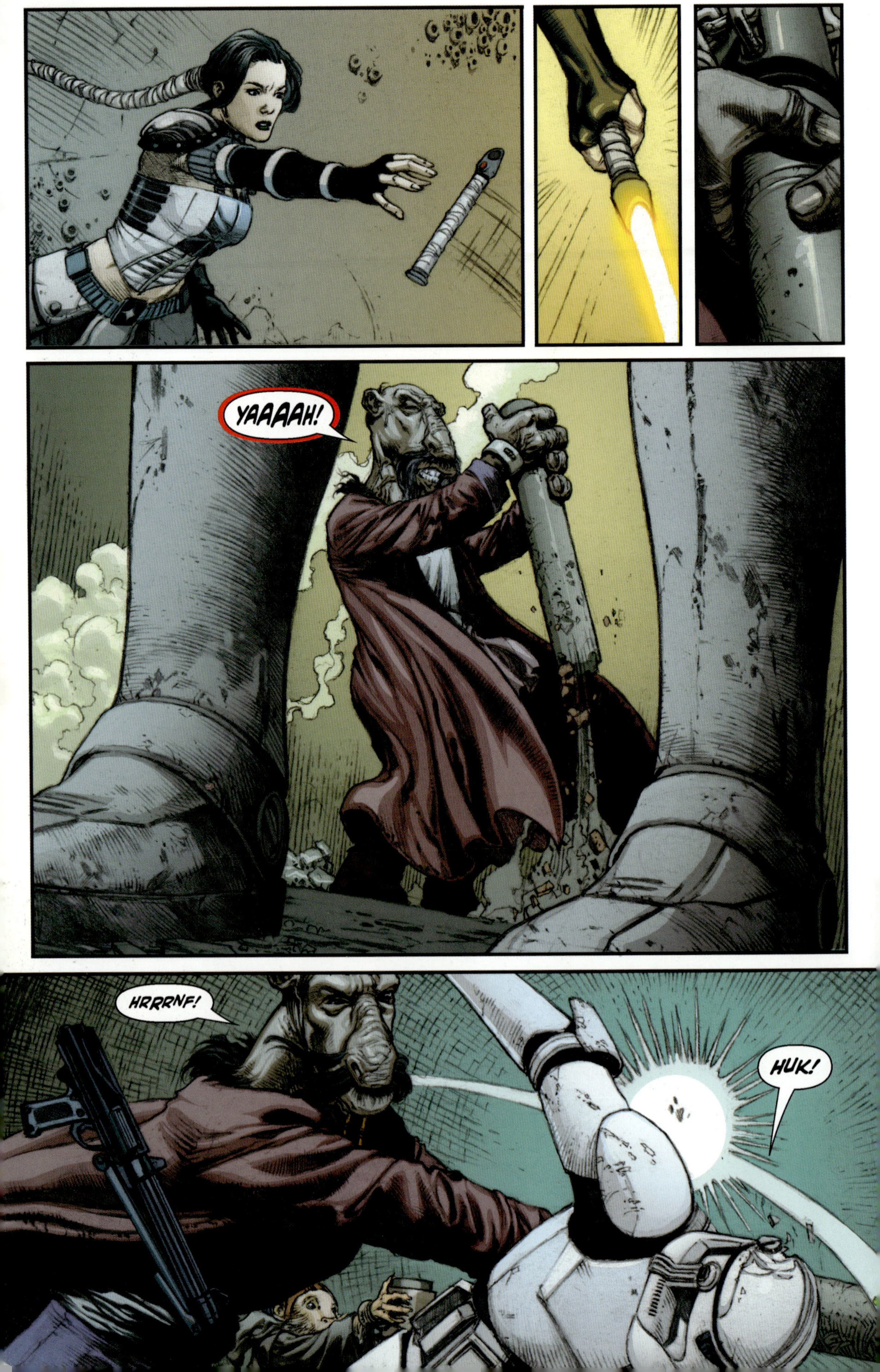
YAAAAH!
HRRRNF!
HUK!

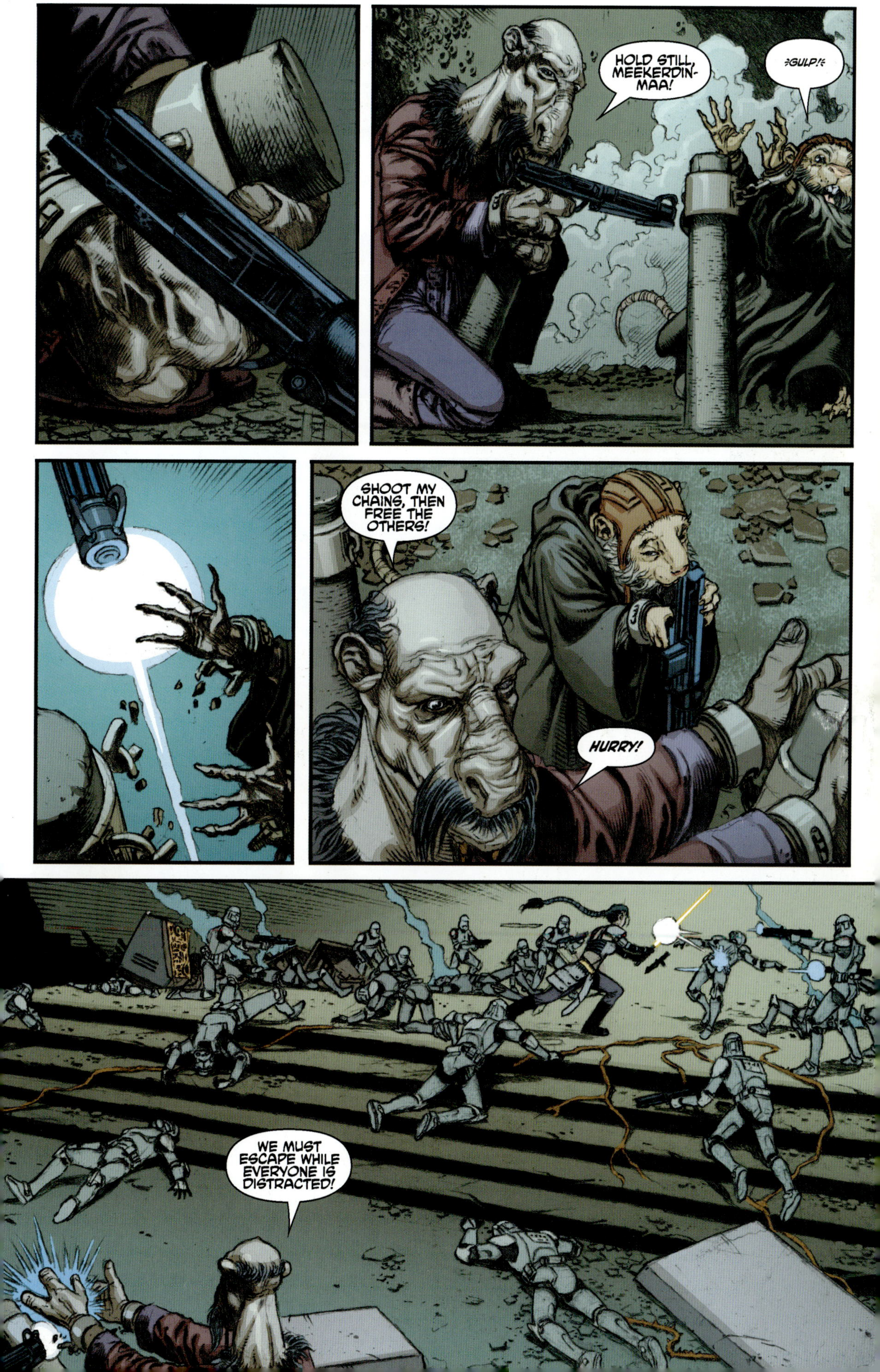
HOLD STILL, MEEKERDIN-MAA!
GULP!
SHOOT MY CHAINS, THEN FREE THE OTHERS!
HURRY!
WE MUST ESCAPE WHILE EVERYONE IS DISTRACTED!

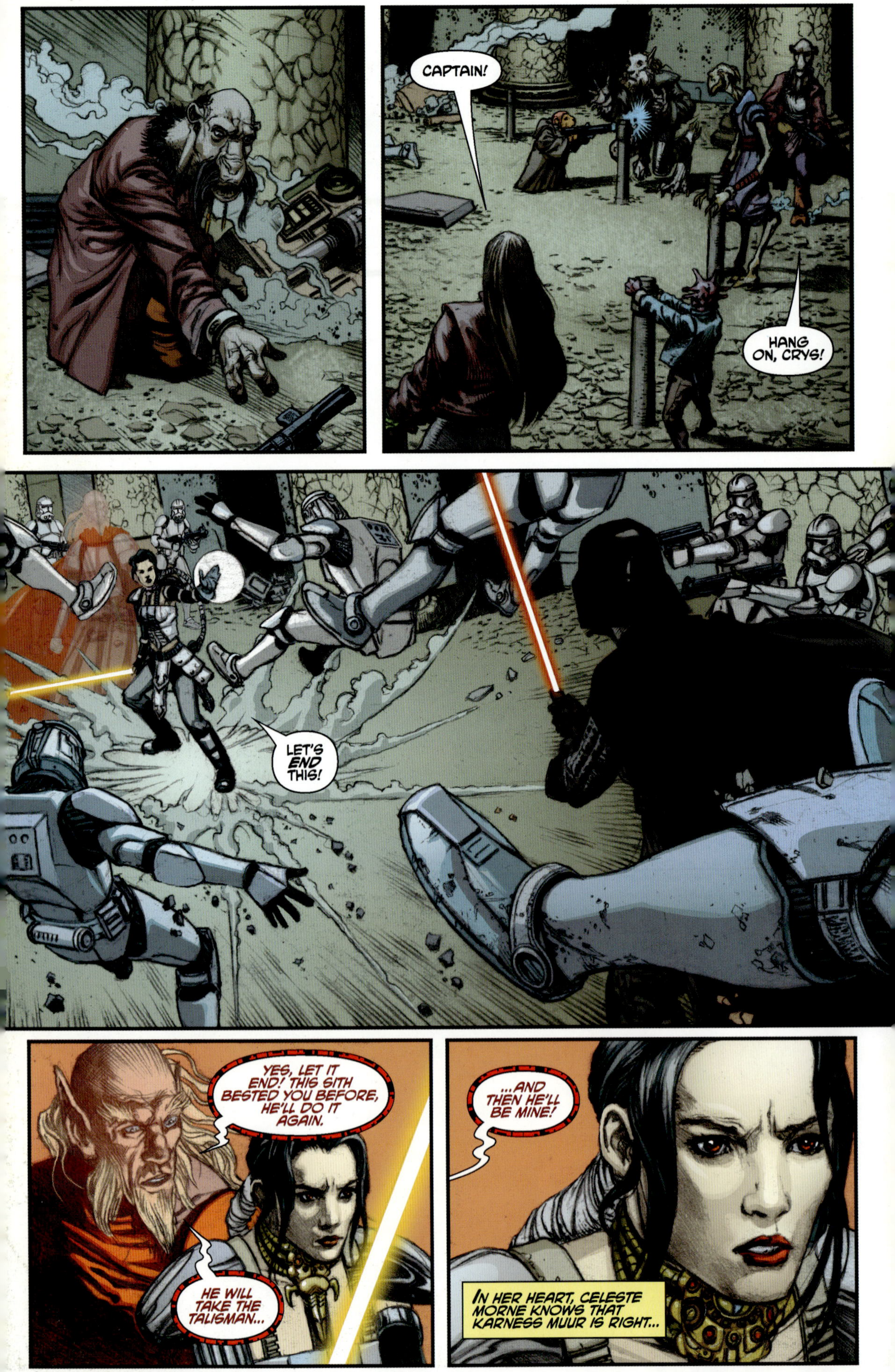
CAPTAIN!
HANG ON, CRYS!
LET'S END THIS!
YES, LET IT END! THIS SITH BESTED YOU BEFORE, HE'LL DO IT AGAIN.
HE WILL TAKE THE TALISMAN...
...AND THEN HE'LL BE MINE!
IN HER HEART, CELESTE MORNE KNOWS THAT KARNESS MUUR IS RIGHT...

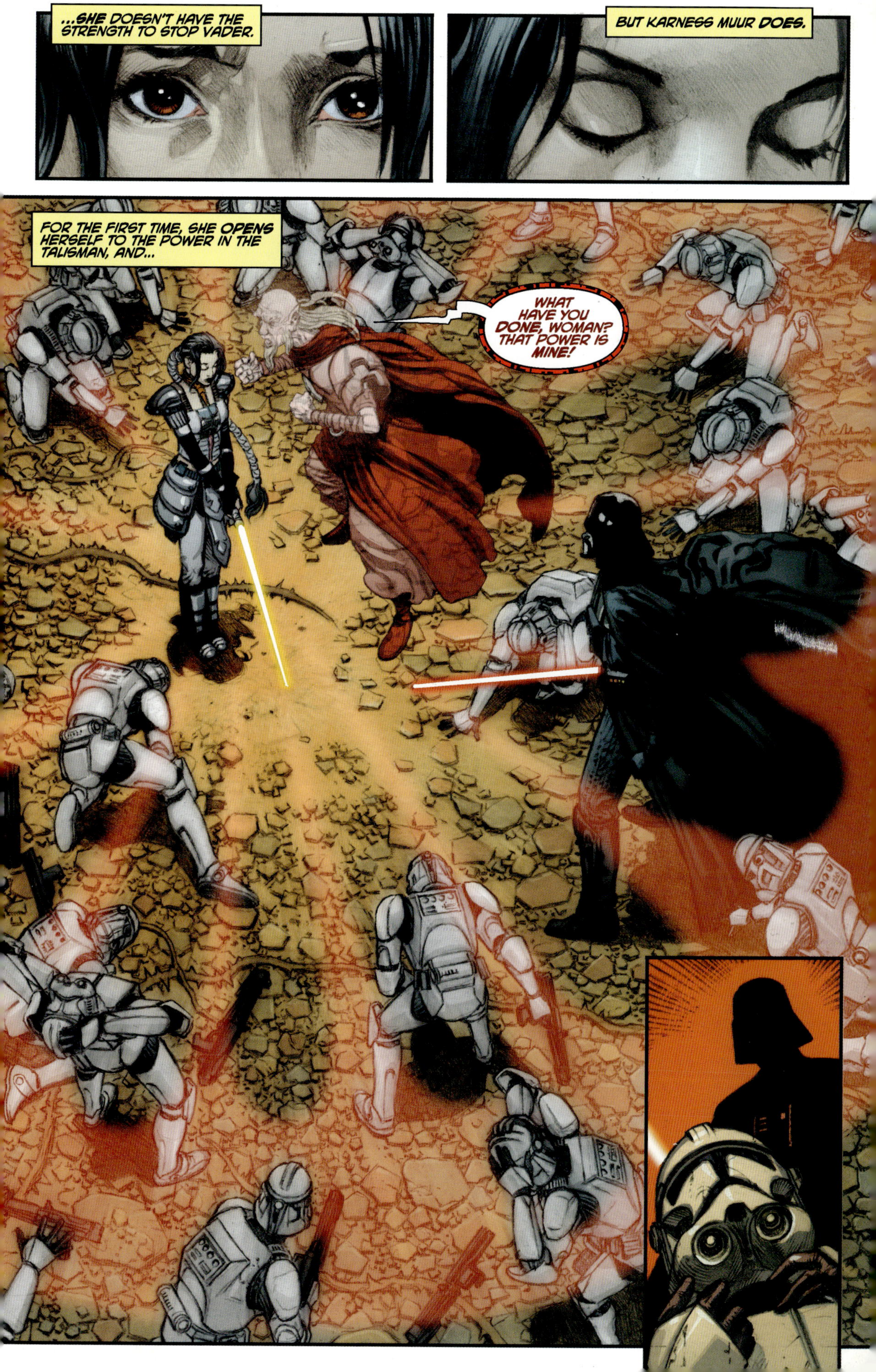
...SHE DOESN'T HAVE THE STRENGTH TO STOP VADER.
BUT KARNESS MUUR DOES.
FOR THE FIRST TIME, SHE OPENS HERSELF TO THE POWER IN THE TALISMAN, AND...
WHAT HAVE YOU DONE, WOMAN? THAT POWER IS MINE!

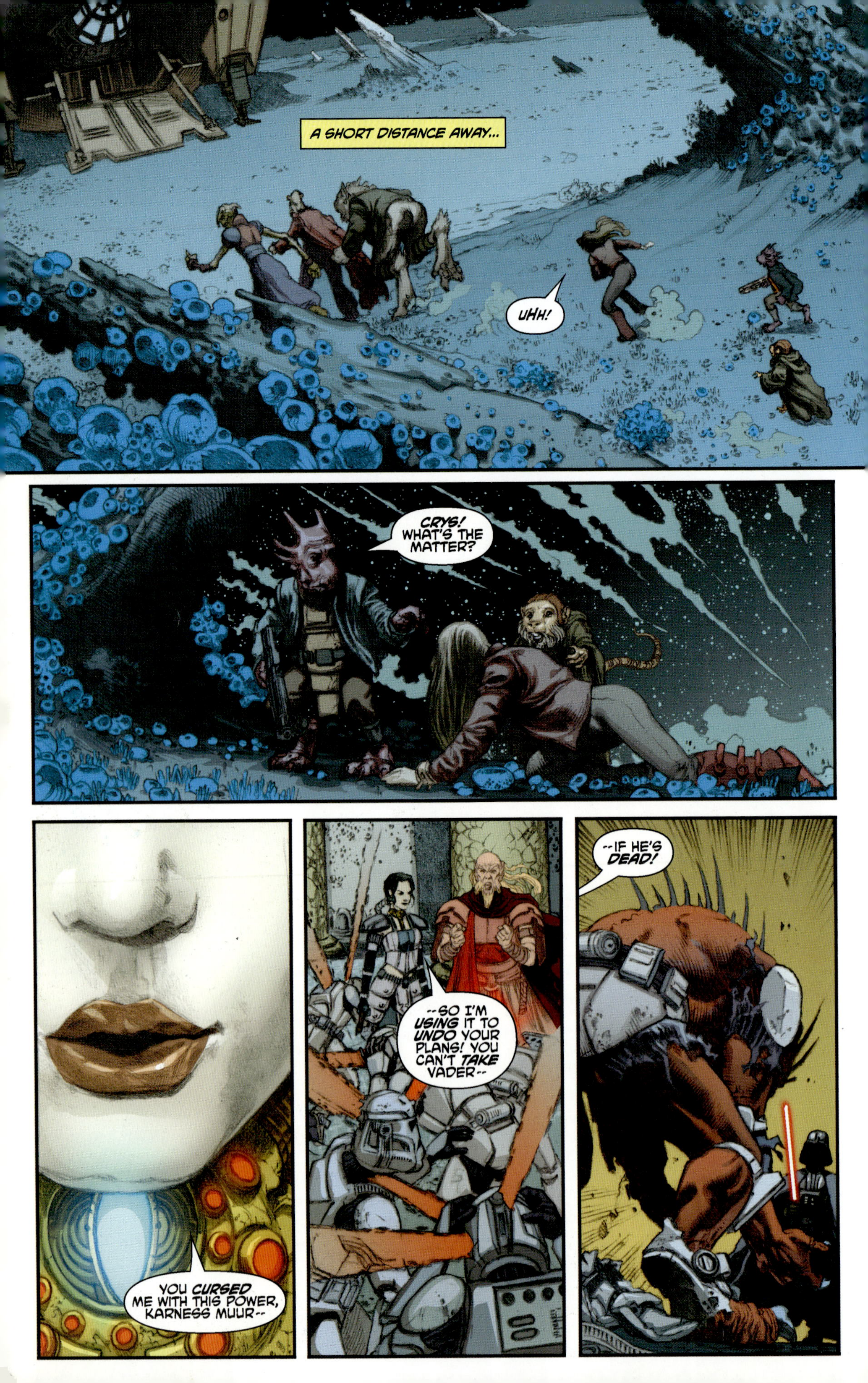
A SHORT DISTANCE AWAY...
UHH!
CRYS! WHAT'S THE MATTER?
YOU CURSED ME WITH THIS POWER, KARNESS MUUR--
--SO I'M USING IT TO UNDO YOUR PLANS! YOU CAN'T TAKE VADER--
--IF HE'S DEAD!

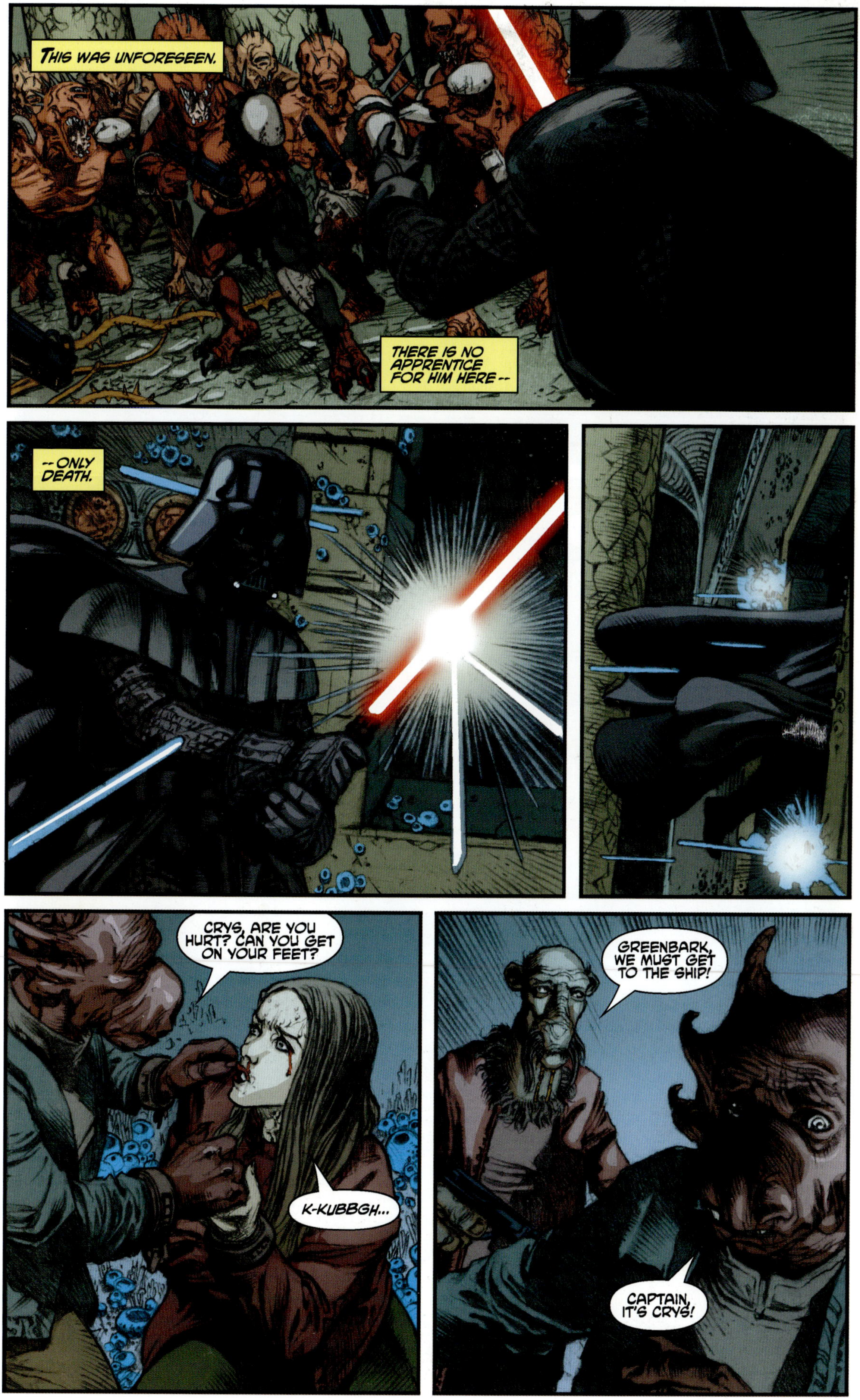
THIS WAS UNFORESEEN.
THERE IS NO APPRENTICE FOR HIM HERE --
-- ONLY DEATH.
CRYS, ARE YOU HURT? CAN YOU GET ON YOUR FEET?
K-KUBBGH...
GREENBARK, WE MUST GET TO THE SHIP!
CAPTAIN, IT'S CRYS!

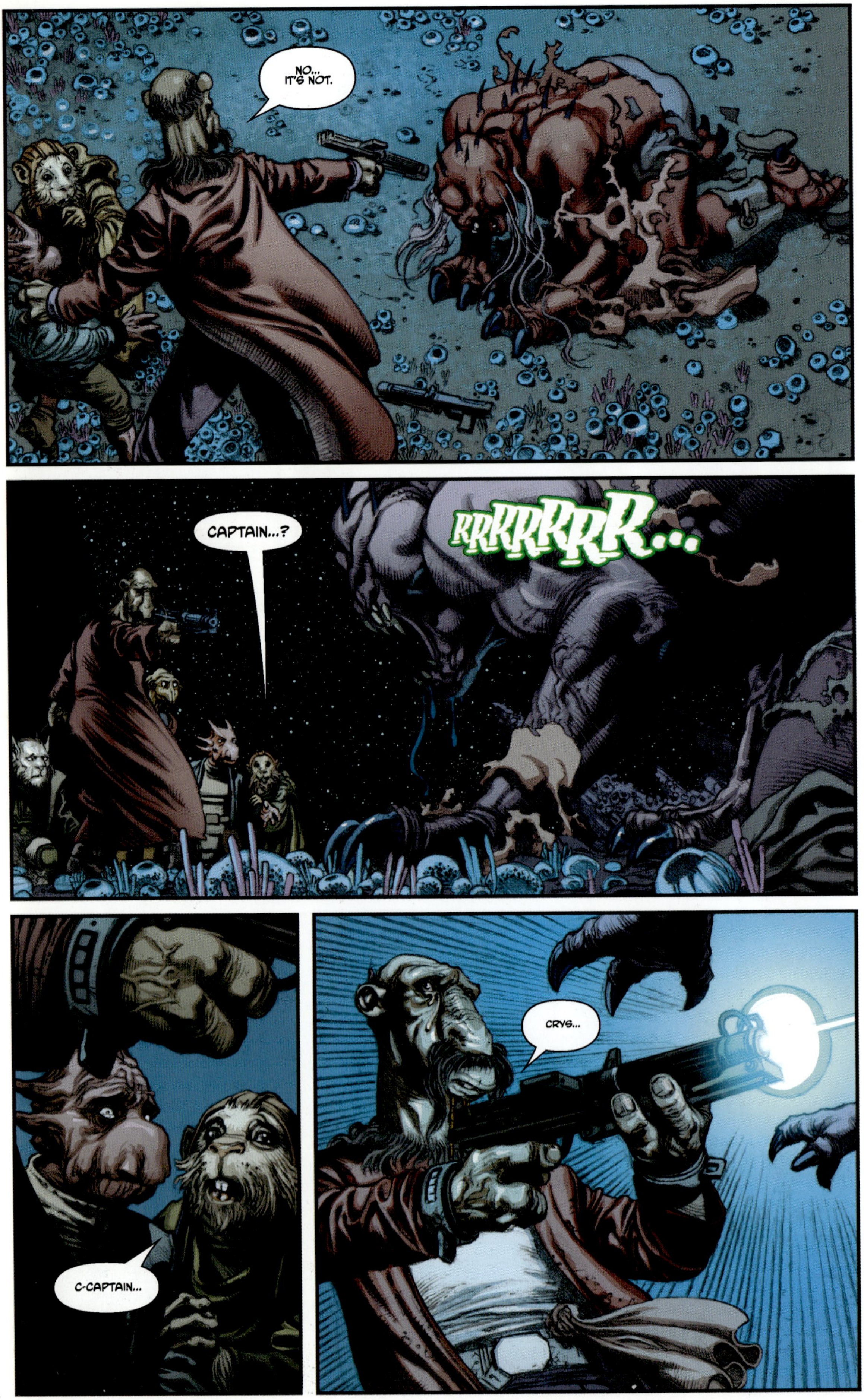
NO... IT'S NOT.
CAPTAIN...?
RRRRRRR...
C-CAPTAIN...
CRYS...

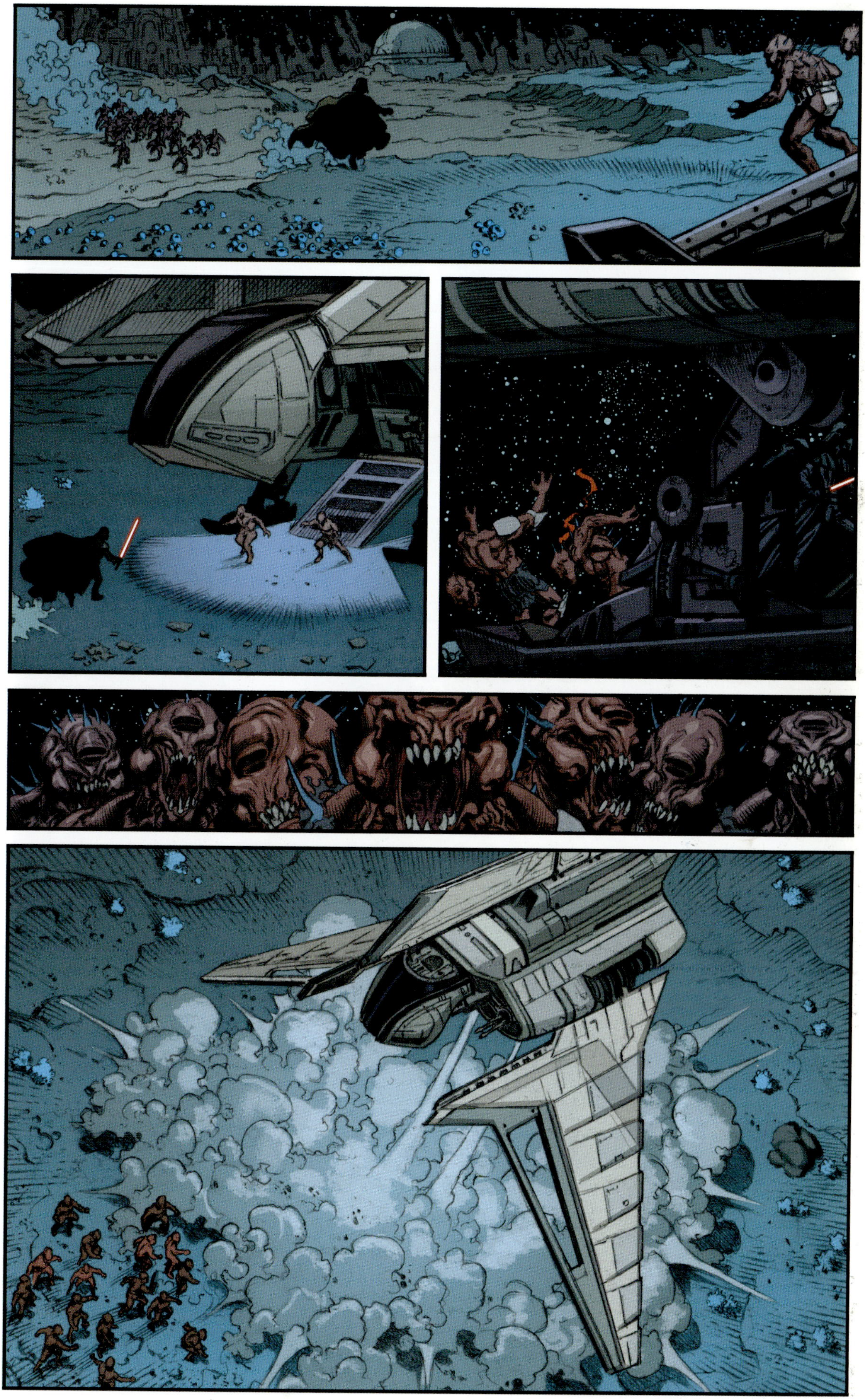

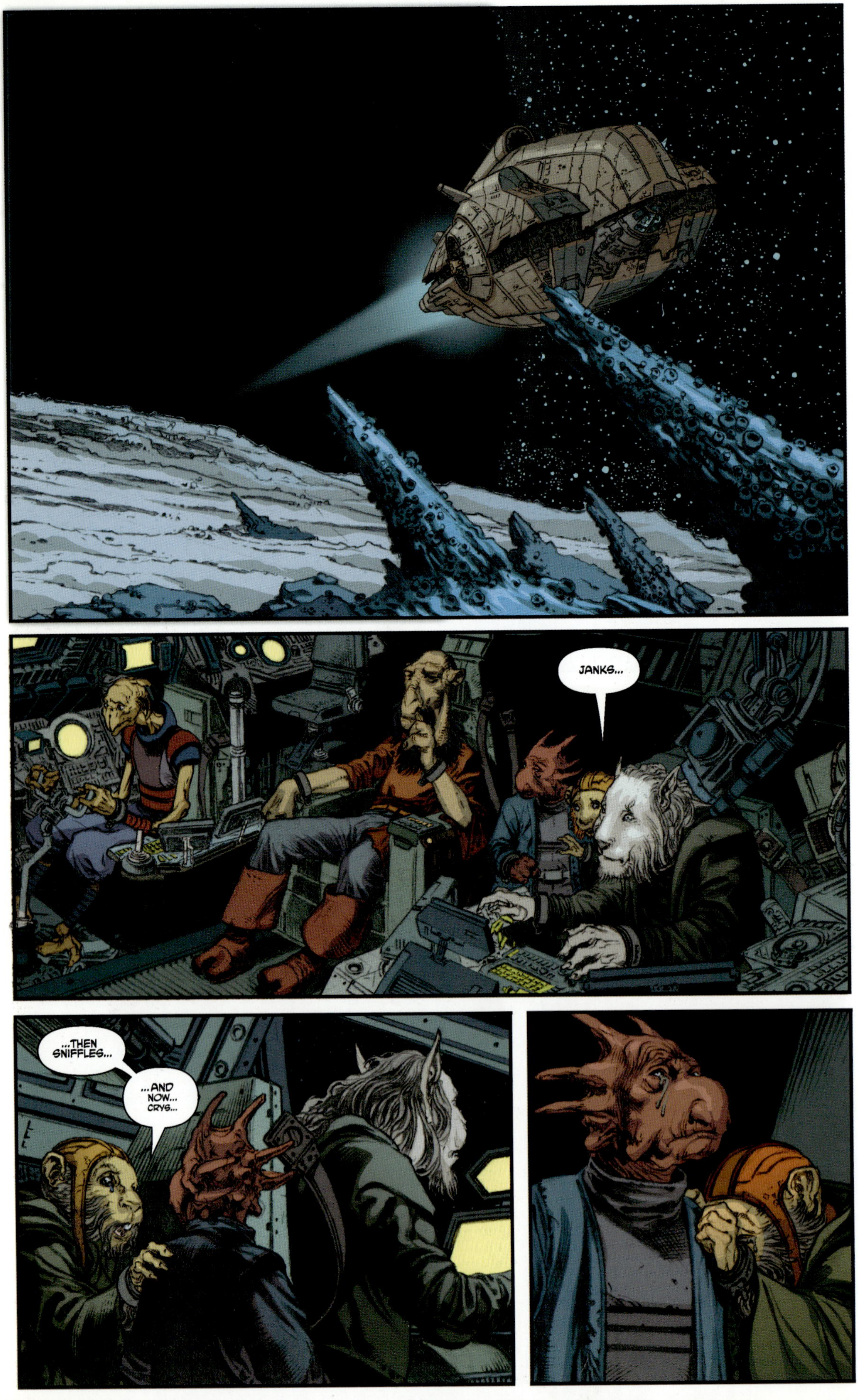
JANKS...
...THEN SNIFFLES...
...AND NOW... CRYS...

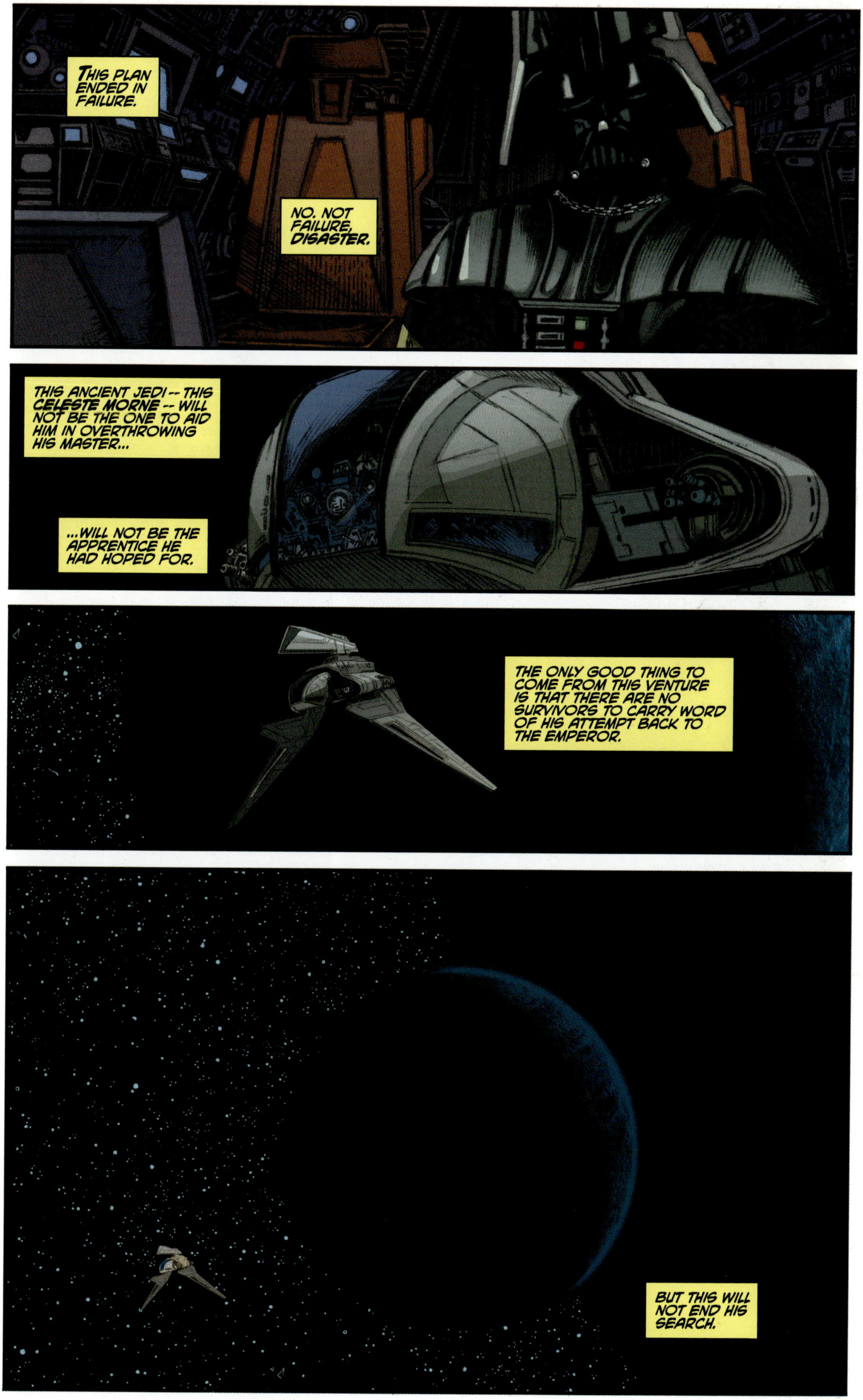
THIS PLAN ENDED IN FAILURE.
NO. NOT FAILURE. DISASTER.
THIS ANCIENT JEDI -- THIS CELESTE MORNE -- WILL NOT BE THE ONE TO AID HIM IN OVERTHROWING HIS MASTER...
...WILL NOT BE THE APPRENTICE HE HAD HOPED FOR.
THE ONLY GOOD THING TO COME FROM THIS VENTURE IS THAT THERE ARE NO SURVIVORS TO CARRY WORD OF HIS ATTEMPT BACK TO THE EMPEROR.
BUT THIS WILL NOT END HIS SEARCH.

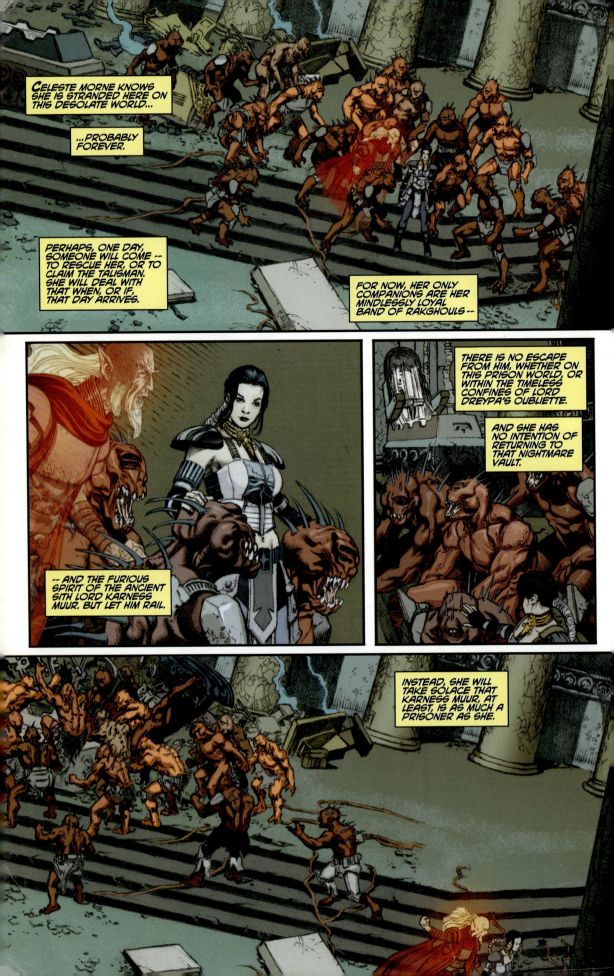

CELESTE MORNE KNOWS SHE IS STRANDED HERE ON THIS DESOLATE WORLD...

...PROBABLY FOREVER.

PERHAPS, ONE DAY, SOMEONE WILL COME -- TO RESCUE HER, OR TO CLAIM THE TALISMAN. SHE WILL DEAL WITH THAT WHEN, OR IF, THAT DAY ARRIVES.

FOR NOW, HER ONLY COMPANIONS ARE HER MINDLESSLY LOYAL BAND OF RAKGHOULS --

THERE IS NO ESCAPE FROM HIM, WHETHER ON THIS PRISON WORLD, OR WITHIN THE TIMELESS CONFINES OF LORD DREYPA'S OUBLIETTE.

AND SHE HAS NO INTENTION OF RETURNING TO THAT NIGHTMARE VAULT.

-- AND THE FURIOUS SPIRIT OF THE ANCIENT SITH LORD KARNESS MUUR. BUT LET HIM RAIL.

INSTEAD, SHE WILL TAKE SOLACE THAT KARNESS MUUR, AT LEAST, IS AS MUCH A PRISONER AS SHE.

STAR WARS VECTOR

An event with repercussions for every era and every hero in the *Star Wars* galaxy begins here! For anyone who never knew where to start with *Star Wars* comics, *Vector* is the perfect introduction to the entire *Star Wars* line! For any serious *Star Wars* fan, *Vector* is a must-see event with major happenings throughout the most important moments of the galaxy's history!

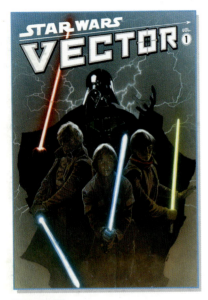

VOLUME ONE
(*Knights of the Old Republic* Vol. 5; *Dark Times* Vol. 3)
ISBN 978-1-59582-226-0 | $17.95

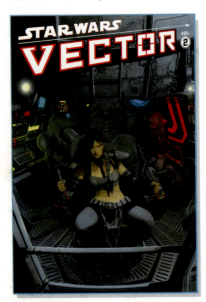

VOLUME TWO
(*Rebellion* Vol. 4; *Legacy* Vol. 6)
ISBN 978-1-59582-227-7 | $17.95

KNIGHTS OF THE OLD REPUBLIC
Volume One: Commencement
ISBN 978-1-59307-640-5 | $18.95

Volume Two: Flashpoint
ISBN 978-1-59307-761-7 | $18.95

Volume Three: Days of Fear, Nights of Anger
ISBN 978-1-59307-867-6 | $18.95

Volume Four: Daze of Hate, Knights of Suffering
ISBN 978-1-59582-208-6 | $18.95

REBELLION
Volume One: My Brother, My Enemy
ISBN 978-1-59307-711-2 | $14.95

Volume Two: The Ahakista Gambit
ISBN 978-1-59307-890-4 | $17.95

Volume Three: Small Victories
ISBN 978-1-59582-166-9 | $12.95

LEGACY
Volume One: Broken
ISBN 978-1-59307-716-7 | $17.95

Volume Two: Shards
ISBN 978-1-59307-879-9 | $19.95

Volume Three: Claws of the Dragon
ISBN 978-1-59307-946-8 | $17.95

Volume Four: Alliance
ISBN 978-1-59582-223-9 | $15.95

Volume Five: The Hidden Temple
ISBN 978-1-59582-224-6 | $15.95

DARK TIMES
Volume One: The Path to Nowhere
ISBN 978-1-59307-792-1 | $17.95

Volume Two: Parallels
ISBN 978-1-59307-945-1 | $17.95

www.darkhorse.com

AVAILABLE AT YOUR LOCAL COMICS SHOP OR BOOKSTORE.
TO FIND A COMICS SHOP IN YOUR AREA, CALL 1-888-266-4226
For more information or to order direct: On the web: darkhorse.com
E-mail: mailorder@darkhorse.com • Phone: 1-800-862-0052 Mon.–Fri.
9 A.M. to 5 P.M. Pacific Time. STAR WARS © 2004–2008 Lucasfilm Ltd. & ™ (BL8005)

DARK HORSE BOOKS